Sustainable and Responsible Business in Africa

Rose Ogbechie • Marvel Ogah
Editors

Sustainable and Responsible Business in Africa

Studies in Ethical Leadership

Editors
Rose Ogbechie
Lagos Business School
Pan-Atlantic University
Lekki, Nigeria

Marvel Ogah
Lagos Business School
Pan-Atlantic University
Lekki, Nigeria

ISBN 978-3-031-35971-2   ISBN 978-3-031-35972-9   (eBook)
https://doi.org/10.1007/978-3-031-35972-9

© The Editor(s) (if applicable) and The Author(s), under exclusive licence to Springer Nature Switzerland AG 2024

This work is subject to copyright. All rights are solely and exclusively licensed by the Publisher, whether the whole or part of the material is concerned, specifically the rights of translation, reprinting, reuse of illustrations, recitation, broadcasting, reproduction on microfilms or in any other physical way, and transmission or information storage and retrieval, electronic adaptation, computer software, or by similar or dissimilar methodology now known or hereafter developed.

The use of general descriptive names, registered names, trademarks, service marks, etc. in this publication does not imply, even in the absence of a specific statement, that such names are exempt from the relevant protective laws and regulations and therefore free for general use.

The publisher, the authors, and the editors are safe to assume that the advice and information in this book are believed to be true and accurate at the date of publication. Neither the publisher nor the authors or the editors give a warranty, expressed or implied, with respect to the material contained herein or for any errors or omissions that may have been made. The publisher remains neutral with regard to jurisdictional claims in published maps and institutional affiliations.

This Palgrave Macmillan imprint is published by the registered company Springer Nature Switzerland AG.
The registered company address is: Gewerbestrasse 11, 6330 Cham, Switzerland

Paper in this product is recyclable.

I dedicate this book to God Almighty, who made it possible to get this done. I would also like to dedicate it to Prof Albert Alos (First Vice Chancellor, Pan-Atlantic University), who inspired me to come to the Lagos Business School for the EXECUTIVE MBA 1 program, and Prof Juan Eligido (Former Vice Chancellor, Pan-Atlantic University), who allowed me to work at the Lagos Business School as a Senior Fellow teaching business ethics and leadership for the past 15 years.

I would also like to dedicate this book to Dr John Bryan of Strathmore University, Nairobi, Kenya, who helped me during my second Master's Degree in Philosophy and Ethics and to all the Professors from IESE Business School who came from Spain for their lectures. In addition, I would like to dedicate this book to my husband, Prof Chris Ogbechie (Dean, Lagos Business School), for his support and for giving me the idea for this book.

Finally, I dedicate this book to my fellow editor, Dr Marvel Ogah of the Lagos Business School, for his hard work and for helping me continue even when I wanted to give up and to my able research assistant, Olusegun Oguntimehin Jr, for his outstanding support and getting things done when needed.

Foreword

The overall business operating environment constantly evolves, and stakeholders' demand for businesses to act responsibly and sustainably has never been this high. As a result, business as usual is no longer acceptable anywhere in the world, Africa inclusive. Several books, mainly from the Western world and a few from other developing countries like India, have attempted to detail how businesses can act responsibly while still serving shareholders' interests. However, the social, cultural, legal, and other peculiarities regarding business operations in Africa have limited African business practitioners' adoption and applicability of these available books.

Driven by this bleak reality, the editors of this book seek to provide informative and practical resources that take into cognisance the peculiarities of Africa's business environment. Therefore, I will encourage every student, academic, and business leader operating or interested in business in Africa to not only read this book with rapt attention but also keep it for future reference for greater benefit. The overall idea of this book is to discuss the appropriate strategies and efficient management techniques organisations can use to build themselves for sustainable strategic advantage. The book's applicability in terms of practical steps will provide insights for local and multinational business organisations operating within the shores of Africa. The book provides ample insights for business enthusiasts and practitioners to understand the opportunities, challenges, and uncertainties in the African business environment.

The authors in this book are great personalities uniquely selected, with the vast majority either operating and consulting for businesses or teaching business-related courses in higher learning institutions across Africa. Given these authors' expertise and experience, the book's opinions and suggestions are quite relatable for business enthusiasts on the continent. This makes this book a useful resource for instructors, business owners, managers, and entrepreneurs interested in comprehending the key concerns in steering firms through the challenging and evolving African operating business environment while keeping an eye on responsible and sustainable business practices.

Another impressive contribution of this book is its focus on almost every sphere of business operation, unlike other books in the same genre, which have been limited to individual subject matters relating to business or industry. This book provides readers with grounded knowledge on varied but interconnected business-related topics such as human resource management, supply chain, marketing, corporate governance, accounting and finance, and strategic management. Most importantly, users of the book will be exposed to the nature, principles, and concerns of global best practices and sustainable business practices and management, especially concerning business operations in Africa.

The book will also be of immense advantage to business practitioners seeking to enhance their knowledge base of state-of-the-art market practices, learn more about ethical leadership, and learn how to operate a responsible business in Africa in terms of the different aspects of the business life cycle, including product development, advertising, culture, pricing, corporate social responsibilities, and accounting strategies as well as understanding and getting the most out of the human components of their organisation. The issues of corporate governance challenges in Africa and how organisations can run effective boards are also not left out of the discussion in this book.

Recently, sustainability made an evolutionary leap and gained popularity across the globe among all societal groups. Africa is also catching up on this trend. Businesses on the continent are now seeking to develop strategies that can reduce social adversities and promote sustainable environmental goals while increasing their performance. A chapter of this book is devoted to how organisations can develop business models and appropriate strategies and techniques that lead to sustainable strategic advantage.

Lagos Business School, Pan-Atlantic University   Chris I. Ogbechie
Lekki, Lagos, Nigeria

Preface

Teaching business ethics and leadership at the Lagos Business School for 15 years has given me an indication of how some businesses are run in Nigeria and Africa. From interactions with corporate executives and students, it was obvious that some businesses needed to be run sustainably, as some business leaders needed help to take responsible actions. Some reasons for this include the notion that many businesses would do anything to maximise profit. Also, there are many challenges in the African business space, and leaders need help to navigate this challenging business space and, at the same time, make responsible decisions.

Profits in the short term are often at the front burner in making decisions; this meant that leaders could take actions that were not responsible and would not lead to the sustainability of the business. Some shareholders drive business managers for maximum returns. Equally, managers want to remain relevant, keep their jobs, and earn bonuses. They tend to keep a blind eye to the possible fallouts of their decisions. Business leaders sometimes tend to act unintelligently even though they think otherwise. This is because they equate acting intelligently to maximising profits at all costs. Acting responsibly also comes with a price, as sacrifices may be needed. Business leaders who do not put sustainability on the front burner could easily fall victim as long as there are short-term gains to be made. I was often delighted when participants and students who have undergone business ethics and other courses at the Lagos Business School, where responsible business practices have always been emphasised, appeared excited and willing to ensure things are done differently in their businesses.

Many indigenous businesses in Africa need to reach the third generation because the businesses collapsed before then due to some irresponsible actions that the organisations had taken in the past. Many African individuals and organisations have suffered dire consequences due to irresponsible business practices. When organisations cut corners, use poor quality materials, sell fake or expired products, dump waste irresponsibly, treat employees and other stakeholders without respect, and bribe their way to get jobs rather than be creative and innovative, sustainability becomes an illusion. This book will help business leaders and managers act more responsibly to achieve sustainability.

The book cuts across the several aspects of business operations. Readers would find it very useful to see how they can better navigate the business space by acting more responsibly and making decisions that could help grow their brands and lead to sustainability.

When responsible business practices become common, many investors will be keen to invest in businesses in Africa, creating more jobs. This would also increase the people's standard of living as they would have more purchasing power. This would lead to more taxes for the government and a more robust economy.

Lekki, Nigeria	Rose Ogbechie
Lekki, Nigeria	Marvel Ogah

Contents

1 Overview of the Chapters 1
Rose Ogbechie and Marvel Ogah

2 Opportunities, Challenges, and Risks: The African Business Environment 11
Franklin Ngwu, Okey Nwuke, and Emeka Agu

3 Opportunities, Challenges and Risks: The South African Business Environment Profiling Opportunities and Challenges of Running Small and Medium-Sized Businesses in the Post-Apartheid Vhembe District of the Limpopo Province of South Africa 41
Amaechi Kingsley Ekene and Tambe-Dede Kelly

4 The Sustainability Challenge: Developing Strategic Advantage 63
Nkemdilim Iheanachor

5 Enhancing Marketing Practices: A Responsible Product for an Engaged Consumer 81
Vanessa Burgal

6	**Responsible Advertising** *Ngozi Okpara*	103
7	**Responsible Pricing** *Louis Nzegwu and Deborah Towolawi*	125
8	**Responsible Financial Accounting Strategies** *Callistus Ekpenga*	141
9	**Understanding, Developing and Supporting Desirable Workplace Behaviour and Careers** *Adeola Yetunde Ekpe*	169
10	**Ethical Leadership** *Rose Ogbechie*	189
11	**Waste Management Issues for Today's African Businesses (Circular Economy)** *Marvel Ogah*	205
12	**Enhancing Corporate Social Responsibilities in Emerging Business Environments in Africa: Challenges and Opportunities** *Silk Ugwu Ogbu*	223
13	**Enhancing Responsible Logistics and Supply Chain Effectiveness: Navigating Current Challenges** *Marvel Ogah*	249
14	**Corporate Governance in Africa: Key Challenges and Running Effective Boards** *Chris Ogbechie and Adebunmi Arije*	265

15	**Concluding Chapter (Summary)**	291
	Rose Ogbechie and Marvel Ogah	

Index 295

List of Contributors

Emeka Agu Lagos Business School, Pan-Atlantic University, Lekki, Nigeria

Adebunmi Arije Lagos Business School, Pan-Atlantic University, Lekki, Nigeria

Vanessa Burgal Lagos Business School, Pan-Atlantic University, Lekki, Nigeria

Amaechi Kingsley Ekene Centre for Youth and Gender Studies, University of Venda, Thohoyandou, South Africa
Department of Business Management, University of Venda, Thohoyandou, South Africa

Callistus Ekpenga Cardinal One Business Services, Lagos, Nigeria

Adeola Yetunde Ekpe Lagos Business School, Pan-Atlantic University, Lekki, Nigeria

Nkemdilim Iheanachor Lagos Business School, Pan-Atlantic University, Lekki, Nigeria

Tambe-Dede Kelly Centre for Youth and Gender Studies, University of Venda, Thohoyandou, South Africa
Department of Business Management, University of Venda, Thohoyandou, South Africa

Franklin Ngwu Lagos Business School, Pan-Atlantic University, Lekki, Nigeria

Okey Nwuke Lagos Business School, Pan-Atlantic University, Lekki, Nigeria

Louis Nzegwu Lagos Business School, Pan-Atlantic University, Lekki, Nigeria

Marvel Ogah Lagos Business School, Pan-Atlantic University, Lekki, Nigeria

Chris Ogbechie Lagos Business School, Pan-Atlantic University, Lekki, Nigeria

Rose Ogbechie Lagos Business School, Pan-Atlantic University, Lekki, Nigeria

Silk Ugwu Ogbu Lagos Business School, Pan-Atlantic University, Lekki, Nigeria

Ngozi Okpara School of Media and Communication, Pan-Atlantic University, Lekki, Nigeria

Deborah Towolawi Lagos Business School, Pan-Atlantic University, Lekki, Nigeria

Abbreviations

AfCFTA	African Continental Free Trade Area
CIPC	Companies and Intellectual Property Commission
CSR	Corporate Social Responsibility
EFCC	Economic and Financial Crimes Commission
EPA	Environmental Protection Authority
ESMA	Environmental and Social Management Account
ESG	Environmental, Social, and Governance
GAAP	Generally Accepted Accounting Principles
GDP	Gross Domestic Product
GRI	Global Reporting Initiative
IFRS	International Financial Reporting Standards
ISO	International Organization of Standardization
MOCs	Multinational Oil Companies
NCSD	National Council for Sustainable Development
PSAS	Public Sector Accounting Standard
ROA	Return on Assets
ROI	Return on Investment
SASB	Sustainability Accounting Standards Board
SEA	Social and Environmental Accounting
SSE	Sustainable Stock Exchange
UNIDO	United Nations Industrial Development Organization

List of Figures

Fig. 4.1	Showing the focus of the sustainability strategies. Source: Author's Presentation	71
Fig. 4.2	Showing areas of applying sustainability strategies. Source: Author's Presentation	72
Fig. 9.1	Maslow's hierarchy of needs (after Maslow, 1943)	177
Fig. 11.1	Waste management service flow. Source: African Clean Cities Platform (ACCF) (2019). Africa Solid Waste Management Data Book 2019	208
Fig. 12.1	Dimensions of CSR definitions. *Source:* James (2012)	227
Fig. 12.2	Pyramid of Corporate Social Responsibilities. *Source:* Helg (2007)	228
Fig. 12.3	Corporate involvement in CSR: a strategic approach. *Source:* Porter and Kramer (2006)	231
Fig. 12.4	Relationship between Stakeholder Theory and CSR. *Source:* Freeman and Dmytriyev (2017)	235
Fig. 12.5	CSR effects on brand trust. *Source:* Aimie-Jade (2011)	241

List of Tables

Table 3.1	Demographic representation of social media marketers	48
Table 4.1	Showing stakeholders of an organisation	65
Table 4.2	Showing execution techniques for sustainability	72
Table 7.1	Pricing strategy objectives example	133

1

Overview of the Chapters

Rose Ogbechie and Marvel Ogah

The book comprises 15 chapters, including the introductory and concluding aspects:

Chapter 2: Opportunities, Challenges, and Risks: The African Business Environment

This chapter examines the opportunities, challenges, and risks in the post-pandemic African business environment. The top ten risks faced by businesses in Africa and practical measures to manage the risks and challenges were examined. Case studies were used to illustrate risk management and opportunity maximisation in the African business environment, focusing on the Rwandan tourism industry, Nigeria's Dadin Hausa Dam/Olam Rice Farmland, and Libya and Nigeria's Crude oil Underproduction.

R. Ogbechie (✉) • M. Ogah
Lagos Business School, Pan-Atlantic University, Lekki, Nigeria
e-mail: rogbechie@lbs.edu.ng; mogah@lbs.edu.ng

The chapter provides insights into what can be done to mitigate the risks and challenges so that the opportunities can be better harnessed for more sustainable growth and development in Africa.

Chapter 3: Opportunities, Challenges, and Risks: The South African Business Environment

This chapter analyses salient opportunities and challenges associated with running Small and Medium-sized Entrepreneurial Ventures (SMEV) in the Vhembe District of the Limpopo Province of South Africa. Drawing from the experience of eight Vhembe-based Small and Medium-sized entrepreneurs, the chapter identifies and discusses what engaging in and sustaining a SMEV in such a context entails. While some of the identified opportunities include an SMEV-friendly environment for start-ups, access to business networking and clientele base, a less complex market, and cheap running costs, some prominent challenges include limited access to finance, lack of basic infrastructure to harness managerial, technical or entrepreneurial skills required for running SMEs, the non-existence of specific entrepreneurial-government policies and insecurity emanating from most violent attacks and theft within South Africa's rural setting. Based on the review, among other things, accelerated efforts to improve rural infrastructures and amenities and provide-friendly policies to foster rural development and entrepreneurial engagement. Such efforts encourage SMEV entrepreneurial start-ups and offer opportunities for SMEV development.

Chapter 4: The Sustainability Challenge: Developing Strategic Advantage

Sustainability is a serious issue that any business that wants to succeed with assured continuity must consider. Internal and external issues can contribute to a company's ability to continue or cease to exist. Making strategic plans and taking critical steps to protect a business's future within its operation's industry and environment is what sustainability in business means. Although this may not be an immediate effect, an unhealthy environment results from unsustainable business practices, eventually affecting the ability and supply of natural materials and the economy. Experts explained that unsustainable practices could reduce employees' well-being and productivity, which will increase effectiveness. Therefore, this chapter discusses the sustainability challenge, identifies sustainability practices, and makes valuable recommendations for strategic advantage in Africa. Consequently, the chapter concludes that sustainability is crucial to the continuity and growth of every organisation. Organisations need to gain a competitive advantage in all aspects of their workforce through sustainable work conditions. Also, organisations must achieve financial stability by making a profit from which their shareholders can profit from their investments, and workers would be paid for their work.

Chapter 5: Enhancing Marketing Practices: A Responsible Product for an Engaged Consumer

African companies should consider consumers as key business stakeholders and protect and develop them. Often African consumers need more resources or the knowledge and education to choose the best products for themselves and their families. Local public institutions lack funds to invest in their populations' education and protect them from dangerous activities, products, and services forbidden outside the continent. To protect consumers and reach customer satisfaction, African companies shall build customer-centric organisations that empower clients and employees. By doing so, marketing teams can guarantee an adequate quality standard for their products and services while developing fully transparent Marketing Mix strategies. We can only protect the consumer if he is aware of the product ingredients, materials, or side effects of its usage. Finally, a responsible marketer should participate in its customers' education to ensure complete customer awareness and understanding. When local African institutions struggle to give their people the required information and to protect them from unethical marketing behaviours, companies can assist and reinforce this learning through the appropriate Marketing Mix tools and activities. An educated consumer will soon become an engaged consumer.

Chapter 6: Responsible Advertising

There is a growing concern about the impact of advertising on African societies. Though advertising has the potential to bring economic growth and development to the region, it can also have negative consequences if not conducted responsibly. This includes promoting unhealthy or harmful products, exploiting cultural values, and perpetuating negative stereotypes. An integral concern about responsible advertising in African businesses is the need to consider the cultural and social context of the region by being mindful of the values and beliefs of different communities and avoiding pirated content. This is to make sure that advertising does not exploit or mislead consumers. Using various theories, this chapter discusses concepts of advertising, types of advertising, functions of advertising, ethical issues in advertising, and various ways businesses can avoid irresponsible and unethical advertising and focus on using responsible business to sell their products and services as well as its brands. The chapter recommends that all advertisements fulfil all ethical approval from regulatory bodies before dissemination. By working on promotion, the advertising industry can play a positive and constructive role in shaping future businesses in Africa.

Chapter 7: Responsible Pricing

This chapter discussed the concept of responsible pricing and how a responsible pricing strategy creates opportunities for businesses in Sub-Saharan Africa to remain profitable in every sales situation and ensure sustainability. Responsible pricing entails setting appropriate value-based prices for an organisation's product or service offering, which is affordable to customers and promotes sustainability for the Orion prices in an ally responsible manner, a business enterprise would be able to can the achieve its objective of sustainability and customer satisfaction. Responsible pricing is mainly achieved by setting prices based on the perceived value of the product/service from a stakeholders' point of view, particularly the consumers. By dynamically modifying pricing in line with customers' perceived value, a business may make efforts to decrease the effect of price sensitivity of consumers, which can positively affect the purchase behaviour of consumers. Businesses that utilise responsible pricing won't set prices lower than necessary because it gives them information on the customers' willingness to pay. On the other hand, setting prices that result in excessive profits or exploits a customer's needs is considered unethical behaviour in pricing practices.

Chapter 8: Responsible Financial Accounting Strategies

This chapter aims to increase awareness of the importance of responsible financial accounting in Africa and contributes to the broader discourse on sustainability in the region. It begins by examining the economic landscape of Africa and the history and development of social and environmental accounting (SEA) in the region. The introduction of Western accounting practices during colonial times greatly impacted how economic activities were conducted and reported on the continent, often leading to neglect of social and environmental considerations. Despite facing challenges such as high levels of inequality, unemployment, and debt, Africa has many pheromonic growth and development opportunities, such as a growing middle class, a youthful population, and abundant natural resources. As a result, SEA is becoming increasingly prevalent as governments, consumers, investors, and other stakeholders demand more transparency and accountability from crucial tools for organisations to navigate the challenges and opportunities of the twenty-first century and contribute to the well-being of both people and the planet. To further drive the development of environmental accounting in the region and influence international standard setting, there is a need for a comprehensive accounting research infrastructure in Africa.

Chapter 9: Understanding, Developing, and Supporting Desirable Workplace Behaviour and Careers

Successful business in Africa requires not only the traditional tools of strategy, structure, and operational processes but a holistic understanding of the environment, the continent's diversity and its intra-continental differences and an effective means of navigating it. The geography, economic, socio-economic factors, culture, and values of Africa are tightly interwoven, and all impact workplace behaviours. However, unlike in the United Kingdom and the United States, there is a need for more published behavioural research in Africa, so mainstreamed Western-based behavioural frameworks are applied with varying degrees of success. The author, who has worked, consulted, taught, and coached executives in African workplaces for over 30 years, draws on her experience and research to highlight crucial issues and challenges affecting and influencing employee behaviour in Africa. She suggests adopting cultural humility when relying on Western frameworks, setting aside preconceptions, and seeking practical ways of working that may differ from perceived norms. She posits that employees must be regarded as key stakeholders in organisational success, suggests building cultural awareness, aligning employee and corporate values, and treating employees sensitively and inclusively. She shares a practitioner's viewpoint, several African examples and valuable insights that should enhance employers' abilities to proffer culturally sensitive strategies for business success.

Chapter 10: Ethical Leadership

Leadership has always been at the heart of management discourse. Still, ethical leadership has gained more prominence following the collapse and scandals that engulfed the corporate world (Enron, WorldCom – Corporate scandals) not too long ago. The performance and culture of an organisation are closely related to its leader's quality, effectiveness, ethical attitude, and approach. This is because leaders do not only inspire but drive the performance and culture of the organisation. Recent studies have also established that ethical leaders are perceived as very effective leaders as they recognise the uniqueness of their people and thus motivate them to more excellent performance. Many unethical behaviours by leaders have had catastrophic effects on the different stakeholders. In contrast, leaders who have built an ethical culture have formed a culture of excellence in their organisations. Leadership is therefore concerned with treating employees and other stakeholders with dignity and building a culture of excellence wherein all the stakeholders can flourish. This chapter focuses on ethical leadership and how organisations can create a culture where employees and all stakeholders can thrive and build a sustainable business.

Chapter 11: Waste Management Issues for Today's African Businesses (Circular Economy)

Successful businesses create products that transform their customers and society for betterment in tandem with the drive to preserve the environment for future generations; this attribute resonates with any business mandate to integrate waste management solutions in its value chain. Responsible African business leaders must be prepared to control and manage their ecosystems regarding the impact of the issues that concern the ethos of the circular economy; the onus rests on African business leaders to navigate responsibly waste management issues and solutions as their businesses evolve and adapt to the future. This chapter will focus on the concept of waste management in Africa, changing waste management issues; challenges, and opportunities of implementing the circularity principle in both industrial and service-based sectors in emerging economies; adoption of innovative measures regarding how emerging economies can transit from the traditional linear approach of production and consumption to a circular path. The scope of the chapter will also entail a discussion of how African leadership in both private and public sectors can sustainably imbibe and integrate the principles and practices of circularity in their value chains amidst the challenges of insecurity and inept business practices abound in sub-Saharan Africa.

Chapter 12: Enhancing Corporate Social Responsibilities in Emerging Business Environments in Africa: Challenges and Opportunities

Corporate Social Responsibility (CSR) is a tool that can be applied to reduce risks, build brand equity, elevate market performance, and drive business sustainability. In developed countries, CSR is becoming a crucial determinant of organisations' ability to deliver expected outcomes to stakeholders and attract future investments. However, in Africa and other emerging markets, the practice of CSR is still evolving, inspired more by the philosophy of charity, philanthropy, and stewardship than business strategy. Against that background, this chapter interrogates the approach to CSR in Africa from ideation to execution/impact and argues for integrating CSR initiatives with business operating strategies to entrench responsible business practices and unlock profit-making opportunities. From a conceptual perspective and the prism of the Stakeholder Management Theory, the chapter draws attention to the shortcomings in the practice of CSR in Africa. It offers suggestions for improvement across the design and implementation protocols. Specifically, the study recommends broadening the corporate social performance spectrum in Africa to incentivise and energise more participation from Micro, Small, and Medium Enterprises (MSMEs) as a pathway to scaling CSR impact in the continent, especially in the post-COVID-19 era.

Chapter 13: Enhancing Responsible Logistics and Supply Chain Effectiveness: Navigating Current Challenges

As critical functional areas of operations, logistics and supply chains have evolved regarding effectiveness. This evolution has implications regarding the dependability of the organisational ability to adapt and adopt relevant metrics to responsibly deliver value to organisational customers and stakeholders. Initiating and sustaining this balance pose a challenge to most organisations regarding enhancing responsible logistics and supply chain effectiveness amidst navigating emerging operational challenges. Organisations operating in emerging economies, like those operating in developed climes, need to leverage internal and external operational capabilities to resolve evolving challenges in tandem with the need to responsibly provide value to their customers. Thus, this chapter will focus on responsible logistics and supply chain framework, critical challenges in driving efficient and effective logistics, and supply chain operations in emerging economies relating to dimensions of green operations. It will also provide a framework for creating a sustainable-cum-responsible logistics and supply chain architecture to adapt to eco-friendly logistics practices; sustainable supply chain architecture is geared towards the responsible, innovative drive for technology, people, and the environment.

Chapter 14: Corporate Governance in Africa: Key Challenges and Running Effective Boards

Globally, businesses and corporate organisations are experiencing unprecedented volatility, uncertainty, complexities, and ambiguity (VUCA), making success a herculean task. How organizations are directed and controlled are important. Corporate governance has become a leading topic among stakeholders in the business world. This is because corporate governance effectiveness has been a factor in achieving sustainable long-term irrespective of the sector, business model, and size. The board is the focal point of corporate governance, and it is responsible for its effectiveness through the board's oversight, leadership, strategic, and other functions. African Boards is not prosaic and most African organization have difficulties with running an effective board due to some cultural, economic, political, and legal factors. This chapter submits that African corporate governance can be strengthened through legal and regulatory reforms; education and training; stakeholder engagement; auditing and monitoring, encouraging meeting international standards, and best practices. However, African organisations seeking to reorganised their Boards must focus on strategy, reinvention, innovation, technological adoption, and board assessment among other things.

2

Opportunities, Challenges, and Risks: The African Business Environment

Franklin Ngwu, Okey Nwuke, and Emeka Agu

Introduction

With 54 countries and a land mass of about 30.37 million km², Africa has abundant and immeasurable opportunities. It is home to about 30% of the global mineral reserves, 8% of the global natural gas, 12% of the worldwide oil reserves, 40% of the worldwide gold, and 90% of the world's chromium and platinum (UNEP, 2022). Africa also has an enormous stockpile of diamonds, cobalt, uranium, and platinum in the world; 65% of the global arable land and 10% of the world's internal renewable freshwater source, hence more than 70% of people residing in Africa rely on forests and woodlands for their livelihoods (UNEP, 2022). There are projections that Africa's extractive resources could account for more than USD 30 billion yearly in government revenue for the next two decades (AfDB, 2016). In addition to the natural resources, Africa's human resource is also immense. It is projected that, by 2030, more than half of

F. Ngwu (✉) • O. Nwuke • E. Agu
Lagos Business School, Pan-Atlantic University, Lagos, Nigeria
e-mail: fngwu@lbs.edu.ng; onwuke@lbs.edu.ng; eagu@lbs.edu.ng

the global under-25 population will be in Africa, which, interestingly, will constitute about 60% of the global workforce (AfDB, 2016).

However, despite Africa's immense potential and opportunities, the continent's sustainable growth seems constrained by many challenges, with poverty and hunger pervasive. Nigeria, the biggest economy in Africa, is ranked as the world's poverty capital, with over 130 of its 220 million population classified as poor and inflation in November 2022 at about 2.47% (CBN, 2022). As it is in Nigeria, so it is in many other African countries with infrastructure deficit, high illiteracy and mortality rate, inequality, weak institutions, and poor leadership common challenges across the continent (World Bank, 2017; Susuman et al., 2015; Owoye & Bissessar, 2014). Even with the benefits of higher trade, mainly how it enhances growth and development, Africa still needs improvement, with intra-African trade at a deficient level of about 15% compared to other regions (UNCTAD, 2022). While intra-American and intra-European trades remain at 60% and 67%, respectively, that of Asia is about 46% (UNCTAD, 2022).

Expectedly, the inherent African challenges cause and manifest in different types of risk, such as insecurity, operational, regulatory, political, foreign exchange, governance, employee attrition, etc. With such a litany of known, emerging, and unknown risks, the African business environment can be described as volatile, uncertain, complex, and ambiguous (VUCA) and, in a cyclic manner, leads to more challenges and risks, consequently further retarding growth and development. Therefore, this chapter aims to critically examine the immense opportunities, challenges, and risks that pervade the African continent and provide insights into what can be done to mitigate the risks and challenges so that the opportunities can be better harnessed for more sustainable growth and development of Africa. The remaining sections of the chapter will proceed as follows. While section "The African Business Environment: Challenges and Risks" will provide detailed insights into the challenges and risks of doing business in Africa, section "Top Ten Risks Faced by Businesses in Africa" will focus more on the immense opportunities. Using the concepts of survival-based theory, value-based leadership theory, and case studies (Libya, Rwanda, and Nigeria), section "The African Business Environment: The Opportunities" will focus on what should be done to mitigate the challenges and risks to tap and benefit more from the abundant opportunities. Section "Managing the Challenges and Risks: Can Survival-Based and Value-Based Leadership Theories Help" will provide additional discussions, recommendations, and concluding remarks.

The African Business Environment: Challenges and Risks

Every continent in the world has its business challenges, risks, and opportunities; however, their degrees are likely dependent on the efforts of different nations to better mitigate the challenges and risks to harness and expand the business opportunities, possibly through simplifying the rules for ease of doing business. The business environment is crucial to any nation's economic growth and development. It offers opportunities for entrepreneurs to venture into various businesses to make a profit and improve their standard of living (Yu et al., 2023). The business environment is the totality of internal and external factors that affect an organisation's operating system, such as the clients, workers, leadership team, demand and supply, and business regulations (Hans, 2018). The unique features of a business environment are its dynamism, unpredictability, complexity, and multifaceted (Hans, 2018). In addition, internal and external factors can constrain the business environment. The external factors are outside the organisation's environment with the potential to affect its processes and performance, while the internal factors are within the organisation's environment with the capacity to influence its activities (Erdi & Bambang, 2021).

A business environment can be conducive/favourable, or hostile. A study has shown that intelligent business environments engender business assurance, reduce institutional costs, enhance investment opportunities (Yin et al., 2022), improve domestic economic growth, and attract high-quality foreign direct investment (Zhaoa et al., 2022). On the contrary, a hostile business environment impedes enterprise growth and productivity (Adamseged & Grundmann, 2020). The increasing difficulties of the business environment have propelled most organisations to make quick and effective decisions (Agostini & Spano, 2021). Hence, instituting a conducive business environment is essential for the growth of businesses and poverty alleviation (Estevão et al., 2022).

Risk is a warning that an event or action will negatively or positively affect the likelihood of achieving targets or goals in business, execution of the goals, and strategic plans (Kiseleva et al., 2018). Internal business risk emanates within the organisation, such as unproductive management, poor marketing policies, misuse of the organisation's position, personnel risk bothering on organisation's workers' professionalism and conduct, ineptitude, inexperience, paucity of information, overconfidence in the organisation's stakeholders, and excessive focus on quick profit with less emphasis on development possibilities, etc. (Belinskaja & Velickiene, 2015).

External risks are environmental factors that affect business effectiveness; hence, business professionals and owners cannot influence external risks but can forecast and consider their likely threats to their organisations (Belinskaja & Velickiene, 2015). External risks could be changes in the government's business regulations, political instability, wars, privatisation, strike, and embargoes on raw materials and finished goods (Belinskaja & Velickiene, 2015). Inadequate management of business risk usually results in the inability of businesses to compete effectively and consequent business failure (Amankwah-Amoah & Wang, 2019). Risks can redirect or reallocate business resources, resulting in cost distortions, supply curve changes, and deviations from business-set goals and objectives (Cavusgil et al., 2020). However, it enhances organisational sustainability when risks are adequately managed (Amankwah-Amoah & Wang, 2019).

Africa's population of more than 1.2 billion people is expected to get to 1.7 billion by 2030, and around 80% of Africa's population growth will occur in cities in the following decades, making it one of the rapidly urbanising continents in the world (Leke & Signé, 2019). It is reported that incomes are rising across the African continent, engendering new business opportunities in the consumer market—it is projected that the annual expenditure by African purchasers and firms will reach $6.66 trillion by 2030 (Signé, 2018). Africa's yearly spending on infrastructure has significantly increased to around $80 billion since the start of this century (Leke & Signé, 2019). Having the world's most enormous free trade territory and a 1.2-billion-person marketplace, Africa is building a novel development pathway and exploring the prospects of its human and natural resources (World Bank, 2022).

Despite the African continent's resources, prospects, and optimistic projections, it has various socio-economic, political, and environmental challenges. The risk associated with doing business in Africa, as identified by Asongu and Odhiambo (2018), include rising costs of starting and running a business, dearth of supporting infrastructures such as energy and electricity, inaccessibility to business loans, excessive taxation, and insignificant cross-border trade. These challenges have been exacerbated by the COVID-19 pandemic and the Russia/Ukraine war. Studies on risks and opportunities in the African business environment have focused on political risks (Meyer & Habanabakize, 2018; Agu et al., 2022); challenges in ease of doing business (Asongu & Odhiambo, 2018); climate risks (Crick et al., 2018); business challenges during COVID-19 pandemic (Gerald et al., 2020; Adeola et al., 2022); and dearth of infrastructure (Kinange & Patil, 2020). Focusing on the COVID-19 pandemic and the on-going Russia/Ukraine war, some of the challenges and risks to Africa include a high increase in food and fuel prices, unsettling trade of goods and services, restricting the financial sector, and limiting the flow of development finance in Africa (Sen, 2022).

Price Shocks

More than 30 countries depend on Russia and Ukraine for at least 30% of their wheat imports. In comparison, at least 20 countries depend on the two countries for over 50% of their wheat imports, consequently leaving these countries to be vulnerable to price shocks caused by scarcity and supply shortages (Hassen & Bilali, 2022). The Russia/Ukraine war has worsened the economic situation of most countries by increasing food prices, causing scarcity, and engendering a global food crisis, particularly in conflict-afflicted nations such as Ethiopia, Sudan, and Nigeria (Hassen & Bilali, 2022). In the Middle East/North Africa (MENA) region, countries such as Algeria, Egypt, Tunisia, and Morocco are not major importers of Russian and Ukrainian wheat. Their high energy revenues may compensate for higher food costs (Blanchard, 2022). However, Northern Africa can experience increased food prices capable of engendering fiscal crises because of the cost of government subsidies for basic foodstuffs (Blanchard, 2022).

Supply Disruption

The prices of wheat, sunflower, and crude oil in the global market have significantly increased, and most African countries are extremely dependent on importing these commodities from Russia and Ukraine (Sacko & Mayaki, 2022). Consequently, Africa is experiencing price hikes and interruptions in the supply chain of these commodities (Sacko & Mayaki, 2022). Though the level of trade between the African continent and Russia/Ukraine may need to be improved, some African nations depend on these warring countries to import wheat, fertilisers, and steel (Sen, 2022). An interruption in imports can, directly and indirectly, affect the African continent. North African countries such as Tunisia, Algeria, Libya, Morocco, and Egypt; South Africa; Ethiopia and Sudan in East Africa; and Nigeria in West Africa account for 80% of wheat imports (Sacko & Mayaki, 2022).

Kenya imported about 30% of its wheat from Russia and Ukraine in 2021; a supply interference would hamper bread production (the third most consumed food item) in Kenya; Cameroon imported 44% of its fertilisers from Russia in 2021, disrupting the supply chain could affect crop yields and worsen food security in West African region; Ghana import about 60% of iron ore and steel from Ukraine, the construction industry in Ghana is expected to face massive challenges because of the war (Sen, 2022). Wheat consumption in Africa is forecasted to reach 76.5 million tonnes by 2025, with 48.3 million tonnes or 63.4% expected to be imported from another continent (Sacko & Mayaki, 2022). Western nations' sanctions on the Russian government have limited trade between Russia and Africa because of port closure and restrictive movement in the Black Sea (Sacko & Mayaki, 2022).

Dwindling Government Revenues

The unforeseen COVID-19 pandemic and the Russia/Ukraine war have drastically decreased most African governments' trade and tax revenues; hence, nations are at risk of spending more with less coming into the national treasuries (Sen, 2022). In response to this, some countries are resorting to borrowing. Africa is borrowing at a high cost, and the detrimental effect of the war in Ukraine is imported inflation; for instance, in Tanzania, where the overall rate of inflation spiked by 34% between February and April 2022; in Namibia, transportation costs increased by 20% between March and April 2022; and in Cameroon, where food prices rose by 26% between February and March 2022 (Sen, 2022). Policy measures to curb inflation, such as increasing government subsidies, could hamper the already weak financial standings. At the same time, the shocking external lending requirements may stimulate capital outflows and add to growth barriers for nations with high debt obligations and massive financing needs (Kammer et al., 2022).

Food Insecurity

The actual effect of the Russia/Ukraine war is on any nation's economy that largely depends on oil and gas imports and exports, imported grain and fertiliser, tourism, etc., meaning that there are long-term consequences such as a potential geopolitical reorganisation, socio-economic instability, and unsustainable debt (Lusigi, 2022). The most glaring effect of the Russia/Ukraine war in Africa is the fuel and food price hikes, inflation, and fiscal instability; the poor and indigent members bore the immense burden as a huge percentage of society their consumption expenditure is on essential commodities and transport (Lusigi, 2022). The shock from the war is set further to complicate the fragile financial balance of most African nations: fiscal authorities are unprepared for more shocks after the COVID-19 pandemic; thus, 50% of Africa's low-income countries are already at a high risk of distress (Selassie & Kovacs, 2022).

Social Tensions

Social tension will arise when most nations have few policy measures to curb the impact of the shock from the Russia/Ukraine war (Kammer et al., 2022). The price hike can engender social tensions in some nations, particularly countries with fragile social safety nets, low job opportunities, and unpopular governments (Kammer et al., 2022). It can also engender conflict, riots, demonstrations, and violence in the food-production and food-consumption space (Burke & McGuirk, 2022). A report indicates that nations with the risk of conflict through the consumer price index (CPI) effect are Rwanda, The Gambia, Sierra Leone, Somalia, Swaziland/Eswatini, Central African Republic, Djibouti, Mozambique, South Africa, Zimbabwe, Ghana, Niger, and Mali (Burke & McGuirk, 2022). Another report revealed that Libya, South Sudan, the Central African Republic, Northern Mozambique, Ethiopia, and Cameroon's northwest and southwest regions are six African conflict zones to watch out for in 2022 (Institute for Security Studies, 2021). The Russia/Ukraine war may not directly impact the crises in Africa, but the shocks and economic and political effects can escalate the problem (Mwansa, 2022).

Poor Rating in the Ease of Doing Business Index

The nature of the business environment is a crucial factor in attracting investors and making investment decisions (Juvonen et al., 2019). Many African countries are ranked low globally in the ease of doing business. Eritrea, Libya, the Republic of the Congo, Chad, the Democratic Republic of the Congo, Central Africa, South Sudan, and Somalia are the lowest-ranked economies in Africa (World Bank, 2020a; and Kamer, 2022), hence designating them as unsuitable environments for investment decisions (Kamer, 2022). Bigger African economies such as Kenya, South Africa, Ghana, Nigeria, and the Democratic Republic of Congo were averagely ranked, attributing it to inefficient port services, poor power supply, and restrictions in cross-border trade (World Bank, 2020a). Mauritius, Rwanda, Morocco, and Kenya top the ranking on the ease of doing business index (Kamer, 2022) by reforming their business environments to become business-friendly destinations (Juvonen et al., 2019).

Top Ten Risks Faced by Businesses in Africa

Studies have examined the risks faced by businesses in Africa. Deloitte (2016) found that the top ten risks in the African business environment are legislation and regulation issues, infrastructure shortage, cyber security and data leaks, disruption in business and supply chain, third party intervention, business model, product adjustment, corporate governance, information management, and loss of business brand value.

A study by KPMG Nigeria in 2020 identified ten risks peculiar to the Nigerian business environment. The study gathered data from large corporations, of which 60% are private sector organisations and 40% are public sector organisations. Findings show that the top ten business risks in Nigeria are:

1. The regulatory risk, with a score of 3.69, depicts the difficulties organisations face in Nigeria's unpredictable regulatory and legislative environment, such as changes in taxation policies.
2. Fiscal and monetary policy risk, with a score of 3.60, is caused by the impact of the COVID-19 pandemic and the decline in oil prices.
3. With a score of 3.56, foreign exchange volatility risk is caused by importation and capital repatriation.
4. Cyber-security risk, with a score of 3.53, is caused by the advancement in digital technology for business innovations and agility.
5. The political risk, with a score of 3.50, is caused by business disruption because of political instability.
6. With a score of 3.43, technology infrastructure risk is caused by insufficient information technology infrastructure to support business needs.
7. Customer attrition risk, with a score of 3.42, is caused by failure to meet customers' expectations.
8. Talent shortage/attrition risk, with a score of 3.37, is caused by the dearth of skilled workers and talent.

9. Business continuity risk, with a score of 3.34, is caused by emergencies in the business environment, such as pandemics, crises, insurgency, climate change, and cyber-attacks.
10. Governance risk, with a score of 3.23, is caused by issues bordering on counterproductive frameworks, systems, or practices for managing organisations.

However, even with the litany of challenges and risks inherent in Africa, there are also immense opportunities. Business opportunities are described as the prospect of attaining a possible economic value by adopting a mixture of new resources and market requirements because of technological knowledge; customer needs changes, or the interdependence between economic players (Urban & Woods, 2015). A business opportunity is the potential of a productive market offer identified by a business owner (Filser et al., 2020). Studies show two business opportunities: innovative and arbitrage (Filser et al., 2020). Innovative opportunities are explored by creating new means or ends, while arbitrage opportunities emerge because of market inadequacies (Shin and Lee in Filser et al., 2020). Efficient management of risk and opportunities is seen as a competitive identifier component, aiding organisations to attain set targets amid turbulent economic environments (Ivascu & Cioca, 2014).

The African Business Environment: The Opportunities

There are massive opportunities in the African business environment for entrepreneurs with innovative ideas and strategic plans to solve Africa's challenges. This section presents such opportunities amid the devastating effects of the COVID-19 pandemic and the Russia/Ukraine war.

Population Growth

Africa's population of around 1.2 billion people is forecasted to rise to 1.7 billion by 2030. Over 80% of Africa's population growth in the following decades will occur in urban areas, projecting Africa as the world's fastest-urbanising continent (Leke & Signé, 2019). It is also projected that the yearly expenditure by African businesses and consumers will reach $6.66 trillion by 2030; these trends are enhancing emerging markets in different sectors where Africans have unfulfilled needs, such as health care, financial services, food, education, and pharmaceuticals (Leke & Signé, 2019). The vast African population can translate to a larger labour force, increasing production capacity, and boosting investment and savings (Bello-Schünemann, 2017). Other opportunities from Africa's vast population size include an increase in the Gross Domestic Product (GDP) and GDP per capita of various African countries, large numbers of wealthy Africans within and outside the African continent, increased number of the middle class in Africa and diaspora, a large number of secondary and university graduates in Africa, the increased political influence of Africa in the international community, and increased diaspora remittances to Africa (Kaba, in Kaba, 2020).

Digital Technology Development

Most studies have revealed that digital technologies are vital to solving socio-economic problems and are regarded as the exclusive component Africa needs to achieve sustainable and inclusive economic development (Duarte, 2021). In most African nations, digitisation has been utilised to overshadow local banking and telecommunications facilities, assisting businesses to innovate and scale up operations (Chivunga & Tempest, 2017). Trade can be stimulated by adopting digital applications throughout the value chain. Machine learning can be used for translation purposes, which presents significant opportunities for businesses domiciled in Africa's multilingual marketplaces; e-learning gives opportunities for both public and private learning and training, which is pertinent to enhancing the skills required; three-dimensional (3D) printing has been seen as a manufacturing solution for Africa—bringing manufacturing plants back to the local environment; e-government can utilise 4IR technologies to minimise bureaucratic bottlenecks for both citizens and organisations; and data analytics can help African governments and organisations make more informed decisions (Chivunga & Tempest, 2017).

With the African Union's digital transformation strategy (2020–2030), African countries are set to enjoy (a) a protected digital single market by 2030, guaranteeing free movement of people, finance, and services to enable entrepreneurs to have access to online activities; (b) create a collaborative environment critical to assuring funding and investment (digital sovereignty fund) to bridge the digital infrastructure gap and provide access to economical and secure broadband; (c) synchronise laws, policies, and regulations to improve digital networks and services and bolster intra-Africa trade, investments, and capital flows (d) execute laws, policies, and regulations to accelerate digital transformation Africa's development; (e) and provision of a significant online e-skills development programme to ICT education and knowledge sharing to 100 million Africans in 2021 and 300 million by 2025 (African Union, 2020).

Abundant Natural Resources

Africa is blessed with enormous natural resource wealth. The continent has the world's largest arable landmass, the longest rivers, and the second-biggest tropical forest (African Development Bank, 2016). It is estimated that the value added of Africa's fisheries and aquaculture sector is over USD 24 billion; 30% of the world's mineral reserves are in Africa; oil reserves make up 8% of the global stock and 7% of natural gas; minerals constitute over 70% of total African exports and 28% of gross domestic product (African Development Bank, 2016). Africa also has the most significant stockpile of diamonds, cobalt, uranium, and platinum in the world; 65% of the global arable land and 10% of the world's internal renewable freshwater source, hence more than 70% of people residing in Africa rely on forests and woodlands for their livelihoods (UNEP, 2022). There are projections that Africa's extractive resources could account for more than USD 30 billion yearly in government revenue for the next two decades (AfDB, 2016). In addition to the natural resources, Africa's human resource is also immense. It is projected that by 2030, more than half of the global under-25 population will be in Africa, which interestingly will constitute about 60% of the global workforce (AfDB, 2016).

African Continental Free Trade Area (AfCFTA)

The AfCFTA is the world's biggest free trade area comprising 55 nations of the African Union (AU) and 8 Regional Economic Communities (RECs) (AfCFTA, 2022). The broad objective of the AfCFTA is to create a sole continental market with an estimated population of about 1.2 billion people and an expected GDP of US$ 3.4 trillion (AfCFTA, 2022). AfCFTA offers an excellent opportunity for African nations to lift bh30 million people out of acute poverty and to increase the incomes of 68 million people who live below $5.50 per day (World Bank, 2020b). Implementing AfCFTA is expected to cut custom bureaucratic procedures and facilitate trade which will drive $292 billion of the $450 billion in expected income gains (World Bank, 2020b).

The AfCFTA is one of the projects of Agenda 2063: The Africa We Want, the African Union's long-term development strategy for transforming the continent into a world powerhouse (AfCFTA, 2022). AfCFTA is mandated to remove trade barriers and increase intra-Africa trade, particularly to facilitate trade in value-added production in all service sectors of the African economy (AfCFTA, 2022) and long-term peace and security (Fofack, 2020). The AfCFTA will enhance the creation of African regional value chains, engendering investment and employment opportunities (Fofack, 2020). AfCFTA can stimulate and boost Africa's competitiveness in the medium to long term (Fofack, 2020). As the COVID-19 pandemic disrupts the world economy, establishing the vast AfCFTA regional market offers a huge opportunity to assist African nations in expanding their exports, stimulating growth, and attracting foreign direct investment (World Bank, 2020b). AfCFTA is expected to alleviate the poverty of about 30 million Africans, increase income by $450 billion, and overly enlarge the size of the single African market to $6.7 trillion in the next 10 years (Sen, 2022).

Managing the Challenges and Risks: Can Survival-Based and Value-Based Leadership Theories Help

The necessity to adequately mitigate the challenges and risks to better harness the opportunities in the African business environment calls for adopting survival-based and value-based leadership theories. The concept of survival-based theory was initially developed by Herbert Spencer (Miesing and Preble, in Abdullah, 2010). The survival-based theory in strategic management perspective argues that organisational survival strategies depend on formulating and executing strategies around managing business operations and expeditiously responding to the changes in the business environment (Khairuddin, Abdullah, 2010). An organisation must evolve in tandem with the ever-changing business environment to ensure it is possible changing for such an organisation to survive; hence, successful businesses in turbulent and rapidly changing environments are those that effectively adapt to their environment (Abdullah, 2010).

The emergence of value-based leadership theory is attributed to the work of House, R. J., Hanges, P. J., Javidan, M., Dorfman, P. W., and Gupta, V., in the year 2004 (House et al., 2004). The beginning of the twenty-first century was beset with large-scale and discouraging leadership deficiency; moral and ethical failures were predominant in most charismatic, dynamic, and transformational leaders in top positions in the public and private sectors (Copeland, 2014). Consequently, leadership and management theorists focused on the imperativeness of ethics and morality in exemplary leaders; hence, the emphasis on values-based leadership (VBL) theories surfaced (Copeland, 2014). VBL encompasses servant, ethical, and authentic leadership and intent to examine the value of providing management value (Lemoine et al., in Chang et al., 2021). Today's leaders must lead with purpose, values, and integrity; build lasting institutions; motivate followers to provide quality service, and create lasting value for shareholders (George, in Copeland, 2014). The VBL concept is significant to nations' socio-political and economic well-being (Sumanasiri, 2020).

The African business environment is characterised by its turbulent and unpredictable nature. In the past decades, African countries have contended with crises, conflicts, wars, famine, droughts, humanitarian issues, economic shocks, leadership challenges, etc. The COVID-19 pandemic and the Russia/Ukraine war further exacerbate these. As such, there is a need for leaders with true purpose, willpower, values, and integrity to find pathways and policy directions, build enduring institutions, and get the best people to implement policies for the interest of Africans. As survival-based theory argues, the African business environment must be flexible to adequately adapt to the ever-turbulent, volatile, and changing climate caused by internal and external factors. In some cases, a better understanding and application of survival-based and value-based leadership theories can be further illustrated.

Case Study 1: The Rwandan Tourism Industry

The tourism industry is one of the mainstays of the Rwandan economy (Geoffrey et al., 2019). The industry has about 7000 hospitality organisations, such as restaurants, hotels, bars, and accommodation establishments in all of the nation, with more than 84,000 employees (Rwanda Hoteliers' Association, in Rwigema, 2020). The Rwandan Meetings, Incentives, Conferences and Exhibitions (MICE) Tourism and the hospitality sector generate an average of 142,000 jobs. Still, due to the COVID-19 pandemic, Hotels in Rwanda reported a loss of over Rwf13 billion (Rwanda Hoteliers' Association, in Rwigema, 2020). As tourism was one of the sectors severely affected by the COVID-19 outbreak, the Rwandan government initiated and executed various strategies to rescue the sector, such as the Rwf100billion Economic Recovery Fund, where 50% of the fund was earmarked to the tourism and hospitality sector (Rwandan Development Board, 2022). This fund and tax relief measures for investors were aimed at assisting hotel owners in balancing their bank loans and recovering financially (Hajbi, 2022).

Once the financial stability of the stakeholders in the tourism industry was nearly achieved, the Rwandan government implemented a mass vaccination drive of the sector's workforce, such as hotels, bars, and restaurants staff, national park agents, and airport workers; suspended various hotel and restaurants in Rwanda for a short period; and imposed fines of 150,000 to 300,000 Rwandan francs (from $145 to $290) for neglecting the established health and safety guidelines (Hajbi, 2022). This was aimed at fostering an atmosphere of assuredness and safety to attract tourists and investors to Rwanda (Hajbi, 2022). These strategies paid off. The total revenue from Rwandan tourism increased by 25%, from US$131 million in 2020 to US$ 164 million in 2021, while the MICE sector brought in US$12.5 million in 2021 compared to US$5.4illion in 2020 (Rwandan Development Board, 2022). The number of tourists in Rwanda rose by 2.8%, from 490,000 in the year 2020 to 512,000 in the year 2021, and this is attributed to the sports events hosted during the year 2021, which led to significant tourist arrivals and massive returns (Rwandan Development Board, 2022).

Over the last ten years, Rwanda has executed a profitable doing-business reform agenda to provide a competitive and conducive business environment. Consequently, Rwanda skipped over 100 places in the World Bank Doing Business Index and now placed 38th and 2nd in the global and African rankings, respectively (Republic of Rwanda, 2022). Zephanie Niyonkuru, the deputy director-general of the Rwanda Development Board (RDB), stated that the authority is poised:

To make Rwanda the best country in Africa, the approach is simple - the country is green, clean and safe. It is open to entrepreneurs and tourists, to whom we roll out the red carpet and for whom access to entry visas has been simplified. (Rwanda Development Board, 2022)

Case Study 2: Nigeria's Dadin Hausa Dam/ Olam Rice Farmland

Nigeria has sufficient surface water bodies and proper dam locations that could be used to construct dams to build storage sites for numerous water uses, such as irrigation, tourism, hydropower generation, flood management, and aquaculture (Ezugwu, 2013). Reports indicate that Cameroon and Nigeria in the late 1970 s were supposed to embark on constructing two dams—Cameroon's Lagdo Dam and Nigeria's Dasin Hausa dam (Abah & Petja, 2017; Aljazeera, 2022; Odifa, 2022; and Abiodun, 2022). The Lagdo dam was successfully constructed between 1977 and 1982 to generate electricity in Cameroon's northern part and assist in irrigation (Abiodun, 2022). The Dasin Hausa Dam, sited in the Adamawa State of Nigeria, still needs to be completed to control the discharged water from the Lagdo Dam and prevent flooding (Odifa, 2022). Consequently, the unavailability of dams to handle the excess water from the Lagdo Dam has resulted in flooding the forefront states and communities along rivers Niger and Benue (Abiodun, 2022).

In 2012, the release of excess water from the Lagdo Dam caused massive flooding with the following devastating effects (Abah & Petja, 2017):

(a) Destruction of 6000 houses and displaced 7 million people, and losses amounted to over $12bn.
(b) Deaths of hundreds of Nigerians and the destruction of hundreds of thousands of hectares of farmland were highly severe.
(c) Humanitarian crisis as internally displaced people (IDP) camps were overpopulated with little or no aid materials.
(d) Food insecurity resulting from losing massive farmlands to flood became pronounced.
(e) Public health challenges from waterborne diseases were rampant.
(f) Migration to neighbouring communities and poverty became the order of the day.

In 2015, there was a report of 53 death, and more than 100,000 people were forced to leave their communities due to flooding; in 2016, 92,000 people lost their houses and businesses, and 38 people died from flooding; in 2017, environmental devastation from flooding affected more than 250,000 individuals in Nigeria's eastern-central region; in 2018, flooding claimed about 200 lives in Delta, Anambra, Kogi, and Niger state, respectively (Odifa, 2022). In 2022, the story did not change; instead, it worsened. Nigeria suffered its worst flooding in the last ten years, with massive hectares of farmland, infrastructural facilities and 200,000 houses, partially or entirely, damaged; hundreds of people have died, over 2400 people injured, and more than 1.4 million displaced (Maclean, 2022; Aljazeera, 2022).

Olam Rice Farm is one of the most prominent private investors in rice farms in West Africa, but it was severely hit by flooding in October 2022. The company is in Rukubi village Doma Local Government of Nasarawa State, with 13,500 hectares of land and over 4400 hectares extensively developed for double cropping of wet and dry seasons (Rabiu, 2022). The agri-business company, in recent times, increased its milling capability from 120 to 240 metric tonnes yearly, aimed at complementing the Nigerian government's effort to ensure food availability and security (Ewepu, 2022). The business head and vice president of Olam rice farm, Anil Nair, said:

> *Over $15 million worth of planted crops are under water as flood submerged 4500 hectares of Olam rice farmland in Nassarawa State. Other damages included infrastructures such as dykes, canals, and drainage worth $8 million. The huge losses can only be estimated once the water recedes.* (Egboboh, 2022)

Case Study 3: Libya and Nigeria's Crude Oil Underproduction

Libya and Nigeria are among the oil-exporting countries in Africa. The resultant effect of the Russia/Ukraine war raised oil prices to an average of $108 per barrel at the beginning of March 2022 (Irede, 2022). Ideally, this presented an excellent opportunity for oil-exporting countries globally, particularly in Africa, to make huge revenues and cushion the devastating impact of the COVID-19 pandemic. Shockingly, Libya and Nigeria still needed to maximise this opportunity fully. A report from USAID's Libya Public Financial Management (LPFM) shows that the projections for Libya's oil revenue in February and March 2022 because of the oil price hike would amount to a $12.5 billion trade surplus (USAID, 2022). However, the political protest led to the closure of oil fields and ports in Libya (Rahman, 2022). Due to the closure of the Al-Feel and Sharara oil fields and the Zueitina and Brega oil ports in April 2022, the LPFM reported that the trade surplus would be considerably lower than that of 2021 because of the hitches; however, the trade surplus of $4.9 billion was considered positive since it was marginally higher than that of 2021's trade surplus of $4.2 billion (USAID, 2022), which is a significant loss to the Libyan government when considering the revenue it would have amassed.

Reports show that Nigeria needs to attain the daily oil production quota assigned by the Organisation of Petroleum Exporting Countries (OPEC). Stats from OPEC reveal that:

(a) Nigeria tops the list of oil-producing nations with the highest deficit globally, producing 1.238 million barrels per day in March 2022 at the expense of OPEC's fixed 1.718 million barrels per day production quota.
(b) With the global oil price at an average of $117.25 per barrel in March 2022 and Nigeria's deficit of 480,000 barrels per day amounting to 14.88 million barrels for the 31 days of March 2022, the country shockingly lost an estimated $1.74bn in March 2022.
(c) Nigeria's OPEC oil quota for April 2022 was 1.735 million barrels per day. With global oil prices at an average of $104.58 per barrel, Nigeria earned around $3.82bn for producing 1.219 million barrels daily, making an estimated loss of over $1.61bn (Irede, 2022).

Studies have shown that the country's inability to meet the OPEC's quota is due to insecurity in the Niger Delta region, illegal refineries, oil theft, poor governance, vandalisation of crucial oil infrastructures, corruption, etc. (Abomaye-Nimenibo et al., 2020; Nwokolo & Aghedo, 2018; Agbana, 2022; Duruji et al., 2019; Okolie-Osemene, 2018; Tantua et al., 2018; Oyewole, 2018; and Chikwem & Duru, 2018).

Discussions

As earlier indicated, the inherent challenges and risks in Africa have been exacerbated by COVID-19 and the ongoing Russia/Ukraine war. While most African countries were addressing the challenges caused by the COVID-19 pandemic and rebuilding their economies in the post-COVID-19 pandemic era, the Russia/Ukraine war has hampered Africa's efforts and optimistic recovery. The import-driven nature of the African economy is a considerable risk as it is susceptible to external shocks. These shocks have resulted in a hike in food and fuel prices, food insecurity, interruptions in the supply chain, inflation, dwindling government revenue, extreme poverty, political and socio-economic instability, unsustainable debt, and unconducive business environments for investment decisions.

The inability of most African countries to manage their risks to tap and expand business opportunities can be linked to leadership and adaptability issues. The chapter's case studies 2 and 3 aptly demonstrate the role of leadership in policy formulation and implementation in solving public problems to achieve socio-economic and political development. The failure of the Nigeria government to complete the Dasin Hausa Dam has destroyed many lives and properties in most regions of Nigeria. The Dasin Hausa Dam project has gone through over ten successive governments in Nigeria (Abah & Petja, 2017) from 1982 to 2022 (40 years) and has yet to be completed.

The leadership tussle in Libya led to the closure of oil fields and ports in a period where the country is expected to earn substantial revenue from global oil price hikes. While in Nigeria, cases of oil pipe vandalism, oil theft, subsidy scam, and militancy have hindered Nigeria's crude oil production from meeting OPEC's daily quota. Consequently, these pose threats to lives, properties, and businesses (the case of Olam Rice Farmland in Nigeria and Libya's low oil trade surplus). Nigeria's national oil company has been unable to generate reasonable revenues into the government account in 2022 as it disburses about $23.8 m daily on fuel subsidy payment, a development the World Bank has depicted as risky, and the IMF projects that fuel subsidy payments can rise to $11.9bn in 2022 (Irede, 2022).

Mauritius and Rwanda are highly ranked in the ease of doing business index because they have reformed their business environments into business-friendly destinations (Juvonen et al. 2022). The chapter's case study 1 aptly illustrated how the Rwandan government was able to revive the tourism sector after a devastating COVID-19 pandemic. By providing incentives to hospitality organisations, the Rwf100billion Economic

Recovery Fund, and other strategies to stabilise the financial base of the tourism stakeholders and build trust and attractive business environments for tourism investors.

Conclusion and Recommendations

The chapter concludes that most African governments, businesses, and individuals struggle to cope with risks and challenges from the post-COVID-19 pandemic and Russia/Ukraine war. However, amid these risks and challenges, opportunities abound in the African business environment for public and private sector organisations genuinely desirous of solving Africa's problems through innovation and value creation.

In line with the theoretical framework of this chapter, African leaders must lead with integrity, willpower, true purpose, and values to find pragmatic solutions to Africa's problems. African leaders must find pathways and policy directions and build effective teams and strong institutions to implement reforms and policies for Africa's socioeconomic and political development.

African governments and businesses must rapidly respond to global and African business environment changes to minimise the threats and shocks currently facing most African economies. Conducive and supportive business environments must be pursued in Africa to attract investors and encourage indigenous businesses. Lastly, African governments and businesses must efficiently capitalise, manage, and maximise the opportunities (population, natural resources, digital technology development, and the AfCFTA) in the continent's environment for a self-sufficient Africa.

References

Abah, R. C., & Petja, B. M. (2017). Increased streamflow dynamics and implications for flooding in the Lower River Benue Basin. *African Journal of Environmental Science and Technology, 11*(10), 544–555. https://doi.org/10.5897/AJEST2015.2069

Abdullah, T. C. M. (2010). Profit maximisation theory, survival-based theory and contingency theory: A review on several underlying research theories of corporate turnaround. *Jurnal Ekonom, 13*(4), 136–143.

Abiodun, A. (2022, October 18). *Quick facts about Cameroon's Lagdo Dam causing floods in Nigeria*. https://thenationonlineng.net/quick-facts-about-cameroons-lagdo-dam-causing-floods-in-nigeria/

Abomaye-Nimenibo, W. A. S., Umana, E. A., & Inyang, I. E. (2020). The snags in post amnesty militancy in the Niger Delta region of Nigeria: The curative therapy by past. *Global Journal of Management and Business Research: B Economics and Commerce, 20*(5), 38–51.

Adamseged, M. E., & Grundmann, P. (2020). Understanding business environments and success factors for emerging bioeconomy enterprises through a comprehensive analytical framework. *Sustainability, 12*, 1–18. https://doi.org/10.3390/su12219018

Adeola, O., Agu, E. R., & Ibelegbu, O. (2022). Stakeholders' communications in online setting: A sub-Saharan African perspective during COVID-19 pandemic lockdown. In P. Foroudi, B. Nguyen, & T. C. Melewar (Eds.), *The emerald handbook of multi-stakeholder communication* (pp. 433–449). Emerald Publishing Limited. https://doi.org/10.1108/978-1-80071-897-520221034

AfCFTA. (2022). *About the AfCFTA*. https://au-afcfta.org/about/

African Development Bank Group (AfDB). (2016). Catalysing growth and development through effective natural resources management. *African Natural Resources Center*. https://www.afdb.org/fileadmin/uploads/afdb/Documents/Publications/anrc/AfDB_ANRC_BROCHURE_en.pdf

African Union. (2020). *The digital transformation strategy for Africa (2020–2030)*. https://au.int/en/documents/20200518/digital-transformation-strategy-africa-2020-2030

Agbana, Z. E. (2022). The uprising militancy as it affects development in Nigeria (a case study of Niger Delta). *International Journal of Peace and Conflict Studies, 7*(3), 78–89. http://journals.rcmss.com/index.php/ijpcs/article/view/645

Agostini, M., & Spano, A. (2021). Big data and business analytics: Definitions and implications in the business environment. In M. S. Chiucchi, R. Lombardi, & D. Mancini (Eds.), *Intellectual capital, smart technologies, and digitalization. SIDREA series in accounting and business administration*. Springer. https://doi.org/10.1007/978-3-030-80737-5_8

Agu, E., Adeola, O., Ibelegbu, O., & Esho, E. (2022). Public relations in Africa's public sector: A crisis situational analysis of South Africa and Nigeria. In O. Adeola, P. Katuse, & K. Twum (Eds.), *Public sector marketing communications, Palgrave studies of public sector management in Africa* (Vol. 1, pp. 147–176). Palgrave Macmillan. https://doi.org/10.1007/978-3-031-07293-2_7

Aljazeera. (2022, October 17). *Nigeria flood death toll tops 600 as thousands evacuated*. https://www.aljazeera.com/news/2022/10/17/nigeria-flood-death-toll-rises-as-thousands-evacuated

Amankwah-Amoah, J., & Wang, X. (2019). Opening editorial: Contemporary business risks: An overview and new research agenda. *Journal of Business Research, 97*, 208–211. https://doi.org/10.1016/j.jbusres.2019.01.036

Asongu, S. A., & Odhiambo, N. M. (2018). Challenges of doing business in Africa: A systematic review. *African Governance and Development Institute, WP/18/057*, 1–16. https://doi.org/10.4324/9780429331961-8

Belinskaja, L., & Velickiene, M. (2015). Business risk management: Features and problems in small and medium-sized trading and manufacturing enterprises. *European Scientific Journal, 2*, 30–58. https://eujournal.org/index.php/esj/article/view/5753/5549

Bello-Schünemann, J. (2017). *African governments aren't investing enough in one of their greatest assets – A young population*. https://issafrica.org/iss-today/africas-population-boom-burden-or-opportunity

Blanchard, C. M. (2022). Middle East and North Africa: Implications of 2022 Russia-Ukraine war. *Congressional Research Service*. https://sgp.fas.org/crs/mideast/R47160.pdf

Burke, M., & McGuirk, E. (2022). War in Ukraine, world food prices, and conflict in Africa. *The Centre for Economic Policy Research (CEPR) Report*. https://cepr.org/voxeu/columns/war-ukraine-world-food-prices-and-conflict-africa

Cavusgil, S. T., Deligonul, S., Ghauri, P. N., Bamiatzi, V., Park, B. I., & Mellahi, K. (2020). Risk in international business and its mitigation. *Journal of World Business, 55*(2), 101078. https://doi.org/10.1016/j.jwb.2020.101078

CBN. (2022). *Inflation rate*. https://www.cbn.gov.ng/rates/inflrates.asp

Chang, S. M., Budhwar, P., & Crawshaw, J. (2021). The emergence of value-based leadership behavior at the frontline of management: A role theory perspective and future research agenda. *Frontiers in Psychology*. https://doi.org/10.3389/fpsyg.2021.635106

Chikwem, F. C., & Duru, J. C. (2018). The resurgence of the Niger Delta militants and the survival of the Nigerian state. *The Round Table, 107*(1), 45–55. https://doi.org/10.1080/00358533.2018.1424074

Chivunga, M., & Tempest, A. (2017). Digital disruption in Africa: Mapping innovations for the AfCFTA in post-COVID times. *South African Institute of International Affairs*. https://www.jstor.org/stable/pdf/resrep28288.pdf

Copeland, M. K. (2014). The emerging significance of values-based leadership: A literature review. *International Journal of Leadership Studies, 2*(8). https://www.regent.edu/journal/international-journal-of-leadership-studies/significance-of-values-based-leadership/

Crick, F., Eskander, S. M. S., Fankhauser, S., & Diop, M. (2018). How do African SMEs respond to climate risks? Evidence from Kenya and Senegal. *World Development, 108*, 157–168.

Deloitte. (2016). *Your essential guide to de-risking Africa: Unlocking the value in Africa*. https://www2.deloitte.com/za/en/pages/risk/articles/de-risking-africa.html

Duarte, C. (2021). Africa goes digital. *IMF Report*. https://www.imf.org/en/Publications/fandd/issues/2021/03/africas-digital-future-after-COVID19-duarte

Duruji, M. M., Olanrewaju, F. O., & Duruji-Moses, F. U. (2019). Youth and Nigeria's internal security management. In O. Oshita, I. Alumona, & F. Onuoha (Eds.), *Internal security Management in Nigeria*. Palgrave Macmillan. https://doi.org/10.1007/978-981-13-8215-4_29

Egboboh, C. (2022). *Olam counts losses as flood submerges rice farm in Nasarawa*. https://businessday.ng/news/article/olam-counts-losses-as-flood-submerges-rice-farm-in-nasarawa/.

Erdi, H., & Bambang, R. (2021). The influence of the external and internal business environment on the marketing strategy and their impact on the marketing performance. *European Journal of Business and Management, 13*(7), 54–61.

Estevão, J., Lopes, J. D., & Penela, D. (2022). The importance of the business environment for the informal economy: Evidence from the doing business ranking. *Technological Forecasting and Social Change, 174*, 121288. https://doi.org/10.1016/j.techfore.2021.121288

Ewepu, G. (2022, October 11). *Flood ravages, and submerges $15m worth of Olam Rice Farm in Nasarawa*. https://www.vanguardngr.com/2022/10/flood-ravages-submerges-15m-worth-olam-rice-farm-in-nasarawa/

Ezugwu, C. N. (2013). Dam development and disasters in Nigeria. *International Journal of Engineering Research and Technology (IJERT), 2*(9), 960–977. https://doi.org/10.17577/IJERTV2IS90087

Filser, M., Tiberius, V., Kraus, S., Zeitlhofer, T., Kailer, N., & Müller, A. (2020). Opportunity recognition: Conversational foundations and pathways ahead. *Entrepreneurship Research Journal*, 1–30. https://doi.org/10.1515/erj-2020-0124

Fofack, H. (2020). Making the AfCFTA work for 'The Africa We Want'. Working Paper: *Africa Growth Initiative at Brookings*. https://www.brookings.edu/wp-content/uploads/2020/12/20.12.28-AfCFTA_Fofack.pdf

Geoffrey, M., Mark, Y., & Odunga, P. (2019). Total economic impact of tourism on Rwanda's economy and its linkages with other sectors of the economy. *Ottoman Journal of Tourism and Management Research, 4*(3), 534–547. https://doi.org/10.26465/ojtmr.2018339526

Gerald, E., Obianuju, A., & Chukwunonso, N. (2020). Strategic agility and performance of small and medium enterprises in the phase of the Covid-19 pandemic. *International Journal of Financial, Accounting, and Management, 2*(1), 41–50.

Hajbi, M. (2022, July 26). Rwanda: How tourism is getting back on track. *The African Report*. https://www.theafricareport.com/226710/rwanda-how-tourism-is-getting-back-on-track/

Hans, V. B. (2018). Business environment – Conceptual framework and policies. *International Educational Scientific Research Journal, 4*(3), 67–74.

Hassen, B. T., & Bilali, E. H. (2022). Impacts of the Russia-Ukraine war on global food security: Towards more sustainable and resilient food systems? *Food, 11*, 2301. https://doi.org/10.3390/foods11152301

House, R. J., Hanges, P. J., Javidan, M., Dorfman, P. W., & Gupta, V. (2004). *Culture, leadership, and organisations. The globe study of 62 societies*. Sage Publications.

Irede, A. (2022, June 30). Missing out: Russia/Ukraine: Nigeria records over $5.6bn revenue shortfall despite rising oil prices. *The African Report*. https://www.theafricareport.com/218845/russia-ukraine-nigeria-records-over-5-6bn-revenue-shortfall-despite-rising-oil-prices/

Ivascu, L., & Cioca, L. (2014). Opportunity risk: Integrated approach to risk management for creating enterprise opportunities. In *2nd international conference on psychology, management, and social science* (pp. 1–5).

Juvonen, K., Kumar, A., Ben, A. H., & Marin, A. O. (2019). Unleashing the potential of institutional investors in Africa. *Working paper series*, 325. African Development Bank.

Kaba, A. (2020). Explaining Africa's rapid population growth, 1950 to 2020: Trends, factors, implications, and recommendations. *Sociology Mind, 10*, 226–268. https://doi.org/10.4236/sm.2020.104015

Kamer, L. (2022, September 13). Ease of doing business in African countries 2020. *Statista Report*. https://www.statista.com/statistics/1227392/ease-or-doing-business-in-african-countries/

Kammer, A., Azour, J., Selassie, A. A., Goldfajn, I., & Rhee, C. (2022). How war in Ukraine is reverberating across World's regions. *IMF Regional Economies Report*. https://www.imf.org/en/Blogs/Articles/2022/03/15/blog-how-war-in-ukraine-is-reverberating-across-worlds-regions-031522

Kinange, U., & Patil, N. (2020). Business environment: The concept and a literature review. In *11th international conference on shifting paradigm in business economy and society: Vision 2050*. Faculty of Management, Pacific University.

Kiseleva, I. A., Karmanov, M. V., Korotkov, A. V., Kuznetsov, V. I., & Gasparian, M. S. (2018). Risk management in business: Concept, types, evaluation criteria. *Revista Espacios Management, 39*(27), 1–18. https://www.revistaespacios.com/a18v39n27/a18v39n27p18.pdf

KPMG. (2020). *Top 10 business risks in 2020/2021*. https://assets.kpmg/content/dam/kpmg/ng/pdf/advisory/top-10-business-risks-in-2020-2021.pdf

Leke, A., & Signé, L. (2019). *Spotlighting opportunities for business in Africa and strategies to succeed in the world's next big growth market*. https://www.brookings.edu/research/spotlighting-opportunities-for-business-in-africa-and-strategies-to-succeed-in-the-worlds-next-big-growth-market/

Lusigi, A. (2022). Africa and the Russia-Ukraine conflict: Seizing the opportunity in the crisis. *United Nations Africa Renewal*. https://www.un.org/africarenewal/magazine/africa-and-russia-ukraine-conflict-seizing-opportunity-crisis#:~:text=The%20most%20visible%20impact%20of,is%20on%20food%20and%20transport

Maclean, R. (2022, October 17). *Nigeria floods kill hundreds and displace over a million*. https://www.nytimes.com/2022/10/17/world/africa/nigeria-floods.html

Meyer, D. F., & Habanabakize, T. (2018). An analysis of the relationship between foreign direct investment (FDI), political risk, and economic growth in South Africa. *Business and Economic Horizons, 14*(4), 777–788. https://doi.org/10.15208/beh.2018.54

Mwansa, R. (2022). Analysis of the Russia-Ukraine war's consequences on sustainable livelihoods of refugees in Africa. *American Journal of Interdisciplinary Research and Innovation, 1*(1), 14–24. https://doi.org/10.54536/ajiri.v1i1.362

Nwokolo, N., & Aghedo, I. (2018). Consolidating or corrupting the peace? The power elite and amnesty policy in the Niger Delta region of Nigeria. *Chinese Political Science Review, 3*, 322–344. https://doi.org/10.1007/s41111-018-0098-y

Odifa, D. (2022, October 24). *Explainer: A tale of two dams and ignored warnings.* https://businessday.ng/business-economy/article/explainer-a-tale-of-two-dams-and-ignored-warnings/

Okolie-Osemene, J. (2018). Nigeria: Perceptions of disarmament, demobilisation and reintegration Modelling. Challenges and prospects for peace in Niger delta. *Conflict Studies Quarterly Issue, 24*, 26–43. https://doi.org/10.24193/csq.24.3

Owoye, O., & Bissessar, N. (2014). *Corruption in African countries: A symptom of leadership and institutional failure.* https://doi.org/10.1007/978-3-319-03143-9_15

Oyewole, S. (2018). Flying and bombing: The contributions of air power to security and crisis management in the Niger Delta region of Nigeria. *Defence Studies, 18*(4), 514–537. https://doi.org/10.1080/14702436.2018.1524709

Rabiu, M. (2022). *Floods: Olam Rice farm rescues 3,805 victims in five Nasarawa communities.* https://leadership.ng/floods-olam-rice-farm-rescues-3805-victims-in-five-nasarawa-communities/

Rahman, F. (2022, April 18). *Libya's NOC shuts down Zueitina oil port and Al Sharara field, warning of more closures.* https://www.thenationalnews.com/business/energy/2022/04/18/libyas-noc-shuts-down-zueitina-oil-port-and-warns-of-more-closures/

Republic of Rwanda. (2022). *Highlight: Economy and business.* https://www.gov.rw/highlights/economy-and-business

Rwandan Development Board.(2022). *RDB records the highest investment registration amid the COVID-19 pandemic.* https://rdb.rw/rdb-records-highest-investment-registration-amid-covid-19-pandemic/

Rwigema, P. C. (2020). Impact of Covid-19 pandemic on meetings, incentives, conferences, and exhibitions (Mice) tourism in Rwanda. *The Strategic Journal of Business and Change Management, 7*(3), 395–409.

Sacko, J. and Mayaki, I. (2022, April 21). How the Russia-Ukraine conflict impacts Africa: An opportunity to build resilient, inclusive Food Systems in

Africa. *United Nations Africa Renewal.* https://www.un.org/africarenewal/magazine/may-2022/how-russia-ukraine-conflict%C2%A0impacts-africa

Selassie, A. A., & Kovacs, P. (2022, April 28). Africa Faces New Shock as War Raises Food and Fuel Costs. *International Monetary Fund (IMF).* https://www.imf.org/en/Blogs/Articles/2022/04/28/blog-africa-faces-new-shock-as-war-raises-food-fuel-costs

Sen, A. K. (2022, June 15). Russia's war in Ukraine is taking a toll on Africa. *United State Institute of Peace.* https://www.usip.org/publications/2022/06/russias-war-ukraine-taking-toll-africa

Sheth, J. N., & Sisodia, R. S. (2006). How to reform marketing. Does marketing need reform?: Fresh perspectives on the future. In J. N. Sheth & R. S. Sisodia (Eds.), *Fresh perspectives on the future* (pp. 324–333). Routledge.

Signé, L. (2018). *Africa's consumer market's potential: Trends, drivers, opportunities, and strategies.* Brookings Institutions' Africa Growth Initiative Report.

Sumanasiri, E. A. G. (2020). Value-based organisational leadership: A literature review. *Journal of Economics Management and Trade, 26*(4), 92–104. https://doi.org/10.9734/JEMT/2020/v26i430259

Susuman, A. S., Ningpuanyeh, W. C., Bado, A., & Abraham, Y. (2015). High infant mortality rate, high total fertility rate and very low female literacy in selected African countries. *Scandinavian Journal of Public Health, 44*(1). https://doi.org/10.1177/1403494815604765

Tantua, B., Devine, J., & Maconachie, R. (2018). Oil governance in Nigeria's Niger Delta: Exploring the role of the militias. *The Extractive Industries and Society, 5*(3), 302–307. https://doi.org/10.1016/j.exis.2018.03.013

UNCTAD. (2022). *Handbook of statistics 2022 - international merchandise trade. Fact sheet #2: Trade structure by partner.* https://unctad.org/system/files/official-document/tdstat47_FS02_en.pdf

UNEP. (2022). *Our work in Africa.* https://www.unep.org/regions/africa/our-work-africa#:~:text=The%20largest%20reserves%20of%20cobalt,50%20percent%20of%20total%20wealth

Urban, B., & Woods, E. (2015). The importance of opportunity recognition behaviour and motivators of employees when engaged in corporate entrepreneurship. *Journal of Business Economics and Management, 16*(5), 980–994. https://doi.org/10.3846/16111699.2013.799087

USAID. (2022). *Analysing how Russia's war in Ukraine impacts the Libyan economy.* https://www.usaid.gov/libya/program-updates/may-2022-analyzing-impacts-russia-war-in-ukraine-libyan-economy

World Bank. (2017). *Why we need to close the infrastructure gap in Sub-Saharan Africa.* https://www.worldbank.org/en/region/afr/publication/why-we-need-to-close-the-infrastructure-gap-in-sub-saharan-africa

World Bank. (2020a). *Doing business 2020 fact sheet: Sub-Saharan Africa.* https://www.doingbusiness.org/content/dam/doingBusiness/pdf/db2020/DB20-FS-SSA.pdf

World Bank. (2020b). *The African continental free trade area.* https://www.worldbank.org/en/topic/trade/publication/the-african-continental-free-trade-area

World Bank. (2022). *The world bank in Africa.* https://www.worldbank.org/en/region/afr/overview

Yin, H., Song, Y., & Zeng, X. (2022). Does a smart business environment promote corporate investment? A case study of Hangzhou. *PLoS One, 17*(7), e0269089. https://doi.org/10.1371/journal.pone.0269089

Yu, L., Tang, X., & Huang, X. (2023). Does the business environment promote entrepreneurship? - Evidence from the China Household Finance Survey. *China Economic Review, 79,* 101977. https://doi.org/10.1016/j.chieco.2023.101977

Zhaoa, X., Yib, C., Zhanc, Y., & Guo, M. (2022). Business environment distance and innovation performance of EMNEs: The mediating effect of R and D internationalisation. *Journal of Innovation and Knowledge, 7,* 100241.

3

Opportunities, Challenges and Risks: The South African Business Environment Profiling Opportunities and Challenges of Running Small and Medium-Sized Businesses in the Post-Apartheid Vhembe District of the Limpopo Province of South Africa

Amaechi Kingsley Ekene and Tambe-Dede Kelly

Introduction

SMEs remain one of the most important business models that enhance socio-economic development in countries around the world (Jayadatta, 2017; Muritala et al., 2012). According to the World Bank's latest study on *Understanding Poverty*, SMEs account for most businesses worldwide. SMEs are important contributors to job creation and global economic development; they also contribute to about 90% of businesses and more

---

A. K. Ekene (✉) • T.-D. Kelly
Centre for Youth and Gender Studies, University of Venda, Thohoyandou, South Africa

Department of Business Management, University of Venda, Thohoyandou, South Africa

© The Author(s), under exclusive license to Springer Nature Switzerland AG 2024
R. Ogbechie, M. Ogah (eds.), *Sustainable and Responsible Business in Africa*,
https://doi.org/10.1007/978-3-031-35972-9_3

than 50% of employment opportunities for youth in communities worldwide (World Bank, 2021).

The value of SMEs to economic development is even more notable in less developed countries, where the majority of their workforce is primarily employed in SMEs. In such economies, formal SMEs contribute up to 40% of national income (Manzoor et al., 2021). SMEs' limited demand for start-up finance and knowledge capital (Tambe-Dede & Amaechi, 2022) and ability to draw from local raw materials (Fatoki, 2014) make them a good resource for new entrepreneurial engagement in such economies. Drawing from easy access to finance and other non-material resources, many low-resource-equipped individuals from such economies can easily explore avenues for self-employment and engagement in entrepreneurial activities (Jayadatta, 2017). The semi-structured business model of SMEV can also serve as a reassurance to individuals, to alleviate anxiety and initial fears associated with starting such ventures in new environments (Amaechi, 2020; Obi et al., 2018; Erdin & Ozkaya, 2020).

This is the case in the Limpopo province and other contexts in South Africa (Moyo & Loock, 2021). In the Limpopo province, local entrepreneurs have often drawn from the unique SME models to develop small businesses, contributing to South Africa's economy (Lekhanya, 2016). In fact, 60% of the province's workforce, across all sectors in post-apartheid South Africa, are employed by SMEs (Ngorora & Mago, 2018). SME employees represent a quarter of job growth in the private sector in the country in the last decade. South Africa's National Development Plan estimated that the country needed to create more than 3 million jobs for young people by 2020 and an additional 11 million jobs by 2030; 90% of these jobs are expected from new and expanding SMEs. This means that SMEs remain the "lifeline" of the Limpopo province's economy (and South Africa in general). It is impossible to imagine significant social and economic growth in South Africa without SMEs.

It is in recognition of the importance of SMEs in the economy that post-apartheid political leaders in South Africa are working towards policy formulations and introducing policies that encourage SMEs. At the dawn of the growing significance of SMEs, they have encouraged engagement in SMEs through the introduction of specific policies that bolster interest and economic opportunities for local and black entrepreneurs

(Irene, 2017; Bek et al., 2004; Rogerson, 1997). Notable examples include the far-reaching Broad-Based Black Economic Empowerment programme that aimed at increasing the participation of black people in the entrepreneurial activities and ownership of businesses (Irene, 2017); the Local Economic Development initiative that sought to bridge the gap in the urban and rural cities divide (Rogerson, 1997); and the Spatial Development Initiatives that aimed to help micro-entrepreneurs through a more meaningful assisted "bottom-up" development and interventions (Bek et al., 2004). These schemes have helped motivate and create a conducive environment for small and medium-sized entrepreneurial engagements to thrive in South Africa.

However, this has only sometimes been the case in most rural areas.[1] Despite the presence of these schemes, SMEs have struggled to fulfil the expected mandate of providing social development through rural communities (Lose & Tengeh, 2015). Part of the reason for this is new entrepreneurs' growing failure and inability to sustain their business ventures within rural environments. New entrepreneurs seem discouraged from entrepreneurial activities within rural communities (Tambe-Dede & Amaechi, 2022). Most who attempt to engage in entrepreneurial ventures tend to find it difficult to sustain such businesses for a longer period (Iwara et al., 2021). The reason remains unclear, as recent literature seems to have paid less attention to articulating the salient factors that hinder and encourage entrepreneurial ventures in such rural contexts. This chapter fills this gap.

The chapter provides a brief analysis of some of the salient challenges and opportunities that inhibit and enhance the running of SMEV in a rural environment. Drawing from the experience of eight SMEs that operate in the Vhembe district of the Limpopo province of South Africa, it identifies and discusses which elements hinder and enhance entrepreneurial engagement in such contexts. This includes providing more

---

[1] "Rurality" in the context of this chapter refers to those areas within the South African communities that are without access to ordinary public services, such as water, sanitation, electricity and tarred roads. Such areas are found mostly in the former indigenous homelands created by the former apartheid South African government. The areas are characterised by inferior infrastructure, low-income habitats, poor site conditions, unreliable water availability, and poor access to health facilities. They make up to 33.14% of South Africa's population.

insight into why such entrepreneurial ventures have continued to fail in this selected South African setting. Such discussion serves as a knowledge resource for prospective entrepreneurs, from both within the South African context and other parts of Africa, who may want to engage in entrepreneurial ventures in the Limpopo region of South Africa.

Understanding Small and Medium-Sized Entrepreneurship in South Africa

In the context of this study, we have adopted a working a definition of SMEV, which is consistent with South African literature.[2] SMEV are, for us, "those separate and distinct business entities and enterprises (together with their branches and subsidiaries), often directly managed and run by one, or up to two hundred and fifty employees within the South African business terrain" (Government Gazette of the Republic of South Africa, 2003). According to the South African Management scholar de Wet (2019), such enterprises have at least an annual turnover of 5 million rand, a significant capital asset, or equipment of less than 2 million rand. Such an enterprise could be in any sector or subsector of the economy, such as information technology, agriculture, communication and production. However, such sectors are often not important; what is important is that there are clearly defined guidelines for how the enterprises are run within such structures.

Further, the creation of such businesses in most cases involves two main stages. First, the start-up phase usually takes 3 months, by which time the individuals identify the products or services to be traded in. Such individuals during this stage also access resources and put in place the necessary infrastructure that is required for the business. In the

---

[2] Drawing a working definition of SMEV from the South African literature is a recognition of the fact that definition of SMEV in the literature is context specific. (Going deep into the philosophical debate about the meaning of SMEs in the literature is outside the scope of this study.) Within the literature, there is no one set definition of SMEV that applies globally. Often, each country set its own definition, which includes the specificity on what is considered a big, medium or small-sized enterprise. For example, while the European Union has a limit of 250 employees, the United States still considers an enterprise with up to 1200 employees as an SME (Small Business Administration, 2020; European Commission, 2020).

second phase, which usually takes 3–42 months, the actors often begin to trade and function within the identified environment(s). During such a period, the business competes with other firms in the marketplace, to find the best ways to become an established firm (Fatoki, 2014).

Around the world, these kinds of enterprises have continued to dominate all sectors of the formal economy. These include the production and manufacturing sectors, communication facilitation sectors, sales and service delivery sectors (Fatoki, 2014). These firms have continued to positively contribute to social and economic growth in the urban areas, mostly through creation of employment, poverty alleviation initiatives and social innovations (Irene, 2017; National Treasury Panel, 2016). Their existence and impact on the economy provide opportunities for increased motivation and engagement in entrepreneurial activities and interest in the maximum use of raw products in rural environments (Lose & Tengeh, 2015).

It is important to note that running SMEs is often more complex. Despite the merits of its business model, running SMEs often entails serious risks and challenges. In many contexts, such challenges have included the unavailability of funds (Mugobo & Ukpere, 2012; Mazanai & Fatoki, 2012), intensified competition that comes with economic and political instability (Cant & Wiid, 2013), and continuous technology change (Akinyemi & Adejumo, 2017; Hakkers, 2020). This also includes a lack of business education for the entrepreneurs (Oyelana & Adu, 2017), insufficient technical and conceptual ability (Sitharam & Hoque, 2016; Leboea, 2017), limited infrastructure including transport and production facilities, productivity and efficiency (Mugobo & Ukpere, 2012; Seeletse & Ladzani, 2012; Sinha, 2015; Jayadatta, 2017; Ashwinkumar & Dignesh, 2019; Rushender, 2020), and inadequate knowledge of information technology in an increasingly digital world (Mamba & Isabirye, 2015). The argument is that the presence of these factors in these rural areas hampers the possibility of running smooth operations of SMEs in rural areas. Rural areas, characterised by limited infrastructural development, must provide the basic amenities and facilities to help entrepreneurs manage and sustain their businesses. As a result of the factors mentioned above, potential entrepreneurs have been discouraged from engaging in entrepreneurial ventures in rural settings (De Wet, 2019).

An analysis of the salient existing opportunities and challenges of individuals who venture into SMEs within the Vhembe district [3] provides an opportunity to understand what opportunities and challenges exist in the sub-Saharan African rural settings. As one of the political districts with the highest number of rural settlements/communities and the lowest number of informal employment and GDP in South Africa (Profile: Vhembe District Municipality 22), Vhembe district also theoretically provides a unique opportunity for understanding how "rurality" empowers or inhibits SME motivation and sustenance.

Theoretically, the conceptualisation of rurality in the study is purposefully broad. Drawing from previous studies, it incorporates all business localities without basic infrastructures and the technologically friendly environment of the urban cities. The argument is that such environments are normally not popular for SMEV. In a South African setting, where about 90% of all registered firms were reported to be SMEs, according to the South African Revenue Service (National Treasury Panel, 2016), new entrepreneurs often prefer urban and semi-urban settings. Most entrepreneurs who establish businesses in these areas often need help to progress. In case they are unable to sustain their businesses over a short period, 50%–80% of small businesses in rural areas fail in the first year. Only about half of the survivors lasted 5 years after being established (Market Research Reports, 2020). These continuous failures and the decline of small and medium-sized enterprises (SMEs) in South Africa's rural areas and indications of uncertainties surrounding running SMEs in such areas lead to disappointment and subsequent discouragement regarding engaging in such ventures, which warrants a systematic discussion of the main challenges and opportunities of running an SME in South Africa's rural setting.

---

[3] Vhembe is situated in the Northern part of the Limpopo province, which also lies in the Northern part of South Africa. With its headquarters in Thohoyandou, the district is composed of four main local municipalities, namely, Makhado, Musina, Thulamela and Collins Chabane. Uniquely, the Vhembe district is one of the only districts that shares borders with three countries: Zimbabwe to the north, Mozambique through Kruger National Park to the east and Botswana to the northwest. The district covers about 21,407 km2 and has a population of over 1.1 million living in 274,480 households.

Communities in the Vhembe district fit perfectly well as examples of rural communities. Before 1994, these communities had existed as part of the independent indigenous community which the South African apartheid government established for the *indigenous people* (Amaechi & Masoga, 2020). Although recognised by the United Nations and a host of institutions in the global community, communities within the current Vhembe district operated as part of the Venda independent state. Hence, they were excluded from the most significant economic development of other parts of South Africa. It was not until post-apartheid in the 1960s that these communities were conscripted into South Africa. For this reason, they infrastructurally remained largely underdeveloped and rural.

Method and Data

In identifying the main challenges and opportunities associated with SME start-ups and sustainability in rural communities, the study adopted an exploratory qualitative approach, which allowed for the interpretation of the data through the eyes of the participants (Ofoegbu et al., 2016). Relying on this research design, it was possible to draw from the experiences of some individuals operating in the cities of the five municipalities within the Vhembe district: Makhado, Giyani, Thohoyandou, Mussina and Malemlele.

Furthermore, participants in the study were chosen through the purposive sampling technique (through the two researchers' contacts) and snowball sampling technique, where the initial participants made referrals to other SMEs based in the district. We conducted telephonic and face-to-face detailed semi-structured interviews with the participants using these two techniques. Telephonic interviews were mainly an alternative means to reach out to the participants due to the South African Corona-19 National Lockdown (as the interviews were conducted during the South African COVID-19 National Lockdown, between March 2020 and August 2020).

Table 3.1 provides a demographic representation of the study participants.

Table 3.1 Demographic representation of social media marketers

1	Total number of participants	8
2	Municipality where business is based	
	Makhado	2
	Thohoyandou	2
	Mussina	2
	Malemlele	1
	Giyani	1
3	Gender	
	Female	2
	Male	6
4	Participants' line of business	
	Health products	3
	Food	2
	Hair pieces	2
	Agricultural products	1
5	Age range	
	Between 30 and 40	1
	Between 20 and −30	5
	Between 16 and −19	2

A few important ethical protocols have also been followed throughout the research process. Firstly, distribution of consent forms and interview request forms provided detailed explanations about the study. The forms also provided honest information regarding the participants' rights, as well as the purpose and the background of the research. Secondly, all information which could potentially give away the identity of the participants in the study was also removed. Dates and times for the interviews were fixed with all the participants who agreed to be part of the study after signing the consent form. No participant was paid for the interviews.

Ultimately, the interview data were transcribed, categorised and thematically coded. The data were analysed using Microsoft Windows 8. Drawing from the data set, the study can generate evidence-based data that describes what it entails to run SMEs in South Africa's rural environment. For clarity in the presentations, we have used the names of the cities where the participants' businesses are based (Mussina, Makhado, Thohoyandou, Malemlele and Giyani), the genders (represented by M/F) and the ages to denote the participants' significant words in the data set.

Running Small and Medium-Sized Ventures in Vhembe District

Given the unique social, economic and political characteristics of the Vhembe district's rural environment, running an SMEV in this location entails unique challenges and opportunities. The discussion below is an analysis of some of these salient challenges and opportunities.

(A) The Challenges: Among the most prominent identified challenges from the participants' narratives are (a) lack of access to start-up finance, (b) lack of access to appropriate entrepreneurial-friendly programmes for harnessing managerial and entrepreneurial skills, (c) non-existent specific rural-targeted favourable entrepreneurial government policies for entrepreneurial development and sustainability, and finally (d) insecurity and local protection of SME businesses.

(I). In analysing the data, *lack of access to start-up finance for entrepreneurial engagement* was the first major challenge identified: Unlike what seems to be the case in urban areas (Rogerson, 2013), most small-scale entrepreneurs in the Vhembe district lack access to finance for entrepreneurial start-ups. The local municipalities often need provisions or budgets that include funds for entrepreneurial start-ups. Worst still, in situations where agencies such as the Department of Small Business Development provide small finance and non-financial support to small enterprises and cooperatives, most entrepreneurs are often either ignorant of their existence or do not know how to approach these agencies for financial assistance. This is how some of the participants explain it:

> *I have a lot of business ideas. I can manufacture and sell mpesu locally....*
> *But how do I get the initial money to start up the business?*

This lack of access to funds (and in some cases, lack of knowledge about the existence of agencies that assist with funds for SME start-ups) kills the desirability for engagement and inhibits SME owners' exposure and opportunities to grow their businesses and sustain them (Adisa et al., 2014; Lekhanya & Mason, 2014; Akinyemi & Adejumo, 2017).

(II). The second challenge described by the participants is the *need for access to appropriate entrepreneurial-friendly programmes for harnessing managerial and entrepreneurial skills.* Much like in other rural contexts in South Africa (Sitharam & Hoque, 2016; Tambe-Dede & Amaechi, 2022), SMEs in the Vhembe district lack exposure to appropriate entrepreneurial-friendly programmes within the district. While the availability of such programmes is supposed to harness managerial and entrepreneurial skills, their lack of availability within the district constitutes a major demotivating factor for entrepreneurial engagement in SMEs. Below are significant statements from two of the participants:

> *How do we learn how to run small businesses in this community? What does the municipality do to encourage us? When was the last time there was a workshop for entrepreneurial development? These are important programmes that help motivate people to engage in small businesses. People need them to be motivated; they also need to know how and where to start. (Malemlele/M/19)*
>
> *I have lived in this town enough to know that one of our biggest problems is government sponsorship. We operate in a context where there is hardly any incentive to train people on how to engage in entrepreneurial ventures. People hardly have the right knowledge to start any good business. They just operate with petty knowledge they have learnt from their friends and family members. Such knowledge is hardly enough to motivate them or help them succeed. (Thohoyandou/M/39)*

The lack of these programmes in the district seems to stem from the fact that they are hardly prioritised within the municipalities. In most cases, the local governments or NGOs which are supposed to deal with such issues are often over-stretched and, as a result, only sometimes prioritise them (Amaechi et al., 2021; Sitharam & Hoque, 2016). As a consequence, the entrepreneurs are left on "their own", operating without such important programmes and with a lack of sufficient funds; they risk the possibility of not learning and accessing new engagement methods and improving their businesses. This, over a period of time, discourages these entrepreneurs from engaging in and sustaining their entrepreneurial activities.

In more practical cases, previous studies on SMEs document how entrepreneurs who operated from rural areas lacked access to activities that helped them to learn about newer approaches and pre-requisite skill for analysing and addressing market needs and entrepreneurial conditions (Tambe-Dede & Amaechi, 2022). In such cases, these deficiencies were also linked to a need for more education by the entrepreneurs. Amid such deficiencies, the entrepreneurs lose their competitiveness and ability to maximise profit. This further translates into the difficulty of sustaining their ventures over a longer period.

These challenges also extend to failure to engage with the advancements in technology and information technology (IT) (Tambe-Dede & Amaechi, 2022; Mamba & Isabriye, 2015). Given that the world has increasingly become more digital, entrepreneurial engagements have correspondingly become more digital. Lack of access to or engagement with such digital advancement results in a tremendous lack of new possibilities for engagement, including a lack of expansion of their consumer base and lack of opportunities through far-reaching and less costly advertisement afforded by technology and service delivery. Thus, entrepreneurs found it difficult to cope.

Comparing SMEs in the Vhembe district to those which operate in more urban contexts in South Africa, there is a clear and significant skill gap. While Vhembe-based SMEs seem to lack the ability to access the basic programmes where they can learn the above-described digital skills, entrepreneurs in the urban areas often have easy access to several institutions that continuously provide training and advisory services. In some cases, these services are offered for free or at affordable prices (Chimucheka & Mandipaka, 2015; Lekhanya & Mason, 2014). And because sustaining SMEs is laden with competitiveness, not having these opportunities for training and upgrading their skills takes away the competitive edge for rural entrepreneurs (Oyelana & Adu, 2015).

(III). Another major challenge confronting rural-based entrepreneurs is the *non-existent rural-targeted entrepreneurial government policies for entrepreneurial development and sustainability*. Admittedly, the South African government has introduced laws and policies which work to protect SMEs, having recognised their ability for job creation and racial equality (National Small Business Act 102 of 1996); however, these policies do not necessarily target SMEs development and sustenance in the rural areas specifically (Mutyenyoka & Madzivhandila, 2014). For example, no policies seek to encourage entrepreneurs to remain in rural environments, amid the inability to stay afloat. Such situations, as some participants rightly described, create an environment of disappointment and desperation (Hakkers, 2020; Musara & Gwaindepi, 2013; Leboea, 2017; Sitharam & Hoque, 2016). This is how one of the participants puts it:

> *The worst thing is that the government is not doing anything to encourage some of us who are venturing into entrepreneurship in this part of the country to remain here. They have done practically nothing regarding policies or laws to make us stay here. In such a situation, what do they expect…? They are simply killing entrepreneurship on this side. (Mussina/M/29)*

(IV) Finally, *insecurity and protection of businesses* was found to be another significant challenge identified by SMEs that operate in the Vhembe district. However, this challenge was not unique to the Vhembe district. Cases of theft or vandalisation of business are well documented in South African business literature (Misago, 2019; Ngcamu & Mantzaris, 2019). In most cases, SMEs in different parts of South Africa are violently targeted and attacked by raging individuals within the communities (Iwara et al., 2018). Criminal elements in the communities, as the participants described, often "use every instance of xenophobic violence as an opportunity to loot business businesses" (Makhado/F/25). Almost all sectors of the country have received their share of this insecurity and criminal looting of businesses.

The difference between the rural and urban areas is the response from the state. While these kinds of attacks are often easily curtailed in more urban areas due to better security infrastructures and other resources, businesses in rural areas are often left on their own. Coupled with the lack of essential facilities such as electricity, water, transportation for conveyance of goods, and other business-friendly equipment that makes it easier for recovery, SME operators often find sustaining their businesses in such a vulnerable environment very difficult (Chimucheka &

Mandipaka, 2015). Worst still, the attacks on a longer range discourage SME ventures, destabilise existing ventures, and make it difficult for them to be sustained over a longer period.

(B) The Opportunities: Despite the challenges, the Vhembe district's rural environment also provides some unique and significant opportunities when it comes to starting up and sustaining SMEs.

(I) The first opportunity described by the participants includes an *SMEV-friendly environment for start-ups*. In most of the participants' narrations, the Vhembe district has a very natural SMEV-conducive business environment that encourages SMEV. The argument is that this is largely a result of the local population's recognition of the invaluable contribution of SMEs to economic development (Jayadatta, 2017; Bek et al., 2004). Given the growing impact of SMEV in providing employment and social development in the local contexts, the local people have, according to the participants, grown to have an "increasingly developed soft spot for SMEs (Mussina/M/28)". Admittedly, this recognition of the role of SMEV in economic development has not materialised in the development of national government policies that specifically target the sustenance of SMEs in rural areas, which has helped improve SME appeal in the rural areas (Mugobo & Ukpere, 2012). In the era of increased calls for equitable redistribution of the country's resources and land reforms, this goodwill provides a substantial platform for desirability and commitment to engage in SMEV.

(II) Secondly, the Vhembe district's rural community provides *a good environment for business networks*. The fact that people within the communities in the Vhembe district still operate in an African communal culture often means that people have good knowledge of other people's (neighbours') business activities. In these communities, there is some interdependency and social lifestyle, making it easier for people to mingle and interact with others within their communities. Within such relationships, they can create links and business associations, which helps SMEV to survive, and encourages knowledge expansion and benchmarking (Mugobo & Ukpere, 2012). Two of the participants described this as follows:

One advantage we have on this side of the world is that we live together. We know the business of everybody around here. I know what my neighbours want, so I factor that in when I bring new products for my business. (Malemlele/M/19)

I do not need to do any internet research to know what to do. My friends are my biggest customers. Before I purchase new stuff, I already know from my interactions with them. I modify my business according to the needs of my community. (Thohoyandou/M/39)

By impacting entrepreneurial adaptability, these types of interactions and linkages described by the participants can also enhance competitiveness in other situations, which helps SMEV survival (De Klerk & Saayman, 2012).

(III) Related to the good environment for business networks discussed above is *easy access to the clientele base*. As the participants rightly described, this often develops from social interaction and loyalty (Akinyemi & Adejumo, 2017; Ngorora & Mago, 2018). Being connected to people within the community creates opportunities for loyalty, which provides a quick clientele base and ensures patronage for the SMEV. In the context of the Vhembe district's rural setting, it also helped ensure certainty and predictability of sales.

(IV) Finally, according to the participants, the Vhembe district's rural environment provides *a less complex market and cheap running costs for products*. These views align with previous studies (Adisa et al., 2014; Amaechi, 2020; Leboea, 2017). In other contexts, studies have pointed out how starting and sustaining an SMEV in South Africa's rural environment could be relatively cheaper and more accessible than in the urban area, not only because of the lack of complexity in running SMEs in such contexts but also because of the generally low cost of living. With limited resources, rural entrepreneurs can often easily rent a location, pay their staff and afford the raw materials needed to sustain their entrepreneurial ventures (Ngorora & Mago, 2018).

This was also described as mostly the case in the communities in the Vhembe district. With the low cost of living and running of businesses in the rural Vhembe communities, SMEs saw starting, running and sustaining SMEV ventures as much easier.

Conclusion

First, this study sought to explore salient opportunities associated with running SMEs in the Vhembe district of the Limpopo province of South Africa. In this light, elements such as a) limited access to finance, b) lack of basic infrastructure to harness managerial, technical or entrepreneurial skills required for running SMEs, c) the non-existence of specific entrepreneurial government policies, and d) insecurity emanating from violent attacks and theft were identified as challenges associated with running SMEs in South Africa's rural environment. We argued that amid these elements in post-apartheid South Africa, local actors running SMEV in rural contexts have found it difficult to operate and sustain their businesses. Secondly, the study also identified: a) an SME-friendly environment, b) access to business networking, c) access to a clientele base and a less complex market, and d) access to a less complex market and cheap running costs. In discussing these opportunities, the chapter argued that new entrepreneurs who wish to engage in entrepreneurship in South Africa's rural environment need to understand these factors. Drawing from such opportunities, they could make informed decisions on how to better engage in SME ventures in South Africa's rural environment.

One theoretical implication is that the rural environment, including communities in the Vhembe district, has unique features. These include poor and less developed infrastructural projects for transport and business logistics, poor technological tools for navigating new business models, and a lower chance of obtaining assistance (in the form of social services). These features serve as demotivating factors for certain entrepreneurial engagements. Yet, in some cases, the features can also serve as a catalyst by which SMEs can develop their SMEV. Without understanding these elements in any given environment, it isn't easy to successfully engage in entrepreneurial ventures within such environments.

Recommendations

Based on these factors, it is therefore recommended that local municipalities in the rural communities adopt practices that target the sustenance of SMEs in their rural communities, drawing from some of the described opportunities. Such practices should not be generic but specific to the needs of SMEs operating within such local municipalities. This could be a provision of compulsory free refresher business courses, provision of cash grants for struggling SMEs, or development of incubation models, which in other contexts has been proven to reduce the failure rate in the first few years for small enterprises (Small Enterprise Development Agency, n.d.). Since there is rarely any collateral security for small and medium-sized entrepreneurs within such communities to take loans from the bank, the government can create special "loans" to be given explicitly to individuals who want to engage in such activities. Such special loans could be given to individuals with signed agreements and documentation to present significant progress and a condition that the only way not to repay the loan is to grow the business towards some measured metrics. This will help SME owners work extra hard to ensure the business succeeds in not repaying the loan. In the contexts where such practices exist, we recommend that there be accelerated efforts in their implementations to encourage desirability in SMEs within such local communities.

Finally, we also encourage accelerated improvements of rural infrastructures such as roads, water, electricity, internet access and other important business-friendly and social amenities in South Africa's rural community. Not only would such improvements encourage business interactions in the rural communities, but they would also foster rural development and create opportunities for employment for people within such communities.

References

Adisa, T. A., Abdulraheem, I., & Mordi, C. (2014). The characteristics and challenges of small businesses in Africa: An exploratory study of Nigerian small business owners. *Petroleum-Gas University of Ploiesti Bulletin, Technical Series, 66*(4).

Akinyemi, F., & Adejumo, O. (2017). Entrepreneurial motives and challenges of SMEs owners in emerging economies: Nigeria & South Africa. *Advances in Economics and Business, 5*(11), 624–633. http://www.hrpub.org. https://doi.org/10.13189/aeb.2017.051105

Amaechi, K. E. (2020). Profiling the sociocultural conditions for Igbo business start-ups and entrepreneurial activities in diaspora: The south African experience. In *Indigenous African enterprise*. Emerald Publishing Limited.

Amaechi, K. E., Iwara, I. O., Musvipwa, F., & Raselekaone, R. (2021). Appraising the Local village leaders 'response to the challenges faced by rural households during the Corona virus 2019 National Lock-down in South Africa. *Sociološki pregled, 55*(4), 1233–1263.

Amaechi, K. E., & Masoga, M. A. (2020). Post-orientalist reflections on the effects of colonialism on political corruption in contemporary South Africa: A review. *Journal of Nation-building & Policy Studies, 4*(2), 143–160.

Ashwinkumar, P., & Dignesh, P. (2019). Rising problems and challenges in rural entrepreneurs. *International Journal for Research in Engineering Application & Management (IJREAM)*. ISSN: 2454-9150. https://doi.org/10.18231/2454-9150.2019.0098.

Bek, D., Binns, T., & Nel, E. (2004). 'Catching the development train': Perspectives on 'top-down' and 'bottom-up' development in post-apartheid South Africa. *Progress in Development Studies, 4*(1), 22–46.

Cant, M. C., & Wiid, J. A. (2013). Establishing the challenges affecting south African SMEs. *International Business & Economics Research Journal (IBER), 12*(6), 707–716.

Chimucheka, T., & Mandipaka, F. (2015). Challenges faced by small, medium and micro enterprises in the Nkonkobe Municipality. *International Business & Economics Research Journal (IBER), 14*(2), 309–316.

De Klerk, S., & Saayman, M. (2012). Networking as key factor in artpreneurial success. *European Business Review, 24*(5), 382.

De Wet, P. (2019). The definitions of micro, small, and medium businesses have just been radically overhauled – Here's how. *Business Insider SA*. https://

www.businessinsider.co.za/micro-small-and-medium-business-definition-update-by-sector-2019-3.

Erdin, C., & Ozkaya, G. (2020). Contribution of small and medium enterprises to economic development and quality of life in Turkey. *Heliyon, 6*(2), e03215.

European Commission. (2020). *Small and medium-sized enterprises (SMEs)*. https://ec.europa.eu/eurostat/web/structural-business-statistics/structural-business-statistics/sme

Fatoki, O. (2014). The causes of the failure of new small and medium enterprises in South Africa. *Mediterranean Journal of Social Sciences, 5*(20), 922–922.

Government Gazette Republic of South Africa. *Vol. 452 Cape Town*. 2003. No. 24576. https://static.pmg.org.za/docs/080610gazette.pdf.

Hakkers, S. (2020). *Explorative research on challenging factors encountered by SMEs operating in developing countries deploying an IT transaction platform* (Bachelor's thesis, University of Twente).

Irene, B. N. O. (2017). The macroeconomic landscape of post-apartheid South Africa: A critical review of the effect of the Broad-Based Black Economic Empowerment (BBBEE) program on the success of female SMEs operators. *Journal of Educational and Social Research, 7*(1), 145–145.

Iwara, I. O., Kilonzo, B. M., Zuwarimwe, J., & Netshandama, V. O. (2021). Entrepreneurs' endogenous attributes necessary for small enterprise success in Vhembe rural areas, South Africa. *The Southern African Journal of Entrepreneurship and Small Business Management, 13*(1), 12.

Iwara, I. O., Obadire, O. S., & Amaechi, K. E. (2018). Xenophobic tendencies in higher learning institutions as impediments to the call for African renaissance. *African Renaissance, 15*(2), 171–191.

Jayadatta, S. (2017). Major challenges and problems of rural entrepreneurship in India. *Journal of Business and Management 19*(9). Ver. II, 35–44. https://doi.org/10.9790/487X-1909023544.

Leboea, S. T. (2017). *The factors influencing SME failure in South Africa* (Master's thesis, University of Cape Town).

Lekhanya, L. M., & Mason, R. B. (2014). Selected key external factors influencing the success of rural small and medium Enterprises in South Africa. *Journal of Enterprising Culture, 22*(03), 331–348. https://doi.org/10.1142/s0218495814500149

Lekhanya, L. M. (2016). Business characteristics of small and medium enterprises in rural areas: a Case Study on Southern region of KwaZulu-Natal Province of South Africa. Problems and Perspectives in Management, 14(3), 108.

Lose, T., & Tengeh, R. K. (2015). The sustainability and challenges of business incubators in the western cape province, South Africa. *Sustainability, 7*(10), 14344–14357. https://doi.org/10.3390/su71014344

Mamba, M. S., & Isabirye, N. (2015). A framework to guide development through ICTs in rural areas in South Africa. *Information Technology for Development, 21*(1), 135–150. https://doi.org/10.1080/02681102.2013.874321

Manzoor, F., Wei, L., & Sahito, N. (2021). The role of SMEs in rural development: Access of SMEs to finance as a mediator. *PLoS One, 16*(3), e0247598. https://doi.org/10.1371/journal.pone.0247598. https://journals.plos.org/plosone/article?id=10.1371/journal.pone.0247598.

Market Research Reports, Inc. (2020). South Africa SWOT analysis market research report. https://www.marketresearchreports.com/market-research-reports-inc/south-africa-swot-analysis-market-research-report

Mazanai, M., & Fatoki, O. (2012). Perceptions of start-up small and medium-sized enterprises (SMEs) on the importance of business development services providers (BDS) on improving access to finance in South Africa. *Journal of Social Sciences, 30*(1), 31–41.

Misago, J. P. (2019). Political mobilisation as the trigger of xenophobic violence in post-apartheid South Africa. *International Journal of Conflict and Violence, 13*, a646–a646.

Moyo, M., & Loock, M. (2021). Conceptualising a cloud business intelligence security evaluation framework for small and medium enterprises in small towns of the Limpopo Province, South Africa. *Information, 12*(3), 128.

Mugobo, V., & Ukpere, W. (2012). Rural entrepreneurship in the Western Cape: Challenges and opportunities. *African Journal of Business Management, 6*(3), 827.

Muritala, T., Awolaja, A., & Bako, Y. (2012). Impact of small and medium enterprises on economic growth and development. *American Journal of Business and Management, 1*(1), 18–22.

Musara, M., & Gwaindepi, C. (2013, April). The impact of the business regulatory environment on the level of entrepreneurship in South Africa: An exploratory view. In *International conference on law, entrepreneurship and industrial engineering (ICLEIE'2013)* (pp. 15–16).

Mutyenyoka, E. M., & Madzivhandila, T. S. (2014) Employment creation through small, medium and micro enterprises (SMMEs) in South Africa: Challenges, progress and sustainability. *Mediterranean Journal of Social Sciences*. https://doi.org/10.5901/mjss.2014.v5n25p65

National Small Business Act 102 of 1996. (1996). https://www.gov.za/sites/default/files/gcis_document/201409/act102of1996.pdf

Ngcamu, B. S., & Mantzaris, E. (2019). Xenophobic violence and criminality in the KwaZulu-Natal townships. *The Journal for Transdisciplinary Research in Southern Africa, 15*(1), 1–8.

Ngorora, P. K. G., & Mago, S. (2018). Prospects of entrepreneurship in South Africa's rural areas: A case study of Eastern Cape Province's Nkonkobe Municipal Area. *African Journal of Hospitality, Tourism and Leisure, 7*(2). ISSN: 2223-814X.

Nicola, M., Alsafi, Z., Sohrabi, C., Kerwan, A., Al-Jabir, A., Iosifidis, C., & Agha, R. (2020). The socio-economic implications of the coronavirus and COVID-19 pandemic: A review. *International Journal of Surgery, 78*, 185.

Obi, J., Ibidunni, A. S., Tolulope, A., Olokundun, M. A., Amaihian, A. B., Borishade, T. T., & Fred, P. (2018). Contribution of small and medium enterprises to economic development: Evidence from a transiting economy. *Data in Brief, 18*, 835–839.

Ofoegbu, C., Chirwa, P. W., Francis, J., & Babalola, F. D. (2016). Assessing forest-based rural communities' adaptive capacity and coping strategies for climate variability and change: The case of Vhembe district in South Africa. *Environmental Development, 18*, 36–51.

Oyelana, A. A., & Adu, E. O. (2015). Small and medium enterprises (SMEs) as a means of creating employment and poverty reduction in Fort Beaufort, Eastern Cape Province of South Africa. *Journal of Social Sciences, 45*(1), 8–15.

Rogerson, C. M. (1997). Local economic development and post-apartheid reconstruction in South Africa. *Singapore Journal of Tropical Geography, 18*(2), 175–195.

Rogerson, C. M. (2013). Improving market access opportunities for urban small, medium and micro-enterprises in South Africa. *Urbani izziv, 24*(2), 133–143.

Rushender, R. (2020). Role of rural entrepreneurship and major problems. Development Professional. *LinkedIn*. https://www.linkedin.com/pulse/role-rural-entrepreneurship-major-problems-rushender-reddy/?trk=read_related_article-card_title

Seeletse, S. M., & Ladzani, M. W. (2012). Social responsibility in the rural businesses of the North-West Province of South Africa: Coerced or business-driven? *African Journal of Business Management, 6*(46), 11457–11471.

Sinha, D. K. (2015). Major problems faced in developing entrepreneurship in rural areas. Next Generation Library. *Your Article Library*. https://

www.yourarticlelibrary.com/entrepreneurship/major-problems-faced-in-developing-entrepreneurship-in-rural-areas/41102

Sitharam, S., & Hoque, M. (2016). Factors affecting the performance of small and medium enterprises in KwaZulu-Natal, South Africa. *Problems and Perspectives in Management, 14*(2), 277–288.

Small Business Administration. (2020). *Table of small business standards marched to North American Industry classification codes.* https://www.sba.gov/sites/default/files/2019-08/SBA%20Table%20of%20Size%20Standards_Effective%20Aug%2019%2C%202019_Rev.pdfPage 36

Statistics South Africa. (2019). *Statistical release. P0302. Mid-year population estimates 2019.*

Tambe-Dede, K., & Amaechi, K. E. (2022). The challenges and effectiveness of social media advertising for rural-based small scale entrepreneurs in South Africa. In O. Adeola, J. N. Edeh, R. E. Hinson, & F. Netswera (Eds.), *Digital service delivery in Africa — A phantomisation perspective.* Palgrave Macmillan.

The World Bank. (2021). *Understanding poverty.* https://www.worldbank.org/en/topic/smefinance

4

The Sustainability Challenge: Developing Strategic Advantage

Nkemdilim Iheanachor

Introduction

The managing director of Nigeria Deposit Insurance Corporation (NDIC), Bello Hassan, disclosed that the corporation paid out about N101.76 billion to about 535,815 insured depositors of liquidated banks (Kano, 2021). Due to certain factors, multinational companies may also fail to sustain their business operations. The famous retail company and market leader in its industry in the United Kingdom, Tesco Plc, attempted to penetrate international markets in Asia. However, it failed to survive in those markets and pulled out of countries like China, South Korea, Japan, and Thailand (Clarke, 2011).

Sustainability is a serious issue that any business that wants to succeed with assured continuity must consider. The 18 banks that liquidated were not started by their founders with the hope of failing. However, various factors can positively or negatively affect a company's survival ability.

N. Iheanachor (✉)
Lagos Business School, Pan-Atlantic University, Lekki, Nigeria
e-mail: niheanachor@lbs.edu.ng

© The Author(s), under exclusive license to Springer Nature Switzerland AG 2024
R. Ogbechie, M. Ogah (eds.), *Sustainable and Responsible Business in Africa*,
https://doi.org/10.1007/978-3-031-35972-9_4

Internal and external issues can contribute to a company's ability to continue or cease to exist. Making strategic plans and taking critical steps to protect a business's future within its operation's industry and environment is what sustainability in business means.

However, sustainability in business is not just about the continuity of a business; it is about doing business in a way that contributes to social, economic, and ecologically sustainable development and removes risks and threats from the environment and the people. Schaltegger and Wagner (2017) explained that achieving sustainability will increase its performance and give it a competitive edge in its sector. Suppose a business conducts its business where the environment is unsafe and unhealthy and the people are unwell. In that case, it will increase the rate of absenteeism in the workforce, reduce productivity, and affect profit.

Although this may not have an immediate effect, an unhealthy environment results from unsustainable business practices, which will eventually affect the availability and supply of natural materials and the economy. Molino et al. (2019) explained that unsustainable practices could reduce employees' well-being and productivity, affecting a company's competitiveness. This chapter discusses the sustainability challenge, identifies sustainability practices, and makes valuable recommendations for strategic advantage in Africa.

Sustainability in Businesses

Sustainability or 'going green' denotes a business doing its operations without negatively impacting the environment or society. It addresses two sections: its effect on the environment and society impacts these sections positively. A business does not exist in a vacuum, but in an environment for its operations, products, and services. Freudenreich et al. (2020) asserted that a good business strategy must promote a good relationship with society and the natural environment, which are part of its stakeholders. This means that sustainability in business is about positively impacting the stakeholders (Table 4.1).

All individuals whose decisions and actions as individuals or collective bodies can affect a company's survival are the primary stakeholders,

Table 4.1 Showing stakeholders of an organisation

Primary stakeholders	• Investors or shareholders • Suppliers • Consumers • Employees • Communities
Secondary stakeholders	• The government • The media • Competitors • Consumer groups • Interest groups and associations

Source: Author's Presentation

including the workers, consumers, suppliers, investors, and communities. They are always concerned about the success of an organisation because they are affected by it (Hörisch et al., 2020). This means that creating sustainable values for these stakeholders will eventually translate into growth and competitive strength for an organisation. Thus, while an organisation benefits the primary stakeholder, it also profits from its positive actions.

The secondary stakeholders, such as the government and the media, can influence the policies and operations of an organisation. Therefore, an organisation must engage in sustainable practices because others are concerned and monitoring. Any unsustainable practice could cause the failure of an organisation. How would the community assess an organisation's sustainability? What if a company decides to hide its practices from the public? Sustainability has gone beyond a private affair of an organisation because there is a standardisation of sustainability report, which requires an organisation to self-report its sustainable practices accurately (Erin et al., 2021).

Severe legal actions could lead to bankruptcy if an organisation fails to report or gives a false report about its sustainability (Nwobu et al., 2017). From the preceding, the only way out for organisations is to improve their sustainability practices in all critical financial, environmental, workforce, and economic areas.

Sustainable Business Practices

Workforce sustainability refers to the sustenance of a workforce to continue functioning for a longer time. This means that workforce sustainability focuses on creating good working conditions for the employees and enabling them to make an excellent living to continue working or remaining in employment for an extended period (Ortiz-de-Mandojana & Bansal, 2016). The wellness of employees is vital to an organisation as they are among its primary stakeholders and the power behind its operations, as society is interested in how an organisation treats its workers.

In developed countries, labour laws protect the employees from employers that may want to focus solely on making profits at the expense of their workers. However, in most developing countries, cheap labour makes foreign investors or companies establish subsidiaries in the host countries (Alamgir & Banerjee, 2019). In such situations, when it seems the policies do not favour workforce sustainability, other frameworks, such as Corporate Social Responsibility and Stakeholder Theory, put pressure on an organisation to respect the rights of its workers (Renouard & Ezvan, 2018).

Environmental Sustainability

Environmental sustainability is not negotiable for organisations in an age of growing concern about climate change. Any organisation that needs to adjust to the trends in environmental sustainability may suffer from future policies the governments are making in different countries or collectively. The activities of businesses in manufacturing, maintenance, packaging, distribution, administration, and other activities have specific effects on the environment, affecting the atmosphere and the water bodies (Sarkis & Zhu, 2018).

The way energy is being used for industrial purposes increases carbon emissions. This is why the UN's SDG 13 is set to fight climate change, SDG 14 is set to protect life under the water, and SDG 15 protects life on land (SDGS UN, 2021). This shows how serious environmental sustainability is to organisations. Business practices must not endanger the water and the natural environment is well preserved. Various projects are capable of causing hazards to the environment, but this does not mean they are dismissible. Instead, it means organisations should measure their projects' impact on society and make efforts to control such risks (Drayson et al., 2015). Hart and Zingales (2017) state that a company must not put profit above other goods, such as treating its employees well and impacting the community.

Financial Sustainability

A company is responsible for making a profit, which is a significant reason for the establishment of an organisation. Although Hart and Zingales (2017) stated that creating value for investors does not mean ignoring others, they still acknowledge that an organisation needs to profit. That means it is essential to make strategies to grow the business, improve sales and revenue, and increase profit. Consistency in profit-making is vital to the survival of an organisation. However, financial sustainability is beyond just making a profit. It also includes making a profit ethically and giving regular reports accurately for the stakeholders to see and make decisions. Oyewumi et al. (2018) argued that if an organisation meets various aspects of corporate social responsibility but needs to disclose its financial activities, its CSR will not impact financial sustainability.

Challenges of Sustainable Businesses

The Challenge of Skilled Labour or Intellectual Capital

To achieve sustainability in business, an organisation needs competent staff, either by recruiting qualified staff with sufficient skill and experience or by training new ones in the field. Whether a company seeks to employ skilled labour or train new employees, it will spend extra funds to achieve it. Bibi et al. (2018) stated that an organisation better avoids the cost of recruiting new workers and training workers through employee retention. That is, workforce sustainability will save an organisation from the extra cost of recruiting new workers and training workers. However, achieving employee retention is also challenging because it requires favourable initiatives that can be costly. In other words, retention, recruitment, and training require extra spending.

Nevertheless, an organisation needs a competent workforce to increase its competitive edge through sustainability. It takes expertise for an organisation to prepare an accurate financial report that will not cause trouble. Every aspect of a company's operations requires experts to work effectively and increase organisational efficiency.

Technology

Organisations need to adopt technology to reduce their unsustainability and enhance their environmental and economic practices to achieve sustainability. However, the cost of some technological equipment upgrades of renewal can be higher, primarily if a company seeks to improve its capacity. Nevertheless, technological advancement brings different opportunities and challenges, and thus organisations must keep improving.

Employee Resistance

When employees are used to a system or practice, the thought of change may unsettle them and cause them to resist change (Caruth & Caruth, 2013). Suppose an organisation uses only a physical model in its business and decides to improve by introducing an online model to allow some workers to work remotely and allow flexible work arrangements. In that case, employees that are familiar and comfortable with the physical model may be threatened by the new model either because they feel incapable of handling the change and they are threatened by the thought of having a new worker brought in with expert power or because they are afraid their incompetence might cause trouble for them.

Government Policy and Political Instability

Valinejad and Rahmani (2018) revealed that political instability and currency fluctuations could affect sustainability. Political change is not limited to Nigeria or Africa. The issue of Brexit in the United Kingdom also caused some sudden changes to businesses as the United Kingdom introduced a new tariff system (Offerman, 2021). However, the decision of the United Kingdom to leave the EU was not suddenly imposed by a government declaration, but it was debated for about four years. In Africa, political decisions can be sudden, affecting organisations' sustainability.

For example, foreign trade policy can affect a business's supply chain. Another example is the ban of Twitter by the Federal Government of Nigeria after Twitter deleted a post by the Nigerian president in June 2021. This decision has led to over 400 billion naira loss between June 2021 and December 2021 which crippled some businesses, leading to a loss of about 2.5 billion naira daily (Anyim, 2021).

The government's decision was unexpected by many businesses using Twitter for different purposes. The incident, however, shows that the government's decision can positively or negatively affect the sustainability of an organisation financially, socially, and economically. If any business had solely relied on Twitter as its platform of existence or operations in Nigeria, the ban would automatically cause the failure of such an organisation. The closure of the Nigerian-Benin border also affected some businesses in Nigeria and other parts of Africa (Abegunde & Fabiyi, 2020). Government policies may be volatile and disrupt organisations' sustainability.

Strategies for Sustainable Businesses

Creating a sustainable business strategy integrates economic, eco-friendly, and social goals into an organisation's objectives, intending to form lasting value for the organisation, stakeholders, and society (Geissdoerfer et al., 2018). Strategy is formed and implemented to protect the present needs of the organisation and stakeholders while securing and sustaining the needed resources in the future (Bocken & Geradts, 2020). To do this, businesses will need to realign their operations and bear responsibility for industrial and social problems they have caused for society, like pollution and bad working conditions. The primary purpose of an accepted business strategy is generating profits (generating value) for both short and long terms. These strategies are designed to create value for the owners and shareholders (Lahti et al., 2018; Oguji & Owusu, 2021).

As organisational strategies for sustainability began to mature, business models changed. A business model encompasses the fundamental logic that an organisation is built on and helps outline the competitive strategy, influences products designs, the value those products deliver and how the organisation captures the value. Initially, the business model will outline a value proposition, value creation, and value capture aspects (Teece, 2010).

An organisation's values must focus on four major divisions of stakeholders. Shareholders need to profit from their investments; an organisation must devise strategies to profit and reduce risks and losses. Also, an organisation must create values for its employees, ensure they are satisfied and retained, and treat them with dignity. Also, the consumers should be respected by creating values that will satisfy the consumers and not endanger them. The government and the public are also interested in the values an organisation creates, and they expect an organisation to conduct business activities to benefit and not endanger the environment (Malik et al., 2018) (Fig. 4.1).

The core belief of every business is value creation; this cannot be compromised. This must be done consistently and be based on specific assumptions (Jain, 2013). Another strategy is embracing change, risk extinction in business, and identifying the value proposition – figuring the marketing strategy that solves customer problems and creates value. There are various areas of applying strategies to achieve sustainability in the four focus areas (Fig. 4.2).

4 The Sustainability Challenge: Developing Strategic Advantage 71

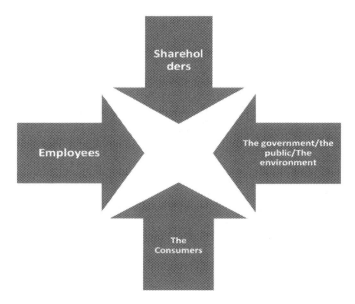

Fig. 4.1 Showing the focus of the sustainability strategies. Source: Author's Presentation

Executing Strategies for Sustainable Businesses

There are various theories and frameworks that an organisation can apply to create strategies in its management. An organisation that wants sustainability needs to apply the best strategies to achieve a competitive advantage in its industry. These strategies will be discussed in detail (Table 4.2).

Adopt the Best Management Strategy and HRM Strategy

According to Uysal (2019), the Contingency HRM paradigm emphasises roles, competence, training, good pay, teamwork, job stability, and performance-based compensation. These practices will assist HRM in

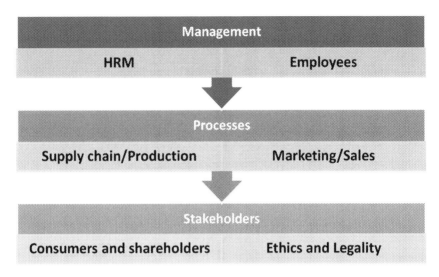

Fig. 4.2 Showing areas of applying sustainability strategies. Source: Author's Presentation

Table 4.2 Showing execution techniques for sustainability

HRM	• Harvard model
	• Contingency model
Career development	• Training
	• Flexibility
Work-life balance	• Flexible working hours
	• Fair and equal compensation for the same work
	• Gender balance
Circular economy	• Recycle
	• Reuse
	• Refurbish
	• Remanufacture
	• Repair
Green energy	• Renewable energy
Waste management	• Proper waste management
	• Avoidance of water, land, and air pollution
Transparency and accountability	• Accurate financial reporting
	• Sustainability report

Source: Author's Presentation

achieving sustainability in its workforce, and it will also achieve improved productivity. The Harvard model is a soft model that focuses on the human element of the business and takes activities such as promotion, job security, career progression, good employer-employee relationship, appraisal system, gender and work balance, and guarantee that employees are satisfied (Uysal, 2019).

Achieve Career Development and Work-Life Balance for the Employees

To achieve workforce sustainability, an organisation must achieve a work-life balance, which will help reduce employee turnover. It will remove work burnout, increase satisfaction, and enhance productivity (Kanwar et al., 2009). Training workers and developing their skills will also increase their commitment and sustainability. Furthermore, fulfilling workers' demands might increase their satisfaction, which will increase their commitment. This can be accomplished by employing Maslow's Hierarchy of Demands, which classifies employees' psychological needs like shelter, food, water, rest, time, and sleep.

The second demand is safety, which refers to protection from threats. It can be met through fair compensation and working conditions, including a solid work-life balance, which will help employees commit and perform better (Johennesse & Chou, 2017). Love is the third human need, and it encompasses social interactions and feelings expressed through interpersonal ways such as friendship, intimacy, affection, love, trust, and acceptance. The fourth need is esteem, which is required for human dignity and the desire for a good reputation and is attained by achievement, mastery, independence; status and prestige.

The last necessity in the hierarchy is self-actualisation. To achieve these, an organisation must adopt flexible work arrangements, giving employees time for career development and work-life balance. Companies must classify their employees according to their tasks and identify suitable for remote employment conditions. If working remotely is not an option, reduced working hours, part-time arrangements, and job sharing can be used to ensure that employees are not burnt out or stressed out (Kanwar et al., 2009).

Circular Economy

Lahti et al. (2018) maintained that a circular economy would help organisations achieve environmental sustainability. This is achieved by designing their products to be suitable for recycling. The circular economy is a response to global climate change. It is achieved through the adoption of strategic Rs such as Reduce, Recycle, Refurbish, and Repair and using these methods will help to reduce wastes by reducing packaging size or removing waste and reusing parts of an old product or recycling it (Farooque et al., 2019; Sodiq et al., 2019). Additionally, a company can make use of renewable energy in their operations. Renewable energy costs less (IEEFA), and green energy contributes to reducing carbon emissions. Organisations must also protect the land and water bodies, reduce or avoid water and land pollution, and manage wastes properly. Improper waste management can make the atmosphere deadly and cause diseases (Siksnelyte et al., 2018).

Financial Reporting

Accurate financial reporting and reporting of sustainability practice is essential. It is ethical and required, and it will also keep an organisation in check and make it consciously engage in sustainability practices. Transparency and accuracy make an organisation avoid unethical business practices (Nwobu et al., 2017). As a result, it will achieve financial and environmental sustainability.

Strategic/Competitive Advantages of Businesses in Africa

Africa is a continent that is blessed with a supply of labour. There is great youth unemployment in the continent of Africa (Chigunta, 2017). The problem of brain drain is common and high in African countries, including Nigeria (Adeyemi et al., 2018). This shows that the labour supply is highly surplus in Africa. That means it is easy for organisations to achieve employee retention by applying sustainability strategies quickly.

Also, various valuable raw materials in Africa can be used for manufacturing and production (Anyu & Dzekashu, 2019). Several multinational companies from Asia and other continents are coming to Africa to exploit its rich natural resources. At the same time, they also take advantage of the developing nature of many African countries to get cheap labour, reducing the cost of production and increasing profitability for these companies (Brautigam et al., 2018). Being close to raw materials and suppliers increases an organisation's sustainability in its supply chain because it is easy to manage suppliers and contribute to safe practices.

Furthermore, Africa is a big market for products and services, and many foreign companies are penetrating Africa to establish subsidiaries in Africa, get raw materials, or use labour in Africa (Anyu & Dzekashu, 2019). This means that there is an opportunity for businesses and entrepreneurs in Africa to grow and enjoy a big market.

Conclusion

Sustainability is crucial to the continuity and growth of every organisation. Organisations need to gain a competitive advantage in all aspects by achieving sustainability in their workforce through sustainable work conditions. Also, organisations must achieve financial stability by making a profit from which their shareholders can earn profit for their investments, and workers would be paid for their work.

Financial sustainability also implies that the organisation contributes to economic growth because it implies growth in a country's

GDP. Environmental sustainability has become a severe concern for decision-makers all over the world. It is crucial to engage in business practices environmentally. As shown in this chapter, various factors, such as government policies, may affect sustainability. Therefore, it is necessary for organisations to conduct adequate and regular research, monitor political trends, and monitor the markets to be able to identify risks and make strategic response plans.

Recommendations

Based on the discussion above, businesses must overcome sustainability challenges and adopt strategies that promote sustainability. Therefore, the following recommendations are made for businesses in Africa.

- Businesses in Africa must not rely on one business model but must adopt a hybrid business model, using the internet and physical models reasonably.
- Businesses in Africa should improve HRM strategies to achieve workforce sustainability.
- Green energy is important in reducing carbon emissions and making the environment safer and healthier.
- Using the circular business model is vital to sustainability because the circular economy reduces waste and leads to materials recycling and reuse.
- Businesses regularly give their financial and sustainability reports but must avoid false financial and sustainability reports to avoid legal actions against financial fraud, leading to bankruptcy.

References

Abegunde, O., & Fabiyi, R. (2020). Nigeria-Benin border closure: Implications for economic development in Nigeria. *Journal of Humanities and Social Sciences Studies, 2*(4), 56–65.

Adeyemi, R. A., Joel, A., Ebenezer, J. T., & Attah, E. Y. (2018). The effect of brain drain on the economic development of developing countries: Evidence from selected African countries. *Journal of Health and Social Issues (JOHESI), 7*(2).

Alamgir, F., & Banerjee, S. B. (2019). Contested compliance regimes in global production networks: Insights from the Bangladesh garment industry. *Human Relations, 72*(2), 272–297.

Anyim, W. O. (2021). Twitter ban in Nigeria: Implications on economy, freedom of speech and information sharing. *Library Philosophy and Practice*, 1–13.

Anyu, J. N., & Dzekashu, W. G. (2019). China's enterprises in Africa: Market entry strategies, implications for capacity building, and corporate social responsibility. *Journal of Economics and Political economy, 6*(2), 172–180.

Bibi, P., Ahmad, A., & Majid, A. H. A. (2018). The impact of training and development and supervisor support on employees retention in academic institutions: The moderating role of the work environment. *Gadjah Mada International Journal of Business, 20*(1), 113–131.

Bocken, N. M., & Geradts, T. H. (2020). Barriers and drivers to sustainable business model innovation: Organization design and dynamic capabilities. *Long Range Planning, 53*(4), 101950.

Brautigam, D., Xiaoyang, T., & Xia, Y. (2018). What kinds of Chinese 'geese' are flying to Africa? Evidence from Chinese manufacturing firms. *Journal of African Economies, 27*(1), i29–i51.

Caruth, G., & Caruth, D. (2013). Understanding resistance to change. *Turkish Online Journal of Distance Education, 14*(2), 12–21.

Chigunta, F. (2017). Entrepreneurship as a possible solution to youth unemployment in Africa. *Laboring and learning, 10*, 433–451.

Clarke, P. (2011). Tesco pull out of Japan. Retrieved December 18, 2021, from https://www.theguardian.com/business/2011/aug/31/tesco-japan-pull-out-philip-clarke

Drayson, K., Wood, G., & Thompson, S. (2015). Assessing the quality of the ecological component of English environmental statements. *Journal of Environmental Management, 160*, 241–253.

Erin, O., Adegboye, A., & Bamigboye, O. A. (2021). Corporate governance and sustainability reporting quality: Evidence from Nigeria. *Sustainability Accounting, Management and Policy Journal.* https://doi.org/10.1108/SAMPJ-06-2020-0185. Accessed 18 Dec 2021.

Farooque, M., et al. (2019). Circular supply chain management: A definition and structured literature review. *Journal of Cleaner Production, 228*, 882–900.

Freudenreich, B., Lüdeke-Freund, F., & Schaltegger, S. (2020). A stakeholder theory perspective on business models: Value creation for sustainability. *Journal of Business Ethics, 166*(1), 3–18.

Geissdoerfer, M., Vladimirova, D., & Evans, S. (2018). Sustainable business model innovation: A review. *Journal of Cleaner Production, 198*, 401–416.

Hart, O., & Zingales, L. (2017). Serving shareholders does not mean putting profit above all else. *Harvard Business Review, 12*, 2–6.

Hörisch, J., Schaltegger, S., & Freeman, R. E. (2020). Integrating stakeholder theory and sustainability accounting: A conceptual synthesis. *Journal of Cleaner Production, 275*, 124097.

Jain, S. (2013). *6 effective ways to build a sustainable business.* Retrieved 11:04 am, December 7, 2021, from https://www.entrepreneur.com/article/252029

Johennesse, L. A. C., & Chou, T. K. (2017). Employee perceptions of talent management effectiveness on retention. *Global Business & Management Research, 9*(3).

Kano, M. (2021). *NDIC pays N11bn to over 500,000 depositors of liquidated banks.* Retrieved December 15, 2021, from https://guardian.ng/business-services/ndic-pays-n11bn-to-over-500000-depositors-of-liquidated-banks/

Kanwar, Y. P. S., Singh, A. K., & Kodwani, A. D. (2009). Work-life balance and burnout as predictors of job satisfaction in the IT-ITES industry. *Vision, 13*(2), 1–12.

Lahti, T., Wincent, J., & Parida, V. (2018). A definition and theoretical review of the circular economy, value creation, and sustainable business models: Where are we now and where should research move in the future? *Sustainability, 10*(8), 2799.

Malik, A., Pereira, V., & Budhwar, P. (2018). Value creation and capture through human resource management practices: Gazing through the business model lens. *Organisational Dynamics, 47*(3), 180–188.

Molino, M., Cortese, C. G., & Ghislieri, C. (2019). Unsustainable working conditions: The association of destructive leadership, use of technology, and workload with workaholism and exhaustion. *Sustainability, 11*(2), 446.

Nwobu, O. A., Owolabi, A. A., & Iyoha, F. O. (2017). Sustainability reporting in financial institutions: A study of the Nigerian banking sector. *The Journal of Internet Banking and Commerce*, 1–15.

Offerman, S. (2021). *Post Brexit Companies face new UK tariff regime.* Retrieved December 22, 2021, from https://tax.thomsonreuters.com/blog/post-brexit

Oguji, N., & Owusu, R. A. (2021). Market entry into Africa: Acquisitions and international joint ventures. Studies of foreign firms' market entry strategies, challenges, and performance in Africa. *Thunderbird International Business Review, 63*(1), 5–9.

Ortiz-de-Mandojana, N., & Bansal, P. (2016). The long-term benefits of organisational resilience through sustainable business practices. *Strategic Management Journal, 37*(8), 1615–1631.

Oyewumi, O. R., Ogunmeru, O. A., & Oboh, C. S. (2018). Investment in corporate social responsibility, disclosure practices, and financial performance of banks in Nigeria. *Future Business Journal, 4*(2), 195–205.

Renouard, C., & Ezvan, C. (2018). Corporate social responsibility towards human development: A capabilities framework. *Business Ethics: A European Review, 27*(2), 144–155.

Sarkis, J., & Zhu, Q. (2018). Environmental sustainability and production: Taking the road less travelled. *International Journal of Production Research, 56*(1–2), 743–759.

Schaltegger, S., & Wagner, M. (2017). Managing and measuring the business case for sustainability: Capturing the relationship between sustainability performance, business competitiveness and economic performance. In *Managing the business case for sustainability* (pp. 1–27). Routledge.

Siksnelyte, I., Zavadskas, E. K., Streimikiene, D., & Sharma, D. (2018). An overview of multi-criteria decision-making methods in dealing with sustainable energy development issues. *Energies, 11*(10), 2754.

Sodiq, A., Baloch, A. A., Khan, S. A., Sezer, N., Mahmoud, S., Jama, M., & Abdelaal, A. (2019). Towards modern sustainable cities: Review of sustainability principles and trends. *Journal of Cleaner Production, 227*, 972–1001.

Teece, D. J. (2010). Business models, business strategy and innovation. *Long Range Planning, 43*(2–3), 172–194.

UN. (2021). *The 17 goals*. Retrieved December 18, 2021, from `https://sdgs.un.org/goals`

Uysal, G. (2019). Quantitative methods in human resource management. *Journal of Modern Accounting and Auditing, 15*(7), 367–370.

Valinejad, F., & Rahmani, D. (2018). Sustainability risk management in the supply chain of telecommunication companies: A case study. *Journal of Cleaner Production, 203*, 53–67.

5

Enhancing Marketing Practices: A Responsible Product for an Engaged Consumer

Vanessa Burgal

Introduction

When discussing consumer empowerment, we think about consumers who can freely choose any product or service of their choice, fully aware and conscious of the consequences of their selection and protected from unfair business actions. Nowadays, companies study their target consumers to develop the most adapted offer to satisfy their clients' needs. As explained by Byrne in the European Commission for Consumers (Byrne, 2003), when focusing on consumer satisfaction, companies enhance market competitiveness, which ensures the development of the best products to answer consumer needs; however, countries need regulations to protect consumer interests and rights. With this consumer satisfaction moment, when consumers choose, acquire, and enjoy the usage and consumption of the product or service they need, we can discuss consumer empowerment.

V. Burgal (✉)
Lagos Business School, Pan-Atlantic University, Lekki, Nigeria
e-mail: vburgal@lbs.edu.ng

But how can consumers make the right choices to satisfy their needs better while taking responsible decisions for themselves and their communities? Is an empowered consumer a potentially responsible and engaged consumer? Are we individually consuming responsibly?

While the world's food and industrial production keep growing, many developed countries are confronted with overproduction problems, while humans are starving in some developing countries. Even in the most sustainable markets, one can see tons of daily food waste, fashion overconsumption, or shoppers running to get the latest version of their smartphone device. For example, Germany is among the most engaged countries with the U.N. Sustainability Goals.[1] While a Bitkom survey from 2021 shows that almost 200 million devices lie unused in German households (Fill, 2022).

Worried by the Earth's climate warming, civil society is putting pressure on governments and companies to take action. Clients and customers push large companies to act on climate change, while smaller businesses feel pressure from regulators (Coppola et al., 2019). Thus, some organisations are transforming their business models towards sustainability, but many still need to be over-producing and influencing customers to overconsume. We can even find companies developing and implementing "greenwashing" strategies to fake a sustainable company image. Indeed, developing greener products and more sustainable lifestyles in the Western regions do not compensate for the negative effects of a capitalist system promoting never-ending economic growth. A growth that requires continuous production for a continuously growing consumption, especially in the developed markets, which externalise the side effects to the poorest economies and less developed countries (Dauvergne, 2010).

Hence, consumption could be seen as a problem. But empowered customers could help rationalise it and protect themselves and their environment. However, to be more responsible, consumers need to be aware of the impact of their shopping behaviours and educated to become sustainably engaged consumers.

---

[1] Germany is ranked 6th over 193 UN Member States in the achievement of the Sustainability Development Goals (SDGs) worldwide. The overall score measures the total progress towards achieving all 17 SDGs (Sachs et al., 2022).

Thanks to the worldwide expansion of the internet and customers' direct access to information, marketers are confronted with well-informed consumers who can easily search about brands, products, and their manufacturing companies. The new "phygital" consumers shop physically at brick-and-mortar retail stores after looking for information online, or the other way around. After visiting shops, many consumers may acquire their products online. Overall, this new "phygital" way of life developing worldwide has many advantages for the African consumer. Indeed, in multiple African markets, customers often need more product and service information access. Besides, they can only sometimes visit different stores, constrained by the local infrastructures and transport problems. Thanks to the internet expansion, primarily accessed through their mobile phones, Africans can better deal with these development issues and confront the market offer better prepared and with more chances to choose the right product. This digital expansion is critical for African consumers to take more responsible decisions and, in the end, ensure complete customer satisfaction.

Is the African Consumer Empowered to Make a Responsible Choice?

The African Consumer

Like most emerging countries, African markets are heterogeneous; they lack resources, suffer from poor infrastructures, and are strongly influenced by socio-political institutions (Sheth, 2011). Indeed, consumption in Africa is directly correlated with the purchasing power of the local populations, who earn meagre salaries for the most part. The poverty disparity between African countries and even within the countries themselves is considerable. Countries such as Burundi register the lowest GDP per capita in sub-Saharan Africa ($792 in 2021), compared to South Africa, with a GDP 20 times higher ($14,420.2) and the highest Gini

Index[2] worldwide (The World Bank, 2021a). About one out of three Africans living in the sub-Sahara region live on less than $2.15 daily (The World Bank, 2019). With this reality, many consumers show a "survival-mode" behaviour, as explained by Maslow in his hierarchy of needs, where humans are meant to cover the most basic and physiological needs, such as health and food, before thinking about higher-level needs such as ethics or self-esteem (Maslow, 1943).

In Africa, purchases are very much concentrated on consumable goods, especially food items (Uzo et al., 2018). Overall, lower-income African consumer shops primarily for affordable essential products. In other words, their purchase decision is influenced by the prices of goods or services (Uzo et al., 2018; Agyenim-Boateng et al., 2015). However, it is also important to note that the perception of value for money and quality differs between countries, economic status, and cultural orientation (Agyenim-Boateng et al., 2015).

The 4As of Marketing

Adapting to consumer demand, companies have produced a range of affordable and accessible products and services that do not always comply with the Sustainable Development Goals from the United Nations (United Nations Department of Economics and Social Affairs, n.d.) but are answering their consumer needs. An excellent example of these African alternatives is the usage of sachets, a small pack containing a single consumption for products such as milk, soap, or even water (Unilever, 2022a). In Nigeria, brands such as Dettol, Baileys, Fresh Yo, and Chivita have joined the "sachetisation" trend (Ifeanyi, 2021). The "sachet concept" is not new to the country. More than 20 years ago, water manufacturers were already selling water in sachets to meet the needs of the poorest segments of the population (Muanya, 2021). Nowadays, after the Covid effects, the rising inflation and the Ukrainian war impact on

---

[2] Gini Index: The Gini index measures the extent to which the distribution of income or consumption among individuals or households within an economy deviates from a perfectly equal distribution. A Gini index of 0 represents perfect equality, while an index of 100 implies perfect inequality (The World Bank, 2023).

the economy, Nigerian's purchasing power continues to decline, increasing their poverty numbers to 133 million Nigerians, exceeding the World Bank projections for 2022 (Trading Economics, 2022; Tuni, 2022). Hence, these small packs have become the day-to-day of numerous Nigerians who need help to afford to buy in larger quantities (often more economical in the long run). Thus, one can see how open-market kiosks are decorated with multi-colour sachets and how the streets and lagoons surrounding Lagos, the economic capital of Nigeria, are covered with a floating garbage patch of non-recycled plastic sachets (Borneo Bulletin, 2022; Agence France Presse, 2022).

For some African markets, the lack of government regulations is often enhanced by the oligopolistic behaviours of some multinational firms, which benefit from government support, trade barriers, and limited foreign competition (Roberts et al., 2017). A good example is the traditional cartels of cement, concrete and fertilisers in the South of Africa (Makhaya et al., 2012; Roberts, 2013), telecommunication markets (The World Bank, 2016), and primary food products such as sugar or rice (Nwuneli, 2018). As mentioned earlier, this situation directly impacts the consumer, especially among lower-income segments who spend most of their income on basic food items. This effect worsens in urban cities such as Abidjan or Lagos, where the average price of essential products such as white rice or white flour can be 24% higher than in other cities worldwide (The World Bank, 2016). Thus, numerous African consumers are handicapped by the limited affordability of essential products.

African consumption is also influenced by product accessibility. Even when they are well-informed, African consumers can only sometimes access ethical and sustainable versions of the products or services they seek. This is due to multiple reasons. First, since African countries are often less regulated than other regions, companies can offer less sustainable versions of their products and services. Sometimes, the non-availability of sustainable products results from limited resources, constraining local companies' manufacturing options. Also, 58% of the sub-Saharan population live in rural areas with inadequate infrastructures, so products are not easily accessible (The World Bank, 2021b).

This lack of accessibility and affordability worsens when the consumer does not have enough information about the product or service and does not know the potential impact of such a purchase. Good product and service understanding require a minimum education, starting with basic literacy and numeracy skills. However, education in Africa is yet a challenge. With only 70% of the students completing primary education in sub-Saharan Africa and an average adult literacy rate of about 67% (World Bank, 2020), how can companies ensure their customers understand the products and services they offer?

Indeed, African consumers need to be made aware of the impact of some products. Often, their expectations differ from the real functional and psychological benefits the products will offer, making the products unacceptable. According to Consumers International, consumers need special support with financial services, food security, energy, household goods, and information and communication technologies (ICT) (Consumers International, 2021). For example, financial services, which are rapidly developing in emerging markets, are supported by digital and mobile expansions. Consumers may adopt these services in those markets, despite partially comprehending them. They often have to deal with contract terms not explained at the point of sale, hidden or inflated charges or fees, and unfair contract terms and conditions (Consumers International, 2021). Another example is how the elevated consumption of ultra-processed foods and drinks boosts the spread of obesity and non-communicable diseases (NCDs), such as hypertension and diabetes, in the region. Unaware of the negative impact of those products, the African consumer replaces traditional food with processed products high in sodium, sugar, saturated fats, and calories (Bopape et al., 2021).

In 1990, after realising the pricing regulations were ineffective, the Botswana government started a programme to educate consumers about their rights and responsibilities. More recently, a study among adolescents in secondary schools from Botswana proved that the consumer education programmes worked effectively among those young consumer segments since the majority were aware of their consumer rights and also responsibilities, and they could act as informed consumers (Makela & Peters, 2004; Wright et al., 2006).

While government initiatives can improve the consumer situation in Africa, companies are co-responsible and can easily support educational programmes to empower consumers. In this new digital world full of marketing content, studies prove that consumers are more likely to buy from a brand immediately after they consume educational content (Stebbins, 2022). Thus, as we will further illustrate, developing educational programmes could be an excellent opportunity for marketers to build authentic customer relationships and empower the African consumer.

From Consumer Protection to Consumer Satisfaction in Africa

The Consumer Rights

Consumers need to be protected. As U.S. President John F. Kennedy announced on 15 March 1962 in a directive to the Consumer Advisory Council, consumers were entitled to the following basic rights (Wood, 2017):

- the right to safety
- the right to be informed
- the right to choose
- the right to be heard

These rights were later extended by the United Nations guidelines (United Nations General Assembly, UNGA, 1985, 2015):

(a) Access by consumers to essential goods and services;
(b) The protection of vulnerable and disadvantaged consumers;
(c) The protection of consumers from hazards to their health and safety;
(d) The promotion and protection of the economic interests of consumers;
(e) Access by consumers to adequate information to enable them to make informed choices according to individual wishes and needs;
(f) Consumer education, including education on the environmental, social, and economic consequences of consumer choice; and
(g) Availability of effective consumer dispute resolution and redress.

Are African Markets Ready to Protect Their Consumers?

Reading the above U.N. guidelines, consumer rights are clear, but how can we ensure the respect of those rights? Moreover, who should be responsible for it?

As explained in the previous section, producing and selling responsible products is difficult in African markets. However, if companies want to build a long-term relationship with their customers, sooner or later, they will also have to act responsibly, even when local governments do not regulate. Companies may have to replace public institutions that sometimes lack the needed resources to invest in the local communities. Overall, "marketers must focus on enhancing customers' quality of life" (Sheth & Sisodia, 2006). Quoting Mallen Baker, "responsible marketing is about building trust between the company and its customers" (Baker, 2009). But can the African consumer trust companies?

History demonstrates that, without supervision or regulation, numerous companies intentionally or unintentionally do not respect those rights. For example, Nestlé in the 1970s, when the company promoted baby formula, especially in developing countries. In those times, mothers' knowledge about baby formula was inadequate to take informed decisions, and the company's communication strategy was unclear, leaving the consumers unprotected. Somehow, this global boycott to protect Third World Mothers influenced the World Health Organisation (WHO) and the United Nations Children's Fund (UNICEF) to develop the International Code of Marketing of Breast-Milk Substitutes (Sasson, 2016).

Another example is the pesticides manufactured and distributed by multinationals such as BASF and BAYER in Africa. Some of those products are officially forbidden in Europe due to their side effects on human health. Nevertheless, despite the scientifically proven research, those companies have continued selling these dangerous products in countries such as South Africa until recently (Bega, 2021).

We can find similar stories around the dirty fuels with high levels of sulphur forbidden in Europe, the used vehicles imported from developed economies, or the lower safety features of some branded cars manufactured for the South African market (BBC News, 2016; DownToEarth, 2018; Le Roux, 2021). Overall, Africa is one of the preferred destinations for occidental waste, reinforced by weak government regulations, consumer poverty, and poor business ethics.

The New Consumer Power

Moreover, the question is, why? These examples prove that consumer rights are rarely respected in low-regulation markets with limited competition.

However, thanks to the digital world expansion and the power of social media, companies have been pushed to be more careful. Many will recall Monsanto, the controversial chemical company, which had to fight legal disputes for more than 20 years with farmers and processors because of the side effects of its chemical and later biotechnological products. Monsanto's famous herbicide, Roundup, and after its genetically modified seeds and cereals were proven unsafe for humans (Mattera, 2020). Consequently, when the multinational Bayer acquired Monsanto, the company decided to rename the group. As president of Bayer's Crop Science Division, Liam Condon stated, dropping Monsanto's name "is part of a wider campaign to win back consumer trust" (Dewey, 2018).

Pushed by regulations, the increasing consumer power, and the need to improve business results, many companies have understood that showing care for the consumer is crucial for their success. Leading companies such as Amazon or Starbucks mention their customer focus strategy as the main reason for their worldwide success. Studies from different sources prove that when the whole organisation's culture aims to create customer value, the business has more chances of success. According to experts, this customer-centric culture should go from the CEO to the organisation's front line. Indeed, when top executives believe in their customer experience, their companies seem more profitable than their competitors (64% of executives, according to the EIU global survey results) (Economist Intelligence Unit, 2015). However, according to the CMO Council, only 14% of marketers believe that customer-centricity is a hallmark of their companies (CMO, 2014). It is true that despite all these trends, many companies are still product-centric or sales-centric, and this is similar in Africa.

Customer-Centric Companies to Achieve Customer Satisfaction

So how can African companies be customer-centric, and what would be the minimum requirements to ensure customer satisfaction?

A consumer-centric vision should start at the leadership level of the company. Studies prove that a truly successful consumer-centric culture requires the total buy-in of the company leaders (The Economist Intelligence Unit, 2015). Indeed, famous business leaders have understood that their company's success is linked to consumer satisfaction, how their teams innovate to solve their customers' problems, and how the whole organisational culture focuses on the consumer experience. Moreover, executives need to care about their employees, creating a sense of belonging and empowering them. To retain employees and ensure they contribute to a great consumer experience, they need to feel loved and valuable with the right tools to bring added value. As experts may say, "the employee experience is the new customer experience" (Franz, 2022) because the employee experiences are the sum of interactions with the company and the customers, and only employees can make consumer experiences unique. In this post-pandemic new digital world, employees are more difficult to retain, especially in sub-Saharan Africa, where talents are moving abroad in search of better living conditions. Thus, as an extension of our consumer understanding, responsible companies should also consider employee understanding.

Marketers should also rediscover the customer-centric essence of marketing, taking their marketing strategy to a new level where African consumers would be aware of the companies' offers, and those products and services would be accessible, affordable, and acceptable for them (Sheth & Sisodia, 2012). A good starting point would be to offer a responsible product, from the raw materials to the point of sale, from the ideation to the commercialisation, to create customer value. Involving consumers during the concept development, conducting consumer research, concept testing, and market testing would also be helpful steps to launch the best-adapted product and services with the ideal marketing strategy and reach consumer delight.

Some Practical Examples

Let me illustrate the above process with the mentioned case of Nestlé's Baby formula in Africa in the 1970s. During those times, the Swiss multinational promoted milk powder as a healthier alternative to mothers' breastfeeding. Consequently, many African mothers decided to replace natural breastfeeding with Nestlé's powder milk. Some families even diluted the formula to make it last longer or used non-potable water to mix the powder (Guasti, 2012; Solomon, 1981). These consumer behaviours caused malnutrition and diseases in numerous infants. Of course, the product packaging included instructions on how to properly use the powder. However, the company did not fully consider the high illiteracy in the regions where the product was promoted. Infant formula is a nutritious product, but only when the shopper can afford sufficient quantities, when they can use clean water and when users can understand the packaging instructions on how to mix the formula correctly. If Nestlé had launched some ethnographic research and observed the target customers using the product, marketers would have identified the limited product comprehension of the poorest customer segments. In other words, the product ingredients were perfect, but the overall product concept did not satisfy the customer's needs. The baby formula needed additional features and a good marketing communication campaign on how and when to use the milk powder, tested adequately with the target audience to validate their understanding.

Once more, looking at the baby formula example, we come across the crucial consumer understanding and the importance of consumer education. Even when the product formulation seems perfect, marketers need to know their clients well enough to predict a potential misusage of the product and prevent it by adapting the concept and building an educational programme.

Another interesting example of how companies can influence customers and educate them through responsible products and campaigns is the case of the skin-lightening cosmetics distributed in multiple African countries, despite global and domestic bans due to their mercury content. Many African women lighten their skin because, in their countries, fair skin is perceived as more attractive and successful (Brown, 2019). Step one for any manufacturing company would be to stop including toxic ingredients in the composition, as major cosmetics companies did, partly pushed by countries' regulations. This should be combined with responsible communication campaigns, especially in regions where darker skin is not perceived as beautiful. In 2020, the multinational L'Oréal decided to stop using words such as "whitening", "fair", and "lightening" from all its skin-evening products as a response to the "Black Matters" worldwide movement (Carr, 2020). Other multinationals such as Unilever and Johnson & Johnson followed. These new respectful attitudes should have been considered while developing this product category. When marketers were brainstorming on how to satisfy the consumers' need for lighter skins, ethics should have come to their minds. Is it right to promote whitening products? Can we help our consumers without promoting unethical products? Moreover, more importantly, could we educate the consumer to understand that all skin colours are beautiful?

Thus, marketing a responsible product can only be successful with transparency and respect for consumers' rights. Consumers can only make responsible choices with balanced product information and education. This balance depends on marketers who understand their target consumers' needs, expectations, and level of product understanding. Quoting Clinton and Chatrah: it is recommended that "Indigenous companies in Nigeria and other Sub-Saharan African countries be proactive in educating consumers, and implementing CSR beyond the philanthropic level and begin to view it as a source of good fortune, novelty and competitive advantage" (Clinton & Chatrath, 2022).

Educating the Consumer: The Right Communication Strategy

Educating the consumer is key. As stated earlier in the general principles of the U.N. Guidelines for Consumer Protection, consumers should have access to "adequate information to enable them to make informed choices" and access to "education, including on environmental, social and economic consequences of consumer choice" (United Nations Conference on Trade and Development, 2016). Different studies also highlight education as one of the best consumer protection strategies. After research on financial services in poor and middle-income countries, the members of Consumers International considered "consumer education and information/awareness" the most relevant factor to help consumers (Consumers International, 2021).

And this needed education can easily come from companies and their marketing departments, especially in countries where local institutions and governments need more resources to develop adapted programmes. To do so, the company should identify the community needs to answer with its brands and products and then create an adapted programme that can educate the consumer and influence its final behaviour in the long run. These programmes can be partial or complete CSR (Corporate Social Responsibility) campaigns. However, they should at least offer a conscious adaptation of the entire Marketing Mix to the local needs, ensuring the brand respects consumer rights and empowers the customer to make a conscious choice. Marketers must guarantee the client is well informed about the product or service characteristics, the pros and cons of acquiring and using it, and the final impact on themselves and their communities. This responsible marketing goes beyond offering the ideal product or service to answer your customers' needs; it implies empowering consumers through education to ensure they can take their own decisions. With this purpose, marketers must consider the local community characteristics, the educational level of its target consumers, their access to new technologies and their knowledge and comprehension of the product or services they are selling.

By simply working on the traditional 4 Ps of Marketing (Product, Price, Promotion, and Place), the professional must guarantee shoppers and consumers understand the category they are purchasing. Take, for example, a mother buying breakfast cereals for her children. In developed markets, packaged consumer products targeting kids are often confronted with country regulations regarding health and promotions to non-adults. Looking at the cereal example, the marketer will probably supervise the composition of the product, mainly the sugar levels and the vitamins written on the front labels, and will check if the advertising campaign is truthful. Those regulations tend to be very rigorous, and multinationals usually apply the same restrictions to the African markets. However, education is not only about regulations but about constructing useful programmes that contribute to a better life for the local community.

In the case of cereals, the marketeer could improve the product by reducing its amount of sugar, which has a tremendous negative impact on the number of diabetics in sub-Saharan Africa (Iwu-Jaja et al., 2020). Furthermore, the marketing team could also contribute by offering complete transparency with a clear and understandable pack label, reminding through social and traditional media that added sugar could have negative health effects, and developing educational programs for local schools, paediatricians, and parents about how sugar can be harmful to health when over-consumed.

A good illustration of the above is how Unilever is nudging consumers to eat healthier, adapting its campaigns to the local community's needs.

In 2015, Unilever launched a programme to compensate for iron deficiency in sub-Saharan African communities such as Nigeria with the brand Knorr and Kenya with Royco (Sidibe, 2020). In Nigeria, Knorr launched iron-fortified seasoning cubes supported by a communication campaign that explained how important iron is for health. This media campaign shows how to mix the seasoning cubes with green leaves such as spinaches, a product rich in iron, creating attractive cooking recipes that directly educate on how to cook and eat healthier. A study evaluating the efficiency of this programme proved that branded behaviour change programmes could influence consumers, in this case, increasing the awareness of anaemia (lack of iron) and changing cooking behaviours (Lion et al., 2018).

In 2019, Knorr developed a similar programme to promote a healthy diet in the Netherlands, where the population needs to consume more vegetables compared to the average intake in Europe. Knorr launched the Knorr Meal Kits to influence consumer behaviour; Knorr, with logos on the front of the pack reminding consumers about eating the recommended amount of vegetables. This was combined with new healthier recipe suggestions on the package and reinforced with social media, in-store activations, and advertisements (Nudging for Good, 2019).

Another demonstration of how marketers can contribute to improved community life is the case of Lifebuoy soap and its "High 5 for handwashing", a social media campaign aimed at celebrating clean and confident hands. Through its campaign, Lifebuoy seeks to change handwashing behaviour in emerging markets such as Kenya and India as part of its commitment to decreasing child mortality. Since 2009, the Unilever soap brand has developed several educational programmes targeting mothers and children to ensure children reach the age of five. A recent study has proven that the programme was successful in its primary objective. As a result, Lifebuoy has developed a strong relationship with its direct consumers (Sidibe, 2020).

Similarly, volunteering employees from Unilever have piloted a container centre to recycle plastic in South Africa. This country produces an average of 41 kilograms of plastic waste per person yearly compared to the global average of 29 kilograms (World Wide Fund for Nature, 2020). Since local populations were not fully aware of what is recyclable, consumer behaviour has been incentivised with R5 airtime rewards and supported with brand communication to educate consumers about the type of plastics they can recycle (Unilever, 2022b).

Another remarkable example is when Carling Black Label, the largest beer brand in South Africa, launched a social campaign to fight against gender-based violence, an extended social problem often related to alcohol abuse. The programme combined the training of community leaders and influencers with the #NoExcuse social media and television advertising, plus sponsored events such as an 8000 men's march and the Soweto Derby soccer match, where the players adhered to the campaign. The brand also partnered with some local NGOs. As well explained by Myriam Sidibe in "Brands on a Mission", the impact of this social campaign is difficult to measure. However, it succeeded in increasing brand awareness, engaging the company employees, and reaching millions across the country, including rural areas (Sidibe, 2020; Makhaya & Roberts, 2013).

The above African examples demonstrate that responsible marketers can build long-term consumer relationships while contributing to people's education. Through their numerous marketing tools, companies can construct adapted educational programmes filling up the lack of resources of the local institutions and producing a common benefit for both the business and the communities.

Key Recommendations

- Build a customer-centric organisation.
- Focus on understanding your target consumer needs.
- Design an educational marketing programme that empowers the consumer.
- Build a relationship of trust and transparency with your clients.

Conclusions

Worldwide, sustainable consumption is a trending topic. Many citizens and societies worry about the increasing temperature of the planet and all the consequences of "Climate Change". Economies are suffering the negative impacts, and numerous governments have started to intervene, considering sustainable consumption to be one of their key international agenda topics (Miniero et al., 2014). Under this environmental crisis, the consumer is more informed than ever and expects companies to lead purposefully, offering more than only products and services. However, this is only sometimes the case in Africa. The African consumer needs to be more aware and empowered to make informed decisions that benefit them and their communities. Through their marketing teams, companies should protect the African consumer, develop marketing programs that empower them, and enhance their marketing practices to create customer satisfaction. With a proper understanding of the consumer and adapted product information and education, marketers can build consumer awareness and develop affordable, accessible, and acceptable products and services that answer consumer needs in Africa. Only responsible marketing practices can create customer value and encourage future consumer engagement. Quoting Mallen Baker, "The responsible marketer is not one that never pushes the boundaries" (Baker, 2009).

References

Agence France Presse. (2022, August 6). From coffee to toothpaste, Nigerians buy small as hardships bite. *The Citizen.* https://www.citizen.co.za/news/news-world/news-africa/toothpaste-nigerians-soaring-prices-2022/

Agyenim-Boateng, Y., Benson-Armer, R., & Russo, B. (2015, July 1). Winning in Africa's consumer market. *McKinsey.* Retrieved December 13, 2022, from https://www.mckinsey.com/industries/consumer-packaged-goods/our-insights/winning-in-africas-consumer-market

Baker, M. (2009, November 17). What is responsible marketing? *Mallen Baker.* We Retrieved December 10, 2022, from http://mallenbaker.net/article/clear-reflection/what-is-responsible-marketing

BBC News. (2016, December 5). Five African countries ban 'dirty fuels' from Europe. *BBC News.* Retrieved November 15, 2022, from https://www.bbc.com/news/world-africa-38210868

Bega, S. (2021, May 9). EU-banned pesticides are harming farmworkers in S.A. *Mail Guardian.* https://mg.co.za/environment/2021-05-09-eu-banned-pesticides-are-harming-farmworkers-in-sa/

Bopape, M., Taillie, L. S., Frank, T., Murukutla, N., Cotter, T., Majija, L., & Swart, R. (2021). South African consumers' perceptions of front-of-package warning labels on unhealthy foods and drinks. *PLoS One, 16*(9), e0257626. https://doi.org/10.1371/journal.pone.0257626

Borneo Bulletin. (2022, August 15). Living on sachets. *Borneo Bulletin* Retrieved November 15, 2022, from https://borneobulletin.com.bn/living-on-sachets/

Brown, O. (2019, January 15). Banning skin-bleaching products will not work as long as fair skin is linked with beauty and success. *CNN.* Retrieved December 20, 2022, from https://edition.cnn.com/2019/01/15/health/banning-bleaching-products-in-africa/index.html

Byrne, D. (2003, October 28) *European Commissioner for Health and Consumer Protection, Consumer General Assembly*, Brussels. Retrieved December 20, 2022, from https://www.europa-nu.nl/id/vgkt1ffuk4wo/nieuws/autom_vertaling_david_byrne_consumenten?v=1&ctx=vgg41g1vojsn&start_tab0=40

Carr, G. (2020, June 28). L'Oréal will remove 'whitening', 'lightening' and 'fair' from skin care products in response to Black Lives Matter protests. *MailOnline*. https://www.dailymail.co.uk/news/article-8466229/LOreal-remove-words-like-whitening-skin-products.html

Chief Marketing Office (CMO) Council. (2014, September 15). Mastering adaptive customer engagements. *CMO Council*. Retrieved December 13, 2022, from http://www.cmocouncil.org/thought-leadership/reports/286/download

Clinton, C., & Chatrath, S. K. (2022). The value of consumer awareness and corporate social responsibility in marketing: An overview. In S. Ogunyemi & V. Burgal (Eds.), *Products for conscious consumers* (1st ed., pp. 49–63). Emerald Publishing. https://doi.org/10.1108/978-1-80262-837-120221004

Consumers International. (2021, March 26). The role of consumer organisations to support consumers of financial services in low and middle income countries. *Consumers International*. Retrieved December 13, 2022, from https://www.consumersinternational.org/media/368720/cgap-ci-repor_26-3-2021.pdf

Coppola, M., Krick, T., & Blohmke, J. (2019, December 12). Feeling the heat? Companies are under pressure on climate change and need to do more. *The Deloitte Sustainability Services*. Retrieved December 20, 2022, from https://www2.deloitte.com/us/en/insights/topics/strategy/impact-and-opportunities-of-climate-change-on-business.html

Dauvergne, P. (2010, May). The problem of consumption. *Global Environmental Politics, 10*(2), 1–10. https://doi.org/10.1162/glep.2010.10.2.1

Dewey, C. (2018, June 4). Why Monsanto is no more. *The Washington Post*. https://www.washingtonpost.com/news/wonk/wp/2018/06/04/why-monsanto-is-no-more/

DownToEarth. (2018, July 23). CSE study exposes massive environmental dumping of old and used vehicles in Africa, and South Asia. *DownToEarth*. Retrieved December 20, 2022, from https://www.downtoearth.org.in/news/energy/cse-study-exposes-massive-environmental-dumping-of-old-and-used-vehicles-in-africa-south-asia-61213

Fill, A. (2022, March 15). How Often Do Users Purchase a New Mobile Phone? *Nevis Security*. Retrieved December 20, 2022, from https://www.nevis.net/en/blog/how-often-do-users-change-their-smartphone

Franz, A. (2022, March 14). Improving employee experience to improve customer experience. *Tymeshift*. Retrieved December 13, 2022, from https://www.tymeshift.com/blog/improving-employee-experience

Guasti, C. (2012). From breastfeeding to bottles: Nestlé infant formula debate and its aftermath. *The Columbia University Journal of Global Health, 2*(2), 1–4. https://doi.org/10.7916/thejgh.v2i2.5018

Ifeanyi, U. J. (2021, April 26). Sachetization: An innovation around poverty? *Nairametrics*. https://nairametrics.com/2021/04/26/sachetization-an-innovation-around-poverty/

Iwu-Jaja, C. J., Kengne, A. P., & Wiysonge, C. S. (2020, November 12). Diabetes is a ticking time bomb in sub-Saharan Africa. *The conversation*. Retrieved December 20, 2022, from https://theconversation.com/diabetes-is-a-ticking-time-bomb-in-sub-saharan-africa-149766

Le Roux, K. (2021, October 6). Unsafe new cars for sale in South Africa that would be illegal in Europe. *CapeTalk*. https://www.capetalk.co.za/articles/429055/unsafe-new-cars-for-sale-in-south-africa-that-would-be-illegal-in-europe

Lion, R., Arulogun, O., Titiloye, M., et al. (2018). The effect of the "follow in my green food steps" programme on cooking behaviours for improved iron intake: A quasi-experimental randomised community study. *International Journal of Behavioral Nutrition and Physical Activity, 15*(79). https://doi.org/10.1186/s12966-018-0710-4

Makela, C., & Peters, S. (2004, September 6). Consumer education: Creating consumer awareness among adolescents in Botswana. *International Journal of Consumer Studies, 28*(4), 379–387. https://doi.org/10.1111/j.1470-6431.2004.00402.x

Makhaya, G., Mkwananzi, W., & Roberts, S. (2012). How should young institutions approach enforcement? Reflections on South Africa's experience. *South African Journal of International Affairs, 19*(1), 43–64. https://doi.org/10.1080/10220461.2012.670402

Makhaya, G. & Roberts, S. (2013, December). Expectations and outcomes: Considering competition and corporate power in South Africa under democracy. *Review of African Political Economy, 40*(138), 556–571. http://www.jstor.org/stable/24858280

Maslow, A. H. (1943). A theory of human motivation. *Psychological Review, 50*(4), 370–396. https://doi.org/10.1037/h0054346

Mattera, P. (2020, September 26). Monsanto: Corporate Rap Sheet. Monsanto (now owned by Bayer). *The Corporate Research Project*. Retrieved December 20, 2022, from https://www.corp-research.org/monsanto

Miniero, G., Codini, A., Bonera, M., Corvi, E., & Bertoli, G. (2014). Being green: From attitude to actual consumption. *International Journal of Consumer Studies, 38*(5), 21–528. https://doi.org/10.1111/ijcs.12128

Muanya, C. (2021, November 3). Why we increased the sachet water price from N100 per bag to N200, by producers. *The Guardian.* https://guardian.ng/news/why-we-increased-sachet-water-price-from-n100-per-bag-to-n200-by-producers/

Nudging for Good. (2019). Retrieved August, 18, 2022, from http://www.nudgingforgood.com/2019/09/13/knorr-meal-kits-helping-people-to-eat-more-veggies/

Nwuneli, N. O. (2018, August 7). The high cost of food monopolies in Africa. *Project Syndicate.* Retrieved December 13, 2022, from https://www.project-syndicate.org/commentary/africa-monopoly-food-prices-by-ndidi-okonkwo-nwuneli-2018-08

Roberts, S. (2013). Competition policy, industrial policy, and corporate conduct. In J. L. Yifu, J. E. Stiglitz, & E. Patel (Eds.), *The industrial policy revolution II: Africa in the 21st century, chapter 4* (pp. 216–242). Palgrave Macmillan. https://doi.org/10.1057/9781137335234_9

Roberts, S., Vilakazi, T., & Simbanegavi, W. (2017). Competition, regional integration and inclusive growth in Africa: A research agenda. In S. Roberts, J. Klaaren, & I. Valodia (Eds.), *Competition law and economic regulation in southern Africa: Addressing market power in southern Africa* (pp. 263–287). Wits University Press. https://doi.org/10.18772/22017070909.17

Sachs, J., Lafortune, G., Kroll, C., Fuller, G., & Woelm, F. (2022). *Sustainable development report.* Cambridge University Press. https://doi.org/10.1017/9781009210058

Sasson, T. (2016). Milking the third world? Humanitarianism, capitalism, and the moral economy of the Nestlé boycott. *The American Historical Review, 121*(4), 1196–1224. https://doi.org/10.1093/ahr/121.4.1196

Sheth, J. N. (2011). Impact of emerging markets on marketing: Rethinking existing perspectives and practices. *Journal of Marketing, 75*(4), 166–182. http://www.jstor.org/stable/41228618

Sheth, J. N., & Sisodia, R. S. (2006). How to reform marketing. Does marketing need reform?: Fresh perspectives on the future. In J. N. Sheth & R. S. Sisodia (Eds.), *Fresh perspectives on the future* (pp. 324–333). Routledge.

Sheth, J. N., & Sisodia, R. S. (2012). *The 4A's of marketing: Creating value for customer, company and society.* Routledge.

Sidibe, M. (2020, May–June). Marketing meets mission. *Harvard Business Review, 98*(3), 134–144. https://hbr.org/2020/05/marketing-meets-mission

Solomon, S. (1981, December 6). The controversy over infant formula. *The New York Times*. https://www.nytimes.com/1981/12/06/magazine/the-controversy-over-infant-formula.html

Stebbins. (2022, April 6). Educational content makes consumers 131% more likely to buy. https://www.conductor.com/academy/winning-customers-educational-content/

The Economist Intelligence Unit. (2015). The value of experience: How the C-suite values customer experience in the digital age. *Genesys*. Retrieved December 13, 2022, from https://www.genesys.com/en-gb/resources/the-value-of-experience-how-the-c-suite-values-customer-experience-in-the-digital-age

The World Bank. (2016). Breaking down barriers: Unlocking Africa's potential through vigorous competition policy. *World Bank Group*. Retrieved December 20, 2022, from https://documents1.worldbank.org/curated/en/243171467232051787/pdf/106717-REVISED-PUBLIC-WBG-ACF-Report-Printers-Version-21092016.pdf

The World Bank. (2019). Purchasing power, Sub-Saharan Africa. *World Bank Group*. Retrieved December 20, 2022, from https://data.worldbank.org/region/sub-saharan-africa

The World Bank. (2020). Literacy rate, adult total, Sub-Saharan Africa. *World Bank Group*. Retrieved December 20, 2022, from https://data.worldbank.org/indicator/SE.ADT.LITR.ZS?view=chart

The World Bank. (2021a). GDP per capita, Sub-Saharan Africa. *World Bank Group*. Retrieved December 20, 2022, from https://data.worldbank.org/indicator/NY.GDP.PCAP.PP.CD?locations=ZG

The World Bank. (2021b). Rural population, Sub-Saharan Africa. *World Bank Group*. Retrieved December 20, 2022, from https://data.worldbank.org/topic/agriculture-and-rural-development?locations=ZG

The World Bank. (2023). Gini index. *World Bank Group*. Retrieved December 20, 2022, from https://data.worldbank.org/indicator/SI.POV.GINI

Trading Economics. (2022, December). Nigerian inflation rate. *Trading Economics*. Retrieved January 2, 2023, from https://tradingeconomics.com/nigeria/inflation-cpi

Tuni, S. (2022, November 18). Nigeria's poverty exceeds World Bank projection, five states lead. *Punch Nigeria*. Retrieved December 20, 2022, from https://punchng.com/nigerias-poverty-exceeds-world-bank-projection-five-states-lead/#:~:text=The%20133%20million%20poor%20Nigerians, projection%20for%20Nigeria%20in%202022

Unilever. (2022a, January). Why do you continue to sell plastic sachets? *Unilever global company website*. Retrieved August 18, 2022, from https://www.unilever.com/news/news-search/2022/why-do-you-continue-to-sell-plastic-sachets/

Unilever. (2022b, June 3). Retrieved August 18, 2022, from https://www.unilever.co.za/news/2022/homecare-africa-making-progress-towards-creating-a-clean-future/

United Nations Conference on Trade and Development. (2016). *Guidelines for consumer protection*. Retrieved December 20, 2022, from https://unctad.org/system/files/official-document/ditccplpmisc2016d1_en.pdf

United Nations Department of Economic and Social Affairs. (n.d.). The 17 goals. *United Nations*. Retrieved January 3, 2023, from https://sdgs.un.org/goals

United Nations General Assembly (UNGA). (1985). Consumer protection. *U.N. General Assembly Resolution 39/248, April 16th,* New York.

United Nations General Assembly (UNGA). (2015). Consumer protection, *U.N. General Assembly Resolution 70/186, December 22nd,* New York.

Uzo, U., Zephania Opati, T., & Shittu, O. (2018). Characteristics of the African Buyer's purchase behaviour. In U. Uzo & A. K. Meru (Eds.), *Indigenous management practices in Africa* (Advanced Series in Management) (Vol. 20, pp. 9–29). Emerald Publishing Limited. https://doi.org/10.1108/S1877-636120180000020002

Wood, J. T. (2017). Consumer protection: A case of successful regulation. In P. Drahos (Ed.), *Regulatory theory: Foundations and applications* (pp. 633–652). ANU Press. http://www.jstor.org/stable/j.ctt1q1crtm.49

World Wide Fund for Nature. (2020). My plastic smart journey. *World wide Fund for Nature (formerly World Wildlife Fund),* South Africa. Retrieved December 20, 2022, from https://www.wwf.org.za/lifestyle_plastic_smart/

Wright, L., Newman, A., & Dennis, C. (2006, September). Enhancing consumer empowerment. *European Journal of Marketing, 40*(9), 925–935. https://doi.org/10.1108/03090560610680934

6

Responsible Advertising

Ngozi Okpara

Introduction

Advertising can be defined as a paid form of mass communication that comprises the specific message sent by a particular sender, which is usually a company or an advertiser to a targeted group of listeners, readers, or viewers for an allotted period, in a way designed to realise the objectives (Jaideep, 2022). Advertising can also be described as an assembled message perceived by the observer to imply a campaign about an idea within the context the observer frames (Karimova, 2012). Advertising is originally derived from the root word, 'adventure', which implies directing a person's attention to an idea, product, or service through a public announcement in either oral or written form (Danesi, 2015). Advertising comprises verbal, written, or audio-visual messages addressed to an audience to inform and persuade them to purchase the products or to have a

N. Okpara (✉)
School of Media and Communication, Pan-Atlantic University, Lekki, Nigeria
e-mail: nokpara@pau.edu.ng

positive perception of an idea. Cohan (2001) defined advertising as a business activity that utilises ingenious methods to create attractive communications in mass media that promote ideas, goods, and services in a way that aligns with realising the advertiser's objectives, delivery of consumer satisfaction, and development of social and economic welfare. Advertising is also defined by O'Barr (2015) as any device that is capable of getting the attention of a potential customer at first glance and then persuading him to accept a mutually beneficial exchange. Advertising can also be viewed as a promotion intended to aggressively portray a business to a target audience (Rehman et al., 2014). Advertising is a one-way communication method in which the packaged message is relayed to its targeted audience.

Advertising is described by The Economic Times (2022) as paid messages designed by a sender to create awareness about products and services to potential customers. Advertising was described by Bovée and Arens (1992) as an impersonal form of paid communication capable of influencing products, services, or ideas by identified sponsors through diverse media forms. Advertising comprises presentation, promotion, and, importantly, persuasion. It is believed that advertising without the element of persuasion should be regarded as ordinary communication. The concept of advertising is described as a non-personal form of communication because it uses mass media forms which implies that its content and presentation do not have to be created at the instance of contact with the customer or prospective customer. The idea for an advertisement can be conceived, revised, modified, and repackaged with every possible initiative to charm the prospective audience. This implies that advertising requires adequate research, including identifying prospective customers, the message elements that would gain their attention, and the best strategy to disseminate such message. Research for making an advertisement is based on ineffectiveness when applied to a large group of customers compared to just one customer. Advertising reaches a larger base of customers in hundreds, thousands, and millions, ultimately bringing down the cost per customer to the barest minimum. Advertising uses mass media to convey its message to the prospective audience by paying for the media's time and space. This payment is made by the advertiser who is also a disclosed entity to the audience for his advertising initiatives.

The types of advertising are categorised based on their penetration level. These include above-the-line, below-the-line, and through-the-line advertising (Thorson, 2011). Advertising is classified as above-the-line advertising when its activities are largely non-targeted and have a broader reach. These include mass media advertisements such as television, radio, and newspaper advertisements. Advertising is classified as Below-the-line advertising when its activities are designed to target specific groups. Examples of this advertising class include billboards, sponsorships, and in-store advertising. The third classification of advertising is Through-the-line advertising which combines the use of the two previous classes of advertising strategies simultaneously. This implies that this class aims to build a business brand using customised advertisement strategies. They include digital marketing strategies, cookie-based advertising, and site advertising.

Advertising can also be categorised using different mediums of dissemination. These include print, broadcast, outdoor, digital, and product advertising. Print advertising includes advertisements made in newspapers, magazines, and brochures. Broadcast advertising includes those conveyed via broadcast media such as television and radio. The outdoor advertising includes hoardings, banners, flags, and posters. Digital advertising includes advertisements displayed over the internet and digital devices. Product advertising includes product placements in entertainment media such as TV Shows and YouTube videos.

Advertising is a form of mass communication in which the advertiser can communicate to consumers. It is highly significant in any business's marketing mix and is a strong marketing tool. Advertising provides promotion for a business, however. However, it is considered costly because a bulky budget must be made for its facilitation (Danesi, 2015). The various functions of advertising to business brands include awareness, promoting sales, and strengthening public relations. Advertising helps to build up the reputation of the advertiser. This is achieved when the accomplishments of the company or business brand are communicated to the general public alongside the efforts of the company to meet consumer satisfaction. Advertising, by its function of informing and persuading potential customers about a product, also helps the sale of goods and services. Advertising has also been proven to be an effective way of introducing new products into the market. It is a recognised way for businesses and companies to introduce themselves and their products or services to the general public.

Advertising plays an important role in Africa, as it helps businesses and organisations promote their products and services and reach new customers. There are many different ways to advertise in Africa, including traditional methods such as print, radio, and television and newer methods such as digital and social media. A study found that television is the most popular medium for advertising in Africa, followed by radio and print (Amegah, 2013). However, digital and social media use for advertising is on the rise, particularly among younger consumers (Amegah & Boateng, 2016). In terms of effectiveness, research has shown that personalised and culturally relevant advertising can be particularly effective in Africa (Oduru & Adeyemi, 2019). In addition, using local celebrities and influencers as spokespeople can also be effective, as African consumers see them as more relatable and trustworthy (Dzanku, 2018). It is, therefore, important for businesses and organisations to carefully consider their target audience and choose the most appropriate channels and strategies for advertising in Africa.

Advertising, like every other business tool, is subjected to ethical principles to ensure no deviation from its intended purpose. It is believed that for advertising to be considered responsible, it must follow a certain set of ethical principles that oversee the type of communication between companies and their potential customers. Advertising is responsible when it appropriately presents true statements. However, the definition of appropriateness may vary from place to place and among persons. This thus poses a challenge in delineating responsible from irresponsible advertising. When a consumer understands the metaphorical implication of an advertisement, another consumer might interpret it literally and perceive it as being deceitful. Since the advent of digital media technologies has given an amplified effect and volume to advertising in business, it is therefore necessarily based on generally accepted ethical principles to identify what responsible advertising is. This chapter seeks to evaluate the concept of responsible advertising using the accepted ethical principles and how companies can effectively market their products without compromising them. The arguments in this chapter are framed by the virtues, utilitarian, and deontologists' ethical theories to define the scope of responsible advertising.

Theoretical Framework

The arguments in this chapter are framed by three ethical theories: the virtues ethical theory, the deontological ethical theory, and the utilitarian ethical theory.

Virtue Ethical Theory

The philosopher Aristotle formulated the virtue ethical theory. It is known as the Aristotelian ethical theory and refers to a habit prepared for action by deliberate choice. Aristotle opined that virtue is a state of character concerned with choice, which is determined by sensible principle, and the principle is a function of applied wisdom. Virtue is not an isolated action but a consistent character of acting well. A virtuous action is believed to be deliberately executed with the actor's consciousness of his acts and also doing it for a good cause. Aristotle opined that a developed attitude could be classified as a virtue to which the act can contribute to the realising ultimate aim of the domain (Onuoha, 2018). The aim of a domain is a natural preference that must be discovered by perception. Aristotle justified that society is the ultimate political reorganisation and humans need the elements of virtue to succeed in that state. This categorically proves that virtue ethics is fundamentally founded on Aristotle's clear distinction between real and ideal human beings. In the frames of this ethical theory, Aristotle identified some cardinal virtues, including fortitude, temperance, prudence, and justice. The virtue of fortitude is implemented when an actor executes his actions for the essence of dignity. This virtue finds the middle ground between extreme conditions of fear and rashness. The virtue of temperance propagates balance about pleasure. A temperate man is balanced on the subject of pleasure and pain. He is able to appreciate pleasure as the right reason calls for. This keeps the desiring part of his mind in check with the voice of reason. The virtue of prudence focuses on spending actions. It involves the appropriation of funds for relevant occasions. Aristotle believes that spending should be done in accordance with merits. The virtue of justice is concerned with the attitude that makes people open to acting justly and desiring what is fair. This virtue classifies people into two major groups: lawful and unlawful persons. Aristotle believes that justice is the greatest virtue and the element that completes virtue because it is the real exercise of the complete virtue. Aristotle opined that a man who possesses this virtue would not use it for himself only but also exercise it towards his neighbour. However, it is possible for a man to exercise justice for himself and not relate it to his neighbours.

The understanding of advertising from the perspective of virtue ethical theory is that each advertisement must be premised on the elements of justice, fortitude, temperance, and prudence. The proponents of virtues theory preach that the message of advertising must be balanced to eliminate fear and rashness in its presentation. It must consider giving pleasure to its recipients without forgetting the purpose or pushing aside its original purpose. The element of prudence will come to play in advertising by allotting funds and budgets to different scales of advertisements. In terms of justice, advertising must be done fairly and inclusive to all members of society. The incorporation of the elements of virtue in advertising would help to maintain relations across borders and cultural differences. Advertising that is void of these elements of virtue is regarded as irresponsible.

Deontological Ethical Theory

The deontological ethical theory was formulated by Immanuel Kant (1724–1804). He formulated the theory as the theory of duty, which was named after him. Kant opined that a good agent is regularly engaged in the right actions and that an action is right when it is done from a sense of duty. Deontology ethical theory is a theory that emphasises actions instead of consequences. It is a theory that believes that there are limitations on broadcasting the best consequences of an action because it is possible that the right actions may not have the most desirable consequences (Borchert, 2006). Deontologists believe an action should be considered right because it inherently carries the imperative to act in such a manner. This is due to the fact that the action allocates an obligatory duty to a moral agent. The theory of deontology propagates that every action possesses intricate characteristics that justify its rightness or wrongness. This implies that in a specific instance, a rational agent would decide to take the same course of action with regard to deontology.

It can therefore be deduced that deontology ethics requires a person or a group of persons or institutions to act from a sense of responsibility. It can be further deduced that this kind of commitment is based on reason instead of experience. A responsible action will thus not depend on experimental data and binding on everyone. Kant described this as the Categorical Imperative. The deontology ethical theory is summarised in the Kantian Categorical Imperative which states that all actions must be conducted from a general principle that applies to any party in similar circumstances.

The principle must be applied to all without exception. Kantian theory prevents the treatment of humanity as a means to some personal gains or ambitions. Kantian theory preaches that no human should be treated as a tool to achieve a goal (Owakah & Aswani, 2011). Therefore, it can be deduced that advertising from a deontologist's perspective will only be regarded as good when done with a sense of duty for consumers' good, regardless of those involved. Advertisers should make sure that the motive for promoting each product and service is not solely profit-oriented but also inclusive of human reasons.

Utilitarian Ethical Theory

The utilitarian ethical theory is a theory from the perspective of a consequentialist that emphasises the result of action instead of the underlying reason behind it. This theory proves that an action should be only judged as wrong or right by considering the eventual outcomes of consequences instead of the original intention. The utilitarian ethical theory supports the principle of utility, which implies that actions are decided as right or wrong based on how much pleasure they can produce (Okiyi &

Eteng-Martins, 2015). This means that the rightness or wrongness of an action is determined by its ability to create more pleasure over pain. Any action that helps people escape any form of suffering and guarantees their pleasure is in alignment with the utilitarian theory.

Advertising from the utilitarian's perspective will be judged as good or bad based on how much satisfaction it can offer its recipients. The eventual consequences of an advertisement will thus determine if it was rightly done or otherwise. The utilitarian believes that advertising is responsibly executed when it guarantees less or no pain, regrets, and loss for the highest number of consumers. On the other hand, the utilitarian advocate also judges advertising as irresponsible when the eventual results are negative and have poor or devastating effects on the highest number of consumers.

Responsible Advertising

Responsible advertising was defined by Borrie (2005) as advertising that is legal, decent, honest, and truthful. It is regarded as advertising communication that is responsibly prepared by adhering to ethical standards and obligations of public communications. Responsible advertising is defined in terms of responsibility to consumers and society at large. According to the Federal Trade Commission (FTC), responsible advertising is fair and accurate (FTC, 2016). This implies that advertisements should not mislead consumers or make false or deceptive claims. It is believed that company or business managers in charge of deciding what is ethically acceptable might encounter challenges if they depend only on the automated application of their company's ethical codes (Hyman, 2009). In addition, advertisers should be transparent about the products or services they are promoting and provide clear and adequate information to consumers so that they can make informed decisions. This is why it is expedient that an ethical principles checklist be used in addition to a company's ethical codes to judge when it is fulfilling its advertising obligations. The work of Kreth (2000) suggested that responsibility in advertising may be decided by asking some right and specific questions.

Advertisers can ensure that their advertising is responsible by conducting market research and gathering sufficient evidence to support the claims made in their advertisements (Sparks et al., 2019). This could include conducting focus groups, surveys, or conducting clinical trials to ensure that products or services are effective as claimed. Ultimately, responsible advertising is crucial for maintaining consumer trust and credibility and upholding ethical business practices. By being transparent and accurate in advertising, companies can build long-term customer relationships and contribute to a healthy and fair marketplace (FTC, 2016).

It is, therefore, believed that responsible advertising is intrinsically good advertising and possesses unforced duty and answerability to do right by consumers and the general public. Responsible advertising must not cause harm to any stakeholder and must be of gain to at least one recipient. This means that advertisements should be created in a way that never promotes destructive behaviours among vulnerable groups. An example of one such brand that leveraged possible behaviour to construct a winning advert creatively is the 4G Blender advert for Airtel Nigeria. The highlighted behaviour was bad blood between the two mothers of a newly wedded couple. One of the mothers is old school and prefers to manually execute tasks, while the other is quite familiar with modern fast-track appliances. The company used this amusing advert to serve a dual purpose of informing its customers about the benefits of the updated 4G in place of 3G and highlighting the need for an allowance for our differing beliefs of one another, just as depicted by the loggerheads' mothers. The advert stated that 3G is good, but 4G is better, thus creating a perception balance (Benson, 2019).

Responsible advertising should also promote values that align with long-term societal well-being in terms of economic and social prosperity. Examples of these would include adverts that encourage family values, sustainable consumption, healthier lifestyles, and a more enlightened society. An example of an advert that promoted family values is that of the Indomie brand. Indomie, one of the leading noodles brands started a campaign to observe the Mother's Day celebration in March 2022. The focus of the campaign was to celebrate the ingenuity of family relationships. The campaign was kick-started online with the hashtag

'Unconditional Love'. It hit the Nigerian market like a storm as it trended for days ranking as the number one online content with people sharing stories of the unconditional love they got from their mother (Nosike, 2022). Another example is an advert focused on achieving economic prosperity through societal enlightenment. This was reflected in the Access Bank advert, 'More than a tag'. The advert was designed to reflect the varying class and status of the bank customers. They included a petty trader, a physically challenged girl, a bus driver, and others, telling them that they matter because they are more than their present situations. The advert reflected that Access Bank believes that economic prosperity can be achieved even by low-income earners. The advert also sent a message of a caring bank to all kinds of customers. It was indeed an inclusive advertisement (Benson, 2019).

A responsible advert is such that it promotes economic and social development. An example of an advert encouraging economic socialisation is the MTN Springboks tagged '5G Your Life'. The advert shows a man watching a nail-biting Springboks rugby match but his screen buffers up at a critical moment. This highlights the basis of the advert, which promotes product marketing by using MTN's sponsorship of the Boks to show the advantage of 5G over using fibre. The advert was a good opportunity to mix the MTN 5G product brief, and a sponsorship Springbok brief since streaming live sports has become very common in South Africa. The advert is full of funny moments featuring the country's rugby team players, such as Siya Kolisi, increasing its receptivity with fans and viewers. The notable features of this advert include its strategy, creative storyline, humour, and production quality (Breitenbach, 2022).

Responsible advertising maintains viewer dignity and autonomy (Sneddon, 2001). This subject of respecting the dignity of persons appeared in the Kantian opinion that humans should be treated as ends in themselves instead of being a means to an end. Responsible advertising includes this element of human dignity, especially in scenarios where the needs of potential consumers are portrayed before considering profit margins. Sasu et al. (2015) believe that responsible advertising is exhibited in a product presentation that respects the rights of an average person to make a responsible choice. Advertising is responsible when it guarantees respect for the dignity of the human person, portraying humans not as objects or numbers but as beings that ought to be served. This thus implies that the human person should do the measurement and completion of all advertising. An example of an advert where the needs of the consumers were prioritised over profit margin was the Zero account opening requirement by Zenith Bank. In prior times, to open an account with Zenith Bank would require a deposit amount of 250,000 naira. However, thanks to the advert, that portrayed the message of consideration of all persons. The advert was one of the trendiest Nigerian adverts that year. The message was very simple and directed straight to the person watching; prospective Zenith Bank customers can now easily open zero balance accounts on their phones by dialling a simple code (Benson, 2019). First National Bank in South Africa set another example. The First National Bank's (FNB) advert, 'Change needs you', brought a new twist to advertisements for South African banking. The campaign was received as smart, engaging, and pulsating with energy, stirring Africans to become agents of change who can in turn build their lives, communities, and country. This campaign has been able to inspire a new shift in purpose and emphasise relevance which helps FNB to stand as a brand beyond banking. The campaign has about 30 to 40 different versions of the same core concept adapted for the presence of FNB in Africa and reflects the bank's customer profiles. The core of the FNB 'change needs you' advert is to deliver a simple and clear message to all individuals to be the change that you want to see in the world (Businesstech, 2021).

Responsible advertising tells the truth by presenting the product to potential consumers in its true form. Statements of truth show the real picture of events, while false statements alter the facts and present the events in an untrue manner (Chukwuma & Ngwoke, 2022). Responsible advertisement passes its message by reporting and recounting to consumers the kind, contents, and producers of a product to persuade consumers to buy these products. The purpose of advertisement to communicate information about a product is actualised through the instrumentality of language, which can deliver both truth and falsity. Responsible advertising thus presents sufficient and accurate information about the content and nature of a product to its consumers. This implies that such an advertisement does not intentionally suppress valuable information away from consumers and buyers of a product. Falling short of this standard is deemed ethically inappropriate (Sasu et al., 2015). The advertising profession allows for figurative expressions to pass messages across but does not encourage them to be used in making intentionally untrue claims about products, especially when the consequences of doing such are obvious. False claims are capable of misdirecting prospective consumers into purchasing products they would later regret, which implies buying products due to untrue persuasion, which may trigger regrets, dissatisfaction, and fight in society. An example of an advert that exhibited plain truth was the I DON PORT campaign launched by MTN. There was a massive buzz in the telecommunication industry in 2013 when the famous MTN Company released an advert on number portability using the popular brand ambassador of a rival company, Saka, to portray the simple message of changing from one network to the other. The advert I DON PORT generated a lot of controversial opinions as some persons perceived it as unethical to have used Saka, the brand ambassador of Etisalat (a rival company), to show people that they could switch brands. However, the evaluation of truth-telling passes as responsible advertising. The advert started with a man dressed in green, the rival brand's colour attacking the audience. The colour changed to MTN's yellow colour when he turned to face while singing the theme song I DON PORT, explaining that users can retain their old numbers even when switching truthful and clearly stating the agenda of the porting initiative to including poaching rival network users. The product was presented in its true manner to the audience, leaving them with the choice of making their own decision (Omisore, 2013).

Ethical Issues in Advertising

Advertising is a profession that requires a number of experts to carry out the conceptualisation, planning, generating, packaging, and placing of advertisements in the media. It is an enterprise themed on thrilling, vibrant, and challenging experiences. Due to the sensitive role, it plays in keeping customers aware of their preferred products and services, it must not fail to fulfil obligations such as honesty, and accountability to avoid having a negative influence on its audiences. Advertising can only be done responsibly when ethical boundaries are justified. The rate at which the practice of advertising has been infiltrated with diverse unethical practices among businesses is so alarming ranging from untruthfulness to doubtful inclinations in the business industry (Chukwuma & Ngwoke, 2022). Society is currently flooded with diverse kinds of advertisements in either print, broadcast, or online media. The broadcast media will probably get people's attention faster due to its usage of images, audio, and video clips. These advertisements can mislead consumers and influence their buying choices, causing mistrust, regret, and panic.

Advertising is considered unethical and irresponsible when it shames a rival product. Identified issues associated with advertising include gender misrepresentation, religious insensitivity, child exploitation, taste and decency, and disputable product advertising, among others.

Gender Misrepresentation

Gender misrepresentation is one of the ethical issues often encountered in advertising. Some adverts misrepresent certain gender, which causes a lot of stir, resulting in negative reviews. An example was the 'mama na boy' advert of the leading telecommunication brand MTN. The advert starts with a man pacing nervously in front of a labour ward in the hospital. A female doctor comes out and gives the man the good news. His wife has just given birth. The man is overjoyed. He calls his mum in the village and delivers the famous line, 'mama na boy!' The mum is elated and gives the villagers the good news. Critics have identified gender bias in the advert when the man tells his mum that his baby is a boy. It is believed that emphasising the gender of the baby is a disservice to the other gender forms.

Religious Insensitivity

Religious insensitivity is another expression of unethical or irresponsible advertising. Different countries have diverse religious practices, and it is unethical for an advertisement to be biased or insensitive toward them.

For example, Nigeria is a country that has gone through diverse phases of religious conflicts and thus strongly reacted to an advert by Sterling bank that likened the resurrection of Jesus Christ to the rising of a loaf of bread. The image was met with huge frowns from the Christian bodies in Nigeria, who publicly demanded that the bank be reprimanded for such an insensitive advert (Stella, 2022).

Children Exploitation

The innocence of children should be protected in advertising. This applies to advertisements that are targeted at children and children's shows. Responsible advertising for children must be void of race, ethnicity, religion, and sexual preferences. Including frightening or distressing images in advertisements for children is also unethical. It is a significant issue in advertising when the children population is targeted as prospective customers for products that might not even favour them as opposed to the older age group of customers (Verma & Gothi, 2017). One such ad that was criticised for wrongly portraying children is Zenith's Bank Children Account (ZECA). The advert encouraged parents to open an account for their children with Zenith bank. However, the advert's concept featured the children as destructive and audacious. Fans believe that the message could have been disseminated with a better concept that did not have to involve children (Nweze, 2019).

Taste and Decency

The advertisement of some products can be challenging due to the controversial nature of the usage of such products. Some people may believe in using some products, while others get offended when advertised, claiming that it does not pass general moral standards. Instances of such products include the advertisement of condoms and other contraceptives. The intention of advertising these products is clearly to spread awareness about responsibly preventing sexually transmitted diseases, but some believe such advertisement only promotes promiscuity. Condom awareness campaigns in Nigeria have been met with opposition and criticism. The Advertising Practitioners Council of Nigeria (APCON) had to issue a buffer statement declaring that 'the condom is not 100% safe and total abstinence of faithfulness is the best option'. There was a need for this due to reactions from the populace about condom advertisements that were perceived to have encouraged indecency and sexual immorality via text, graphics, and sound. All condom advertisements were henceforth stipulated to carry health warnings and not to be aired on children's programmes before 8 pm on television and radio or displayed on billboards close to places of worship, schools, and hospitals (The New Humanitarian, 2006).

Disputable Products Advertising

Another issue worthy of mention about advertising is the issue of disputable products. Advertisers must consider the need for consumers to understand the difference between their needs and weaknesses. Advertisements can target the weaknesses of their consumers such as gambling and consumption of harmful substances such as tobacco and cigarettes (Verma & Gothi, 2017). The advertising of such products is even completely prohibited in nations like India. In Nigeria, tobacco control advocates crusaded for immediate enforcement of the ban on Tobacco Advertising Promotion and Sponsorship (TAPS) in the National Tobacco Control (NTC) Act 2015 and the NTC Regulations 2019. They lamented that the lack of enforcement of the ban has encouraged the tobacco industry to continue to entice kids through movies and other entertainment sectors (Abade, 2021).

Preventing Irresponsible Advertising by Companies

The influence of advertising cannot be overemphasised in the marketing industry. Companies and business brands have to engage in advertising at different levels to promote their business to the general public. It can be said that advertising has, over time, proven to be a thriving component that is necessary for businesses. Regardless of the numerous benefits of advertising campaigns, there are significant concerns about the possible adverse consequences, especially when done irresponsibly. Some of these concerns include its tendency to promote materialism, influence consumer purchasing choices, and exploit children's innocence and others (Chukwuma & Ngwoke, 2022). This implies that the benefits and positive impacts of advertising can only be harnessed when standard ethical principles execute it for the common good of consumers and society at large.

Irresponsible advertising can have negative impacts on both individuals and society as a whole. In Africa, it is essential to prevent irresponsible advertising due to the region's diverse cultures and vulnerabilities to certain types of messaging. Irresponsible advertising in Africa can be prevented by implementing advertising standards and regulations. An instance, the Advertising Standards Authority of South Africa (ASASA) has established a code of conduct for advertising in the country, which includes provisions against misleading or deceptive advertising and the exploitation of superstition and cultural beliefs (ASASA, 2019). In addition to regulatory approaches, self-regulation by the advertising industry can also play a role in preventing irresponsible advertising. Another instance is the Association of Accredited Advertising Agencies of South Africa (AAAASA), which has a code of conduct for its member agencies, including provisions against offensive or irresponsible advertising (AAAASA, 2017). This implies that preventing irresponsible advertising in Africa requires a combination of regulatory and self-regulatory measures and ongoing efforts to educate and raise awareness among advertisers, consumers, and other stakeholders.

In the digital age, more advertisements are getting scrutinised by consumers and the general public. There have been cases of individuals or entities filing lawsuits against business brands due to unethical advertisements that damaged their well-being and intruded on their privacy. It has, therefore, become highly expedient for companies to make efforts to execute responsible advertising campaigns. Companies can act responsibly with their advertising campaigns by avoiding elements that propel segregation or alienate a specific group. It is unethical to intentionally alienate potential consumers from relevant information that could guide their purchasing choices. Business brands must package their advertising campaigns as direct, straightforward, and informative without alienation or misguidance. Alienation in advertising campaigns can lead to a psychosomatic gap between business brands and potential consumers.

In their awareness campaigns, companies should refrain from using statements or comments that are defamatory in nature. This is because such statements or concepts can damage the reputation and image of their competitors. The strategy of slander involves denigrating other brands by emphasising their weaknesses and flaws. This means that a company can engage in unethical advertising by making misleading comparisons to highlight the superior qualities of their products, creating the impression that they are superior to similar products from competitors.'

Advertising campaigns must be founded on the principle of truth and creatively planned to expose only the true nature of products to potential consumers. Companies can prevent irresponsible advertising when they ensure that their campaigns present sufficient and accurate information about the content and nature of a product to prospective consumers (Sasu et al., 2015). Figurative expressions can be used in advertising content but must be guided to avoid false claims and misleading ideas. The principle of truth-telling must be implemented to correct irresponsible advertising.

Conclusion

Advertising provides communication capable of convincing viewers, readers, and listeners towards a cause. It performs the duty of informing customers and potential customers about the nature and characteristics of their desired products. This implies that it is heavily relied upon by the general public to make purchasing choices about similar and new products in the market. The varying preferences of diverse persons across different borders and cultures can be sieved and sorted with responsible advertising in making their choices. It can, thus, be said that advertising can be held accountable as a determinant of the product experiences a consumer can have.

The modern market is, however, saturated with different advertising campaigns that are borderline unethical and deterrent to the good of the public. Digital technologies have made it easier for advertisers to reach a wider audience, as fewer barriers or constraints exist. This can lead to an amplification of the message being promoted. Therefore, companies and advertising agencies must ensure that ethical principles are inculcated in their advertising campaigns. The principles needed to achieve responsible advertising include truth-telling, dignity, clarity, fairness, prudence, temperance, fortitude, and non-alienation. Companies and advertising agencies can build on these principles to plan and execute advertising campaigns effectively and responsibly. These ethical principles will help us justify what qualifies as responsible advertising.

Recommendations

It is thus recommended that.

- Advertising regulatory bodies must ensure that only advertisements that fulfil all ethical obligations should be approved for dissemination.
- Approved advertisements must fulfil the obligation of informing the public of the pros and cons of the product or service advertised to give people a chance to choose responsibly.
- Advertising agencies should conduct regular internal revision sessions to be updated on relevant laws regarding advertising.
- Government and Regulatory bodies need to intensify their efforts at overseeing that advertising agencies adhere to the culture of decent content and principles adherence.
- Advertising agencies should create awareness among the general public about an advertisement's ethical obligations.

References

Abade, E. (2021). *Advocates seek enforcement of bam on tobacco advertising, promotion, and sponsorship.* Retrieved October 12, 2022, from https://guardian.ng/news/advocates-seek-enforcement-of-ban-on-tobacco-advertising-promotion-sponsorship/

Advertising Standards Authority of South Africa (ASASA). (2019). *Code of conduct for advertising in South Africa.* https://www.asasa.org.za/code-of-conduct/

Amegah, A. (2013). Advertising and the mass media in Africa. *Journal of African Media Studies, 5*(2), 143–157.

Amegah, A., & Boateng, F. (2016). Social media and advertising in Africa: Opportunities and challenges. *African Journal of Communication, 13*(2), 148–162.

Association of Accredited Advertising Agencies of South Africa (AAAASA). (2017). *Code of conduct.* https://www.aaaasa.co.za/about-us/code-of-conduct/

Benson, E. (2019, August 22). *See the top ten adverts in Nigeria at the moment.* Retrieved October 10, 2022, from https://nairametrics.com/2019/08/22/top-ten-adverts-in-nigeria-at-the-moment/

Borchert, D. M. (2006). *Encyclopedia of philosophy* (2nd ed.). Thomas Gale.

Borrie, L. (2005). CSR and advertising self-regulation. *Consumer Policy Review, 15*(2), 64–68.

Bovée, C., & Arens, W. (1992). *Contemporary advertising* (4th ed.). Irwin.

Breitenbach, D. (2022). *#BehindtheCampaign: Touch, pause…engage with MTN's Springbok TVC.* Retrieved January 8, 2023, from https://www.bizcommunity.com/Article/196/12/230872.html

Businesstech. (2021). *FNB launches its new #TheChangeables brand campaign with refreshed bank cards.* Retrieved January 8, 2023, from https://businesstech.co.za/news/industry-news/497863/fnb-launches-its-new-thechangeables-brand-campaign-together-with-refreshed-bank-cards/

Chukwuma, J. N., & Ngwoke, H. C. (2022). Moral and ethical issues in advertising. *Journal of Legal, Ethical and Regulatory Issues, 25*(3), 1–13.

Cohan, J. A. (2001). Towards a new paradigm in the ethics of women's advertising. *Journal of Business Ethics, 33*(4), 323–337.

Danesi, M. (2015). Advertising discourse. In K. Tracy, C. Illie, & T. Sandel (Eds.), *The international encyclopedia of language and social interaction* (1st ed., pp. 1–10). John Wiley & Sons.

Dzanku, F. M. (2018). Celebrity endorsements in advertising: A review of research on their effectiveness in Africa. *Marketing Intelligence & Planning, 36*(6), 663–680.

Federal Trade Commission (FTC). (2016). *Truth in advertising*. Retrieved from https://www.ftc.gov/tips-advice/business-center/advertising-and-marketing/truth-advertising

Hyman, M. (2009). Responsible ads: A workable ideal. *Journal of Business Ethics, 87*(1), 199–210.

Jaideep, S. (2022). *Advertising: Its definitions, characteristics and objectives.* https://www.yourarticlelibrary.com/advertising/advertising-its-definitions-characteristics-and-objectives/48658

Karimova, G. Z. (2012). *Bakhtin and interactivity: A conceptual investigation of advertising communication.* Academica Press, LLC.

Kreth, M. (2000). Exploring "responsibility" in advertising: Health claims about dietary supplements. *Business Communication Quarterly, 63*(3), 66–70.

Nosike, M. (2022). *Indomie celebrates mothers, unveils 'Unconditional Love' campaign.* Retrieved October 10, 2022, from https://www.vanguardngr.com/2022/04/indomie-celebrates-mothers-unveils-unconditional-love-campaign/

Nweze, E. (2019). *Worst ads of 2019 by Live with Lynda.* Retrieved October 12, 2022, from https://lists.ng/worst-ads-of-2019-by-live-with-lynda/

O'Barr, W. M. (2015). What is advertising? *Advertising & Society Review, 16*(3), 7–11.

Oduru, O., & Adeyemi, T. (2019). Personalisation in advertising: A review of effectiveness and implications for Africa. *African Journal of Marketing Management, 11*(3), 41–48.

Okiyi, G. O., & Eteng-Martins, C. (2015). Professionalism: An imperative for the ethical practice of advertising in Nigeria. *Journal of US-China Public Administration, 12*(1), 71–79.

Omisore, I. (2013). *MTN's I DON PORT Campaign: Why managers have sleepless nights!* Retrieved January 8, 2023, from https://idowuomisore.wordpress.com/2013/04/25/mtns-i-don-port-campaign-why-managers-have-sleepless-nights-by-idowuomisore/

Onuoha, J. (2018). The morality of the Aristotlean virtue ethics to the contemporary Nigerian man: A philosophical reflection. *Research on Humanities and Social Sciences, 8*(10), 126–131.

Owakah, F. E., & Aswani, D. R. (2011). The ethics of deontology in corporate communication. *Thought and Practice: A Journal of the Philosophical Association of Kenya (PAK), 3*(1), 115–129.

Rehman, F. U., Javed, F., Nawaz, T., Ahmed, I., & Hyder, S. (2014). Some insights in the historical prospective of hierarchy of effects model: A short review. *Information Management and Business Review, 6*(6), 301–308.

Sasu, C., Pravat, G., & Luca, F. (2015). Ethics and advertising. *SEA Practical Application of Science, 3*(7), 513–518.

Sneddon, A. (2001). Advertising and deep autonomy. *Journal of Business Ethics, 33*(1), 15–28.

Sparks, B., Duncan, T., & O'Reilly, N. (2019). *Principles of marketing*. John Wiley & Sons.

Stella, G. (2022). *Like Agege bread, He rose: Sterling Bank MD lands in trouble as CAN calls for his removal over 'ungodly' Easter message*. Retrieved October 12, 2022, from https://www.gistlover.com/like-agege-bread-he-rose-sterling-bank-md-lands-in-trouble-as-can-calls-for-his-removal-over-ungodly-easter-message/

The Economic Times. (2022). *What is advertising*. Retrieved October 3, 2022, from https://economictimes.indiatimes.com/definition/advertising

The New Humanitarian. (2006). *Condom ads stir passionate debate*. Retrieved October 11, 2022, from https://www.thenewhumanitarian.org/news/2006/03/27/condom-ads-stir-passionate-debate

Thorson, E. (2011). *Advertising*. Retrieved from https://www.oxfordbibliographies.com/view/document/obo-9780199756841/obo-9780199756841-0016.xml

Verma, A., & Gothi, T. (2017). Ethics in advertising. *International Education and Research Journal, 3*(6), 330–332.

7

Responsible Pricing

Louis Nzegwu and Deborah Towolawi

Introduction

From Oscar Wilde, who once described a cynic as 'a man who knows the price of everything and the value of nothing', to La Rochefoucauld who believed that 'the height of ability consists in knowing the price of things', the price was, is, and without a doubt always will be a significant factor in many aspects of human interaction. The same is true in business, where setting prices for goods and services involves much more than simply figuring out what amount will draw in and maintain customers while also covering costs and earning a profit. It requires a thorough grasp of the product or service value to the consumer to reach the right conclusions.

Price is the value that consumers associate with the sum of money they exchange for a product or service. It can be said to be the marketing mix element that captures the value produced by the other elements. Agwu

L. Nzegwu (✉) • D. Towolawi
Lagos Business School, Pan-Atlantic University, Lekki, Nigeria
e-mail: lnzegwu@lbs.edu.ng; dtowolawi@lbs.edu.ng

and Carter (2014) claim that among the marketing mix's four Ps, price is the only one that generates revenue. It is interest to lenders, service charged by the banker, premium to the insurer, fare to the transporter, honorarium to the guest lecturer, etc. (Kotler and Armstrong 2008). Thus, pricing reflects the value a business' product or service delivers to the consumers and the value it captures for the business.

Pricing is part of almost every consumer purchase decision, and it is also one of the most important strategic decisions businesses generally face, including businesses in Sub-Saharan Africa (Kumar and Steenkamp 2013). However, pricing in today's market is not as easy as in the majority of history. The set amount shown in stores and advertisements now was not the norm historically; rather, prices were discussed between a buyer and a seller. Sellers who just consider their own perspectives and disregard those of their customers or sellers who see their consumers as prey to be manipulated may succeed at one time but were unlikely to maintain their success in the long run. Consequently, setting prices in a responsible manner was necessary for businesses that expect to grow successfully and sustainably.

The basic idea behind responsible pricing is that the price of goods should reflect the value to the consumer rather than the actual costs of production plus a margin. Responsible pricing entails setting appropriate value-based prices in such a way that is affordable to customers and promotes sustainability for the business. Usually, prices frequently fluctuate abruptly in response to changes in the market conditions, which creates room for unfair pricing practices (Lindsey-Mullikin and Petty 2011). More often than not, responsible pricing necessitates the cautious and continuous management of how pricing decisions are made taking into account customers' willingness to pay. Responsible pricing is mainly achieved by setting prices based on the perceived value of the product or service from a stakeholders' point of view, particularly the consumers.

The basis of customer perceived value is equity theory, which deals with a customer's assessment of what is fair, right, or merited for the cost of the organisation's product or service offering. Customer perception of value is determined by weighing the relative benefits and costs of the offering. If customers believe that the ratio of their output (what is given) to inputs (what is received) is comparable to the ratio of output to inputs that the business experiences, they are more likely to feel treated fairly. The notion of customer perceived value is used to link customer's satisfaction, which directly impacts repurchase behaviour (Parasuraman and Grewal 2000). Customers' purchase intentions will rise if they believe they are receiving a fair price for the benefits they receive (Grewal et al. 1998). In other words, gaining a grasp of how customers perceive the value of a product or service is one of the key criteria for responsible pricing.

Purchase and Pricing Nexus

Customers' Purchase Decisions and Responsible Pricing

Taking into account the variations in purchasing behaviour in different countries of Sub-Saharan Africa, customers are separated based on their various preferences to analyse the best pricing and sustainable strategy for a business. Pricing is not the only factor influencing customers' purchasing decisions (Duarte et al. 2019). Getting a good value is typically one of the most crucial factors customers take into account when making a purchase (Dutta and Snehvrat 2020). Under normal conditions, consumers simply won't buy an item if its price is too expensive, or a business might come up with a price against competition from a supplier who believes it can undercut its price. At the same time, a business might not turn a sufficient profit if prices are set low.

Finding the right price requires striking a balance between the customer's need for a good value and the business need to cover costs and generate a profit. A business must recognise and address the needs of its customers in order to offer the desired value to the customers they serve; for instance, in Sub-Saharan Africa where we have unmet needs, including food, beverages, pharmaceuticals, financial services, health care, and education (Acha and Landry 2019), creates great value to support purchases at prices that generate adequate profitability.

A customer's willingness to pay for a product or service is not exclusively based on its economic value but considers how reasonable or fair the price is. Bolton and Lemon (1999) claim that a customer becomes more sensitive to the price of a product when the product's price goes beyond the range the customer considers fair or reasonable, given the purchase context. The standard pricing is no longer acceptable if customers start to anticipate that altering their purchase habits would allow them to obtain the same product or service for an even better price. For instance, a customer at a retail store can think that a new fashion wear is well worth the price that was requested for it in a particular month but decides against purchasing it if he/she anticipates that the store, based on its previous actions, will hold a 20 per cent off sale in the following month.

According to Nagle and Holden (2002), customers become less sensitive to the price of a product the more they value any unique feature that sets the product apart from competing offerings. Businesses that ignore this reality and set prices solely based on costs frequently fall short of realising their full potential for profit. For instance, high prices are charged by luxury companies like Mercedes as part of a profit-maximising strategy that depends on a consumer's willingness to pay more for a product to which they attach a greater value. However, customers may choose an alternative good or service if a business charges prices that are more than what they value in a product or service.

By dynamically modifying pricing in line with the customer's perceived value, a business may make efforts to decrease the effect of price sensitivity of consumers, which can positively affect the purchase behaviour of consumers. On the other hand, because of individual variances in their financial capacity, subjective preferences, and level of familiarity with the product category, consumers will value differentiating qualities of goods and services quite differently (Monroe 1990). A strategic approach to responsible pricing is rarely to charge the same price among the different customer segments. A price structure that aligns with the variations in economic value and cost of service among customer segments is necessary for such a pricing strategy.

A customer's decision to purchase a product is also influenced by whether the product is of high quality in addition to the product's price (Gwinner et al. 1998). Prices and perceived quality play a big role in influencing African customers' purchase decisions. For instance, Bett et al. (2013) researched how Kenyan customers react to price increases on locally produced chicken items and what they are ready to pay for them on the open market. The findings indicated that because local chicken and eggs were thought to be of higher quality than imported ones, customers were willing to spend around a quarter more for them.

In reality, customers are the ones who determine a product or service's final price (Aulia et al. 2016). When making a purchase choice, customers' perceptions about the prices of the offered goods and services are crucial (Bayad and Govand 2021). Because of this, businesses in Sub-Saharan Africa must first determine what customers anticipate to get for their money before setting a price that reflects the offering value of their goods. In order to satisfy customers, businesses must have a thorough grasp of their needs and take proactive steps to meet both present and future demands. Customers value a product or service pricing as being in line with the perceived value if they believe it will satisfy their needs (Heskett et al. 1990).

Businesses Communicate Their Product's Value Through Pricing

Price is one of the most significant factors driving value perceptions (Varki and Colgate 2001). Consumers' perception of a product or service is influenced by the price the business set for it, which results in a perceived value. For businesses, it is crucial to develop an understanding of how customers perceive value. Customer perceived value is arrived at when the customer weighs a business' offering based on the trade-off between perceived benefits and sacrifices (Ulaga 2003). Usually, when making purchases, customers choose those products/services that they perceive will provide them with the highest value (Kotler and Armstrong 2008). Customers who do not realise a product differential value are susceptible to purchasing substandard products at cheaper rates that are backed by vague performance guarantees (Khan et al. 2020). Therefore, the purpose of value and price communications is to convince customers of a product value offer to achieve three objectives: enhance the possibility of a sale, increase customers' willingness to pay, and enable them to completely appreciate the benefits (Nagle and Muller 2018).

A company's pricing goal is unsuccessful if its product price does not convey value to the customers. Effective value and pricing communications involve a thorough understanding of consumers' perceived value in addition to an understanding of how and why consumers make purchases. Cöster et al. (2020) claim that finding the unique value proposition for consumers is very important, in order to generate communication that truly affects purchasing behaviours. If a business' product or service provides value that is not immediately apparent to potential customers, communicating that value can significantly impact sales and price realisation (Nagle and Muller 2018).

The likelihood that a customer will not realise or completely comprehend the value of a product or service increases with the level of market experience or the uniqueness of a product's benefits. The level of value communication can alter as customers gain knowledge (Nagle and Muller 2018). For instance, a technophile can rapidly determine how a laptop will carry out different activities by reading its feature specifications. To draw the same conclusions, however, a more ordinary customer would need to conduct a lot more investigation and evaluate a variety of products. Through pricing and marketing activities, a business must demonstrate to its customers the value of its products. Note that it is erroneous to believe that consumers will instantly recognise the value of a truly new and superior product. Before customers will be willing to pay for value, they must first identify it, as opposed to making their purchasing decisions simply based on price. Although many businesses in Africa can create and launch high-quality products, most of them completely fall short when it comes to communicating the value of these products to potential customers. Businesses must educate their customers and convey their product superiority before tying a product's worth to its price.

Pricing Strategies and Objectives

The Success of a Business Hinges on Its Pricing Strategy

Pricing strategies are the procedures and methods that companies employ to determine the prices of their goods and services (Chan et al. 2015). Market conditions, consumer demand, and the cost of goods all have a role in pricing strategies. Businesses employ different pricing strategies for their products and services for a variety of purposes including increasing earnings, gaining market share, or lowering a firm's inventory (Hamilton and Chernev 2013). There are numerous pricing strategies; however, some of the most common ones include:

Penetration pricing: The penetration pricing technique is setting a price substantially lower than competitors' offering in order to get initial sales. The business may lose money by offering such low pricing while gaining new customers and brand recognition (Alexandre and Jean-Marie 2010). This approach won't work for a business' long-term success; it is designed to kick-start sales. A business should prepare for some consumers to leave as they continue to hunt for the cheapest choice when the business finally raises prices to be more in line with the market. For example, an online news website offering one month free for a subscription-based service.

Competitive pricing: When a business uses a competitive pricing strategy, it bases prices on what the competition is charging; the products or services will be priced at the going rate in the market. If a business operates in a saturated market, the pricing of all other products in the sector determines its product's price, which helps the business maintain a competitive edge. As long as it remains within the price range established by the competitors in the sector, the business is free to price its products above or below the going market rate. This technique may work well under some certain conditions such as when a company is just getting off the ground, but it doesn't allow much room for expansion.

Cost-plus pricing: With cost-plus pricing, the final price is calculated by adding a predetermined percentage to the cost of producing the good. By initially determining how much profit to make from each sale of a product, a business may work backward to estimate the markup percentage for a product. This is one of the simplest pricing strategies (Dudu and Agwu 2014). Although basic, it is not the best option for anything other than tangible goods.

Premium pricing: In this kind of pricing, a business sets a price that is greater than that of its competitors to gain a premium position or create perceived value, quality, or luxury. Companies employ this pricing strategy when their product or service has certain distinctive characteristics or core advantages or when the business has a distinctive competitive edge over its rivals. If the business' target market comprises early adopters who enjoy being in the lead, this kind of pricing strategy excels. Premium pricing is a common tactic employed by businesses that market high-end, innovative, or exclusive goods, particularly those in the fashion or technology sectors.

Economy pricing: Economy pricing consistently undercuts competitors' prices with the intention of turning a profit through high sales volumes. The goal is to price a product cheaper than the competition while making up for it with higher sales. Typically, low production costs go hand in hand with this kind of price strategy, which works well in the commodity goods sector.

Value-based pricing: This pricing strategy is a worth-based pricing approach that largely bases prices on what consumers believe a product or service is worth. According to Dholakia (2016), value-based pricing is the process of price setting through which a business determines and attempts to earn the differentiated worth of its product for a certain customer segment in comparison to its competitors. Value-based pricing necessitates the identification of all the crucial purchasing criteria that determine how much a product is worth to a specific consumer, an awareness of how those criteria compare with offerings from other companies, and the ability to quantify the value created for the customer.

Responsible pricing: Responsible pricing entails setting appropriate value-based prices for an organisation's product or service offering in such a way that is affordable to customers and promotes sustainability for the organisation. Value-based pricing puts the customer first; thus, businesses choose their prices based on a consumer's perceived value of a product or service. According to Ingenbleek et al. (2003), value-based pricing is increasingly viewed as being superior to all other pricing strategies.

Specific Example in Sub-Saharan Africa: Botswana

Advertising firm NW Ayer & Son developed the most well-known instance of a successful value-based pricing campaign for the De Beers diamond corporation in 1947. De Beers Company, owned 85 per cent by Anglo American and 15 per cent by the Government of the Republic of

Botswana, specialises in diamond mining, exploitation, retail, and diamond trading. Following a series of pre-war and post-war economic downturns, the price of diamonds had significantly decreased, and NW Ayer & Son was briefed to make them desirable again. With the genius slogan, 'A diamond is forever' they led young men into believing that the size and quality of the diamond in their fiancées' engagement rings was a clear reflection of their love. And thus, the value and price of diamonds skyrocketed.

Businesses that utilise value-based pricing won't set prices lower than necessary because it gives them information on the customers' willingness to pay. Second, because value-based pricing allows businesses to reflect perceived benefits in the price, these businesses can promote a product/service whose perceived value and benefits matches. Thus, choosing a pricing strategy that aligns with the customer perceived value can result in increased sales and profit margins.

The Objectives Behind Pricing Strategy

Roos et al. (2004) describe strategy as a number of planned activities that will help a company reach its objectives. According to Avlonitis and Indounas (2006), pricing strategy objectives provide directions for action: 'to have them is to know what is expected and how the efficiency of operations is to be measured'. Pricing strategy objectives should describe what a business hopes to achieve through pricing. For example Table 7.1 shows;

Table 7.1 Pricing strategy objectives example

Profit maximisation	Achievement of satisfactory profits
Sales maximisation	Achievement of satisfactory sales
Market share maximisation	Achievement of a satisfactory market share
Maintenance of the existing customers	Customers' needs for satisfaction
Long-term survival	Achievement of social goals
Return on investment (ROI)	Return on assets (ROA)

The goal of profit maximisation is to increase profits for each unit sold. Profit maximisation is based on the premise that consumers value a product's distinctive features and are willing to pay more to benefit from them. The other components of the marketing mix must be used by businesses to ensure the product is manufactured, distributed, and marketed in a way that clearly distinguishes it from the rival products for profit maximisation to be effective. Sales maximisation aims to increase a business' volume and income. It is the practice of lowering prices to stimulate more sales (George and Kostis 2005). A company needs a large cost or resource advantage over rivals to maximise sales in the long run. For instance, sales maximisation has helped make Wal-Mart the largest retailer in the world.

Most businesses consider and strategise for market share, profit, and sales volume. Gaining market share is what they believe will lead to long-term profitability. According to economic theory and empirical data, profitability appears to rise with market share. Take the example of a business with a fixed plant size. In this instance, the company's earnings rise as sales volume does. Now think about the business that can grow its plant and market. This typically allows for economies of scale in marketing, distribution, and production. A larger business may afford more automation or better equipment, which reduces unit costs. Market share provides information about a company's size and is a valuable indicator of its competitiveness and dominance in a certain industry. The prices that a business can charge for its goods or services can all be strongly impacted by its market share.

On the other hand, customers' needs satisfaction is a tactical tool for acquiring and maintaining customers in the present customer-centred business environment. According to research, consumers assess their satisfaction with a product purchase based on its features. The first category is the functional attributes, which are the features and qualities connected to what the product actually does or is anticipated to perform. The second category is psychological attributes, which refer to how transactions between the consumer and seller are performed. These augmented features go above and beyond the expectations of the buyer and improve customer satisfaction. The most fundamental of all price objectives is survival. The survival objective is designed to maximise cash flow over the short term. It involves lowering prices to the point at which revenue just covers costs, allowing the firm to survive during a difficult time for the sake of long-term viability. In order to be effective, survival pricing must only be employed occasionally or temporarily.

Conclusion: *Customer's Perceived Value Is a Signal to Responsible Pricers*

Instead of only focusing on what the customer is willing to pay, responsible pricers examine, 'What is our offering worth to this consumer and how do we communicate effectively that value, therefore justifying the price?' On the other hand, when the value for some customers is insufficient to justify the price, responsible pricers think about how to service these consumers while not compromising the perceived value to other customers by segmenting the market with distinct products or delivery methods (Wang et al. 2004). Due to rising price pressure, businesses are working harder to understand their customer's perceptions of value in their business environment (Ulaga 2003). Using value-based pricing, businesses establish their prices by taking into account what customers believe a product is worth. In customer value-based pricing, the value that a good or service provides to a particular group of customers serves as the primary determinant of price (Hinterhuber 2008). To boost the perceived value of the products and services from the customer's perspective, businesses should offer products and services based on customers' needs (Kotler and Armstrong 2008).

In addition, companies must switch from the conventional perspective of viewing their business as a collection of functional operations to an externally focused perspective concerned with viewing the business as a means of value delivery (Bower and Garda 1985). As opposed to being a collection of internally focused functions, the value delivery sequence shows the business as seen from the consumer's perspective. According to Berghman et al. (2006), creating and delivering value is the basis of a sustainable pricing strategy. Understanding every possible way that a business' product or service could provide the customer with more value than a competitor's, as well as every possible way that a change in a customer's purchase behaviour could increase or decrease the value to the company, is key for a successful pricing strategy. Buyers and sellers primarily participate in exchange relationships to mutually create value for both parties. Also, it is in the customer's interest for a business that generates value for the customer to establish pricing that optimises the organisation's profitability since that would offer the business the best chance of continuing to create that value. On the other hand, the setting of prices that result in excessive profits or exploit a customer's needs is considered to be unethical behaviour and against responsible pricing practices.

Key Recommendations: *How Businesses Can Set Up Responsible Pricing for Long-Term Growth*

Businesses in Sub-Saharan Africa differ widely in their geographic and sector focus, however, a responsible pricing strategy creates opportunities for businesses to remain profitable in every sales situation and ensure sustainability.

Customer Research

Businesses should perform buyer-value interviews to find out why their current consumers buy from them and how much they would pay if they realised what the business offers. A business should research its entire addressable market to determine the price range each segment is prepared to pay for its core offerings and particular features. The research should incorporate both demographic and qualitative information and questions, including what problem the business is solving, how customers benefit from the use of the product, and what they are willing to pay to solve that problem.

Competitive Analysis

The worth of a company's product is only relative to the market. Therefore, a business should conduct a competitive analysis to determine its customers' next best option. Where would they go if you weren't in the market? The competitor? What are they offering for sale, and how much do they charge? The business must fully comprehend how much more valuable they are than the next best alternative. Does the business' product perform more efficiently, look better, or last longer than the competitive products? Does it offer additional features? The answers to these questions will help a business in raising its customers' perceived value.

Pricing

At this point, a business divides its offering into distinct product categories. It sets the price as per the 'customers' willingness to pay' of each segment for the features the business provides. In order to determine the prices to charge for each pricing bundle, a business must first identify and assess its consumer personas to define prices and selling price objectives. A business should also establish how its offering is valued in relation to other products on the market and how factors such as customer willingness to pay, business profit, and market objectives determine the ultimate price.

References

Acha, L., & Landry, S. (2019, January 11). Spotlighting opportunities for business in Africa and strategies to succeed in the world's next big growth market. *The Brookings Institution.* https://www.brookings.edu/research/spotlighting-opportunities-for-business-in-africa-and-strategies-to-succeed-in-the-worlds-next-big-growth-market/

Agwu, M. E., & Carter, A. L. (2014). Mobile phone banking in Nigeria: Benefits, problems and prospects. *International Journal of Business and Commerce, 3*(6), 50–70.

Alexandre, D., & Jean-Marie, P. (2010). Pricing strategies and models. *Annual Reviews in Control, 34*(1), 101–110. https://doi.org/10.1016/j.arcontrol.2010.02.005

Aulia, S. A., Sukati, I., & Sulaiman, Z. (2016). A review: Customer perceived value and its dimension. *Asian Journal of Social Sciences and Management Studies, 3*, 150–162.

Avlonitis, G. J., & Indounas, K. A. (2006). Pricing practices of service organizations. *Journal of Services Marketing, 20*(5), 346–356. https://doi.org/10.1108/08876040610679954

Bayad, J. A., & Govand, A. (2021). Marketing strategy: Pricing strategies and its influence on consumer purchasing decisions. *International Journal of Rural Development, Environment and Health Research, 5*(2), 26–39. https://doi.org/10.22161/ijreh.5.2.4

Berghman, L., Matthyssens, P., & Vandenbempt, K. (2006). Building competences for new customer value creation: An exploratory study. *Industrial Marketing Management, 35*(8), 961–973. https://doi.org/10.1016/j.indmarman.2006.04.006

Bett, H. K., Peters, K. J., Nwankwo, U. M., & Bokelmann, W. (2013). Estimating consumer preferences and willingness to pay for the underutilized indigenous chicken products. *Food Policy, 41*, 218–225.

Bolton, R. N., & Lemon, K. N. (1999). A dynamic model of customers' usage of services: Usage as an antecedent and consequence of satisfaction. *Journal of Marketing Research, 36*(2), 171–186. https://doi.org/10.2307/3152091

Bower, M., & Garda, R. A. (1985). The role of marketing in management. In V. P. Buell (Ed.), *Handbook of modern marketing* (2nd ed., pp. 34–36). McGraw-Hill.

Chan, K., Jubas, K., Kordes, B., & Sueling, M. (2015, March 1). *Understanding your options: Proven pricing strategies and how they work*. McKinsey & Company. https://www.mckinsey.com/business-functions/growth-marketing-and-sales/our-insights/understanding-your-options-proven-pricing-strategies-and-how-they-work

Cöster, M., Iveroth, E., Petri, C. J., & Westelius, A. (2020). Strategic and innovative pricing. Pricing. https://doi.org/10.4324/9780429053696.

Dholakia, U. M. (2016). A quick guide to value-based pricing. *Harvard Business Review*. Retrieved April 29, 2021, from https://hbr.org/2016/08/a-quick-guide-to-value-basedpricing

Duarte, P., Yamasaki, V., Rocha, T. V., & Silva, S. C. E. (2019). Evidence of a global marketing strategy: A case study in the Brazilian telecommunication market. *International Journal of Business Excellence, 19*(3), 364–380. https://doi.org/10.1504/IJBEX.2019.102820

Dudu, O. F., & Agwu, M. E. (2014). A review of the effect of pricing strategies on the purchase of consumer goods. *International Journal of Research in Management, Science & Technology, 2*(2), 88–99.

Dutta, S. K., & Snehvrat, S. (2020). A componovation perspective of innovation in emerging markets: Evidence from Indian organisations. *Thunderbird International Business Review, 62*(1), 65–75. https://doi.org/10.1002/tie.22100

George, J. A., & Kostis, A. I. (2005). Pricing objectives and pricing methods in the services sector. *Journal of Services Marketing, 19*(1), 47–57. https://doi.org/10.1108/08876040510579398

Grewal, D., Monroe, K. B., & Krishnan, R. (1998). The effects of price-comparison advertising on buyers' perception of acquisition value, transaction value, and behavioural intentions. *Journal of Marketing, 62*(2), 46–59. https://doi.org/10.2307/1252160

Gwinner, K. P., Gremler, D., & Bitner, M. J. (1998). Relational benefits in services industries: The consumer's perspective. *Journal of the Academy of Marketing Science, 26*(2), 101–114. https://doi.org/10.1177/0092070398262002

Hamilton, R., & Chernev, A. (2013). Low prices are just the beginning: Price image in retail management. *Journal of Marketing, 77*(6), 1–20. https://doi.org/10.1509/jm.08.0204

Heskett, J. L., Sasser, W. E., & Hart, C. W. L. (1990). *Breakthrough service*. The Free Press.

Hinterhuber, A. (2008). Customer value-based pricing strategies: Why companies resist. *Journal of Business Strategy, 29*(4), 41–50. https://doi.org/10.1108/02756660810887079

Ingenbleek, P., Debruyne, M., Frambach, R., & Verhallen, T. (2003). Successful new product pricing practices: A contingency approach. *Marketing Letters, 14*(4), 289–305. https://doi.org/10.1023/B:MARK.0000012473.92160.3d

Khan, A., Yang, A. J. F., & Chen, Y. J. (2020). Impact of buying counterfeit brands on the brand image of original brands. *Asia Proceedings of Social Sciences, 6*(1), 89–94. https://doi.org/10.31580/apss.v6i1.1281

Kotler, P., & Armstrong, G. (2008). *Principles of marketing* (12th ed.). Prentice Hall.

Kumar, N., & Steenkamp, J. E. M. (2013). *Brand breakout: How emerging market brands will go global*. Palgrave Macmillan. https://doi.org/10.1057/9781137276629

Lindsey-Mullikin, J., & Petty, R. D. (2011). Marketing tactics discouraging price search: Deception and competition. *Journal of Marketing, 64*(1), 67–73. https://doi.org/10.1016/j.jbusres.2009.10.003

Monroe, K. B. (1990). *Pricing: Making profitable decisions*. McGraw-Hill.

Nagle, T., & Holden, R. (2002). *The strategy and tactics of pricing* (3rd ed.). Prentice-Hall.

Nagle, T., & Muller, G. (Eds.). (2018). *The strategy and tactics of pricing*. Taylor & Francis Group.

Parasuraman, A., & Grewal, D. (2000). The impact of technology on the quality-value loyalty chain: A research agenda. *Journal of the Academy of Marketing Science, 28*(1), 168–174. https://doi.org/10.1177/0092070300281015

Roos, G., von Krogh, G., & Roos, J. (2004). *Strategy – An introduction*. Student Literature.

Ulaga, W. (2003). Capturing value creation in business relationships: A customer perspective. *Industrial Marketing Management, 32*(8), 677–693. https://doi.org/10.1016/j.indmarman.2003.06.008

Varki, S., & Colgate, M. (2001). The role of price perceptions in an integrated model of behavioural intentions. *Journal of Service Research, 3*(3), 232–240.

Wang, Y., Lo, H., Chi, R., & Yang, Y. (2004). An integrated framework for customer value and customer-relationship-management performance: A customer-based perspective from China. *Managing Service Quality, 14*(2/3), 69–82. https://doi.org/10.1108/09604520410528590

8

Responsible Financial Accounting Strategies

Callistus Ekpenga

Introduction

Gone are the days when financial accounting was solely about numbers and profit. Today, responsible financial accounting strategies are about much more—building trust, transparency, and long-term sustainability. Imagine a world where businesses not only focus on maximising profits but also consider the long-term impacts of their activities on society and the environment. This is the world of responsible financial accounting, where businesses take actions to mitigate their negative impacts on the environment, ensuring they are engaging in ethical practices, giving back to their communities, prioritising diversity and inclusion in their workplaces, investing in renewable energy, and promoting sustainability.

In Africa, even though social and environmental accounting (SEA) practices are still largely understudied (Tilt, 2018), there are several reasons why they are becoming more prevalent. One reason is that consumers, investors, and other stakeholders demand more transparency and

C. Ekpenga (✉)
Cardinal One Business Services, Lagos, Nigeria

accountability from organisations. In addition, many African countries face significant social and environmental challenges, such as climate change, pollution, and inequality. Social and environmental accounting can help provide the information that will assist organisations in identifying and addressing these issues in their operations.

Also, in the face of increasing competition and rising costs, many businesses want to adopt a more sustainable business model. To that end, they're turning to traditional financial accounting to manage their finances. While these methods can be used for various purposes, such as credit management, allocation of resources, and financial reporting, they are not generally suited for ongoing operations and operations-focused businesses. This is because traditional financial reporting does not consider the impacts of allocating resources and fair use of natural resources. In other words, it disregards how its actions may affect society and the environment. This has created an opportunity for a new approach: sustainability reporting.

In this chapter, we will explore the current state of SEA practices applied by businesses in sub-Saharan Africa. While there is increasing interest in how African countries provide social and ecological disclosures within annual reports, there still needs to be more scholarly attention on how African businesses engage with social and environmental accounting forms. The chapter will trace the history and development of social and environmental accounting from the middle of the twentieth century until now. This summary aims to show the intersections between accounting practice and sustainable development and, more importantly, how accounting disclosures can be used to demonstrate organisational commitment to social and ecological well-being. The next part of the chapter will discuss the history of accounting research in the sub-Saharan region. Though the region's recorded history of accounting practice is rooted in colonialism, there is some development in mandating sophisticated forms of SEA, such as sustainability reporting and integrated reporting. The South African reporting environment will be discussed in detail due to the country's history of mandating integrated reporting. The last part of the chapter will reflect on the future of social and environmental accounting for businesses on the continent.

The chapter hopes to achieve some goals. Firstly, it aims to raise awareness of the importance of responsible financial accounting practices among African businesses, encouraging more companies to adopt these practices. Secondly, the chapter hopes to contribute to the broader discourse on responsible financial accounting and sustainability in Africa, providing insight and expertise on the challenges and opportunities faced by businesses in this region. Overall, the chapter's goal is to contribute to developing a more sustainable and responsible business environment in Africa, which is important for the long-term prosperity and well-being of the region.

The Context: Economic Landscape of Africa

Africa is a continent with immense potential for economic growth, but it also faces several challenges that hinder its economic advancement. Key economic indicators that provide insight into the continent's economic health include population, GDP, GDP per capita, inflation, unemployment, and foreign direct investment.

In terms of population, Africa is home to 1.3 billion people, which is projected to double by 2050 (The Economist, 2020). This population growth has been accompanied by a rapid increase in urbanisation, with over 40% of the population living in cities. This growth presents opportunities and challenges, which can lead to increased economic activity and increased demand for resources and services. In terms of GDP, the African continent has seen strong economic growth in recent years, averaging approximately 5% in 2017. It has the world's second-fastest growing economy, with a projected growth rate of 3.9%. It has been driven by improved macroeconomic policies, increased foreign direct investment, greater access to technology, and increased domestic spending. The continent's GDP per capita remains low, at an estimated $2182 in 2022 (International Monetary Fund, 2022). Inflation in Africa is estimated to be around 6.7%, which is low compared to other regions. However, this could be due to the continent's limited access to credit and financial services, which makes it more difficult to finance investments and spur economic growth. Unemployment in Africa is estimated to be around 7.6%

(World Bank, 2021), which is significantly higher than the global average. This is partly due to a lack of skilled labour and job opportunities in key sectors, such as agriculture and manufacturing. In recent years, Africa has seen a surge of foreign direct investment, with countries such as Nigeria, South Africa, Kenya, and Ethiopia receiving the most investment. This investment has helped to spur economic growth and development in the continent, although it has not been evenly distributed across countries.

A mix of challenges and opportunities characterised the economic landscape in Africa in 2021. Africa has also faced many economic challenges, including high levels of inequality, unemployment, and debt. The COVID-19 pandemic has also significantly impacted the African economy (Mugano, 2020; Hamann et al., 2020), with many countries experiencing economic downturns and disruptions to trade and supply chains. However, the pandemic also highlighted the need for African countries to diversify their economies and reduce their reliance on exports. Many are making efforts to promote domestic production and consumption. Other challenges facing the African economy include a need for more infrastructure, a reliance on natural resource exports, political instability, and a need for greater economic diversification. Despite these challenges, Africa has many opportunities for economic growth and development. These include a growing middle class, a youthful population, and abundant natural resources.

It is important to consider the role of the informal sector in the African economy. The sector is a major source of employment in many African countries, and it is estimated that this sector generates up to 40% of the continent's GDP. It is also an important economic growth and development source, providing employment opportunities and access to basic goods and services for many people (Grey-Johnson, 1992). Overall, Africa is a continent with immense potential for economic growth, but it also faces some challenges that need to be addressed for the continent to realise its potential.

History and Development of SEA

Social and environmental accounting, also known as sustainability reporting, refers to identifying, measuring, and disclosing a business's social and environmental impacts. Responsible businesses are increasingly adopting sustainable financial accounting strategies to manage their financial resources in a financially successful, environmentally and socially responsible way. This approach helps businesses to consider and report on their non-financial performance, such as their impact on the environment and their relationships with stakeholders like employees, customers, and local communities.

It is an increasingly important area of corporate responsibility, particularly in Africa, where the potential for negative impacts on local communities and the environment is often more significant due to weaker regulatory frameworks and limited resources. In recent years, African businesses have increasingly adopted SEA practices to measure and report their impacts (Zulkifli, 2008). This information is essential for decision-making, as it allows organisations to identify areas where they can improve their performance and make more sustainable choices. It also helps organisations to be more transparent and accountable to stakeholders. In addition, social and environmental accounting can support the development of African economies by promoting sustainable business practices and creating a more equitable and sustainable society. It is a crucial tool for organisations in Africa to navigate the challenges and opportunities of the twenty-first century and contribute to the well-being of both people and the planet.

Early Attempts at Social and Environmental Accounting in Africa

Before the arrival of European colonisers, many African societies had developed their resource management and accountability systems. These systems often involved using traditional forms of knowledge, such as oral history, storytelling, and spiritual beliefs, to guide the responsible use of natural resources. Many of these systems also included mechanisms for holding individuals and communities accountable for their actions, such as community meetings and using elders or spiritual leaders as mediators.

The introduction of Western accounting practices during the colonial era significantly impacted the way economic activities were conducted and reported on the continent. These practices originated in Europe and North America and were often imposed on African societies without considering their unique cultural, social, and environmental contexts.

One of the main goals of colonial powers was to extract resources and profits from Africa, and Western accounting practices played a key role in this process. They were used to track and report on the financial performance of colonial enterprises, such as plantations, mines, and factories, with little regard for their social and environmental impacts. This narrow focus on financial performance often led to the exploitation of natural resources, the degradation of the environment, and the exploitation of local communities. In addition to serving the interests of colonial powers, Western accounting practices also significantly influenced the development of African economies. They shaped how business was conducted and influenced the priorities of African governments and businesses. This emphasis on financial performance often led to a neglect of social and environmental considerations, which negatively affected African societies' welfare.

The concept of environmental accounting first emerged in the 1970s as a way to measure and report on the environmental impacts of organisations. This was primarily in response to growing concerns about the negative impacts of industrialisation and development on the environment and the need for more transparent and accountable reporting on these impacts. It initially focused on the direct environmental impacts of organisations, such as the use of natural resources and the generation of waste. In the 1980s, social accounting began to emerge, focusing on the social impacts of business activities. This included labour practices, human rights, and community relations. Social and environmental accounting eventually merged to become known as "sustainability accounting," which includes social and environmental considerations. One of Africa's earliest examples of social and environmental accounting was the introduction of the "triple bottom line" concept in the 1990s.

This concept focuses on measuring an organisation's financial, social, and environmental performance.

Adoption of Sophisticated Forms of SEA in Africa

In recent years, businesses in Africa have started to report on their social and environmental performance with more transparency and accountability. This has been made easier by creating numerous reporting frameworks and rules, including those from the International Accounting Standards Board, the Global Reporting Initiative, and the International Integrated Reporting Council (IASB). The Sustainable Development Goals (SDGs) of the United Nations, which seek to promote sustainable development throughout the world, are another significant endeavour. Many African nations have committed to attaining the SDGs and have implemented policies and initiatives to help them do so. Adopting SEA methods as a way to track and report on progress towards the SDGs is frequently a part of these initiatives. These frameworks provide guidelines for what information should be given in a social and environmental report and how it should be included.

Regional frameworks have also been created and implemented in Africa to support social and environmental accounting practices in addition to international frameworks. For instance, the Environmental and Social Assessment Procedures (AfDB, 2015) that the African Development Bank has developed explain the standards for environmental and social analyses of investments and projects that the bank sponsors. Agenda 2063 (African Union, 2015), a framework for African development with several objectives linked to sustainability and environmental preservation, has also been accepted by the African Union. The goal of "A Prosperous Africa Based on Inclusive Growth and Sustainable Development" is another one of Agenda 2063's particular objectives. It calls for incorporating environmental, social, and economic factors into all initiatives, programmes, and policies. With the help of these policies, projects should be carried out sustainably, responsibly, and with effective management and mitigation of their social and environmental repercussions.

In 2003, the South African government released the King Report on Corporate Governance, which mandated that businesses report on their social and environmental performance. This report paved the way for adopting sophisticated SEA practices like sustainability reporting in African nations. The International Integrated Reporting Framework (IIRF) was unveiled in 2009 after that. Companies must report on their financial, social, and environmental performance under the IIRF, a global accounting standard. Since then, Kenya and other African nations like Nigeria have enacted comparable requirements. Companies must report on their social and environmental performance under the Nigerian Code of Corporate Governance. Under Kenya's Corporate Governance and Sustainability Regulations, they must report on their advancement towards sustainability objectives.

Additionally, several NGOs and civil society organisations are attempting to encourage the implementation of SEA procedures in Africa. These organisations frequently offer businesses and governments in Africa technical aid and capacity-building support, assisting them in implementing SEA practises and disclosing their effects on the economy, society, and environment.

SEA Research in African

According to Wise (2021), "Africa needs a comprehensive accounting research infrastructure to fulfil the desire to embrace IFRS and drive the development of accounting in Africa and influence the international standard setting." However, several factors, such as the expanding significance of accounting in the global economy and the growing awareness of the need for research pertinent to the unique context and requirements of African countries, are fuelling the expansion of accounting research in Africa. The subject matter of study has changed throughout time, but it has frequently centred on issues like corporate governance, social and environmental accounting, and financial reporting. The environmental concerns and threats that impact Africa and Africans have not yet been thoroughly investigated in existing studies on environmental accounting (Denedo & Egbon, 2021).

A wide range of topics have been the subject of recent research in social and environmental accounting in Africa, including corporate environmental management, corporate social responsibility, corporate governance, climate change, the role of voluntary disclosure, the impact of cultural and institutional factors on accounting practises, the role of external assurance in fostering trust in corporate sustainability reporting, and the impact of climate change on accounting standards. Developing integrated reporting for Africa, using technology to improve sustainability reporting, and the effect of accounting rules on business performance are some other research areas. Research has also been done on the use of environmental accounting to measure environmental performance; the use of stakeholder engagement to improve sustainability reporting and development (Agyemang et al., 2017; Denedo et al., 2017); the function of accountability and transparency in promoting sustainability in African companies; the drivers behind and obstacles to environmental, social, and governance (ESG) reporting in African nations; and the quality and usefulness of such reports for stakeholders.

In addition to earlier studies, research on how social and environmental accounting can be utilised to inform decision-making and promote sustainability in African countries is becoming increasingly important. Research can, for instance, concentrate on the creation of integrated reporting standards, the application of technology to sustainability reporting, and the possibility of encouraging African businesses to adopt more sustainable business practices. Research may also examine how institutional and cultural factors affect accounting procedures and how external assurance helps to build public confidence in company sustainability reporting.

African accounting research output is unimpressive (Negash et al., 2019). Due to many reasons, including the fact that social and environmental accounting is a relatively new topic, this inevitably results in less scholarly attention being paid to African enterprises' engagement with sustainability reporting (Tilt et al., 2020). There are also practical obstacles to implementing social and environmental accounting in African enterprises, such as a need for more funds for research, resources, education, or competence, access to information or data, and interest in the topic relative to other business research fields. Because there is increased interest in sustainable accounting, more research will be done on this subject in the future.

SEA Practices in Africa

African businesses are increasingly adopting SEA practices to meet the needs of stakeholders while remaining profitable. But the regulatory environment in the region varies from country to country, as each country has its system of laws, regulations, and government agencies responsible for enforcing them. These environments in which businesses operate are shaped by various factors, including each country's level of development, political system and level of governance, economic goals and priorities, and cultural and historical context. Some African countries have relatively well-developed regulatory frameworks and strong institutions to enforce them, while others have weaker regulatory systems and less effective enforcement. Countries with robust regulations have implemented policies to promote sustainable development, protect the environment, and encourage corporate social responsibility.

Increasing Interest in SEA Disclosures

In recent years, there has been increasing interest in social and environmental accounting disclosures in African countries. This is due to the growing awareness of environmental issues such as climate change, environmental degradation, and the depletion of natural resources. As a result, African countries have been implementing various policies and practices to promote transparency, accountability, and public disclosure of information related to social and environmental issues.

For example, in Kenya, the Companies Act of 2015 requires all companies to disclose information about their social and environmental activities in their annual reports. Similarly, in Nigeria, the Companies and Allied Matters Act of 2020 requires companies to include information about their social and environmental policies, initiatives, and performance in their annual reports. Still, companies intervene primarily in the areas of education, health, and security while neglecting the environment (Okaro & Okafor, 2021). The Sustainable Development Goals (SDGs) have also acted as a driving force for social and environmental accounting in African countries. They provide a framework for countries to monitor and measure their progress in achieving their goals. To this end, some African countries, such as Ghana, Kenya, and Nigeria, have introduced legislation that requires companies to disclose their social and environmental impacts in their financial reports (see Ghana, 2017; Kenya, 2017; Nigeria, 2017). Ultimately, the increased interest in social and environmental accounting disclosures in African countries is helping to promote the sustainable development of these countries.

The Role of External Stakeholders in Promoting SEA in Africa

External stakeholders play a significant role in promoting social and environmental accounting (SEA) practices in Africa, which can lead to greater sustainability and improved economic performance for businesses. Government bodies, development organisations, non-governmental organisations, and academic institutions work together to develop and implement standards and frameworks for SEA. They support research and development initiatives to increase understanding of SEA, raise awareness of SEA among businesses, investors, and other stakeholders, provide technical and financial support and incentives, such as tax breaks or grants to businesses that are interested in implementing SEA, and act as catalysts for collaboration between different actors in the SEA ecosystem, as well as help to create an environment of trust and shared value. Ultimately, external stakeholders play a key role in advancing and promoting SEA in Africa by working together.

For example, the South African government has created a tax incentive to encourage businesses to adopt SEA practices. Additionally, the government of Nigeria has established a legal framework that requires businesses to report on their SEA practices. In Kenya, the government has provided funding for developing SEA systems and made access to data and other resources available to businesses. The government created a training and certification programme in Ethiopia to help businesses understand and implement SEA practices. Likewise, the government of Ghana has launched a public campaign to promote the importance of SEA.

Development organisations such as the African Development Bank and the World Bank have also provided financial and technical assistance to African businesses for SEA initiatives. Non-governmental organisations such as the United Nations Environment Programme (UNEP) have created awareness campaigns to promote SEA in African businesses. Academic institutions such as the Institute of Social and Economic Research have engaged in research and development initiatives to increase understanding of SEA. Also, investors have provided technical support and capital to businesses interested in implementing SEA. Finally, local communities have provided input and feedback to businesses on their SEA initiatives. Altogether, external stakeholders play a key role in advancing and promoting SEA in African businesses.

Impact of Social and Environmental Accounting

As a result, SEA practices are advancing in Africa at a slower pace than in developed economies. Firstly, it enables African countries to monitor their progress towards achieving sustainable development goals. It provides organisations with the information they need to assess their performance and identify areas of improvement. It ensures that organisations comply with relevant laws and regulations, which can help ascertain that they are following best practices and ethical standards. Also, it reduces opportunities for corruption and other unethical behaviours. Moreover, it helps identify areas of potential waste, fraud or abuse, enabling organisations to take corrective actions before the problem becomes more serious. Finally, it ensures that resources are used appropriately and that funds are allocated to benefit the organisation and society as a whole.

Intersections Between Accounting Practice and Sustainable Development

Social and environmental accounting seeks to align sustainability corporate sustainability goals with the principles of financial accountability. This creates intersections and emphasises the close link between accounting practices and sustainable development, which are essential in today's world, as companies need to ensure that their operations align with the global goals for sustainable development.

On the one hand, accounting practices provide a means of measuring and monitoring progress towards sustainable development goals, which helps to ensure that resources are being used sustainably and that progress is being made towards achieving the desired outcomes. On the other hand, sustainable development provides a framework for accounting practice, as it outlines the principles and objectives that should be considered when making decisions about resource allocation and accounting practices. Moreover, sustainable development also guides how to measure and report on performance, which helps ensure that accounting practices align with the principles of sustainability.

Although the adoption of social and environmental accounting practices by businesses has been relatively low compared to other regions of the world, companies are beginning to engage with social and environmental accounting forms, providing social and ecological disclosures within their annual reports. Businesses increasingly consult with external stakeholders like local communities, governments, and other organisations to ensure that their SEA forms align with their interests. This has resulted in some SEA project successes across industries and nations.

For example, the International Finance Corporation (IFC) launched an initiative in Ghana to support small and medium-sized enterprises (SMEs) in the adoption of SEA practices (IFC, 2016). In South Africa, the Financial and Accounting Services Board (FASB) launched a SEA initiative to improve financial reporting in the mining sector (Federica et al., 2016). In Uganda, the Uganda Investment Authority (UIA, 2021) launched an initiative to promote adopting SEA practices among SMEs in the manufacturing sector. Additionally, in Kenya, the National Climate

Change Adaptation Programme (NCCAP) launched an initiative to increase climate change resilience and promote the adoption of SEA practices among businesses in the agriculture sector. Kenya has also developed a regulatory framework for SEA through its Public Sector Accounting Standard (PSAS) and Environmental and Social Management Account (ESMA) guidelines. The PSAS requires public sector entities to report on their economic, social, and environmental performance. At the same time, the ESMA guidelines guide how to register and write on environmental and social issues. In Tanzania, the Ministry of Finance has launched an initiative to promote the adoption of SEA practices among businesses in the retail sector. In Zimbabwe, the Ministry of Environment and Tourism has launched an initiative to encourage SEA practices to address the impacts of climate change. In Nigeria, the Economic and Financial Crimes Commission (EFCC) has launched an initiative to promote SEA practices to combat financial crimes and money laundering. In Ethiopia, the Environmental Protection Authority (EPA) has launched an initiative to promote SEA practices for companies in the energy sector. In Cote d'Ivoire, the National Council for Sustainable Development (NCSD) has launched an initiative to promote SEA practices for companies in the tourism sector. In Morocco, the National Bank of Morocco (NBM) has launched an initiative to promote SEA practices among companies in the banking sector.

Also, some companies in Africa are leading the way in sustainability reporting, while most continue to lag (KPMG, 2017). Companies such as Sasol (South Africa), Dangote Cement (Nigeria), Safaricom (Kenya), Orascom Telecom (Egypt), and MTN (Ghana) have implemented a range of initiatives to improve their sustainability practices. These initiatives include developing sustainability strategies, investing in renewable energy and energy efficiency initiatives, improving water management practices, improving waste management and recycling, improving employee working conditions and benefits, investing in sustainable supply chain management, and providing transparency in financial reporting. Furthermore, many of these companies have also developed internal sustainability targets and indicators to measure the progress of their sustainability efforts, as well as external reporting frameworks such as the Global Reporting Initiative (GRI) to provide transparency to stakeholders.

The South African Reporting Environment

The South African sustainability accounting and reporting environment is the most advanced in the region (Denedo & Egbon, 2021) and similar to the disclosures made by companies in industrialised nations (Ackers, 2009). Most other African countries, such as Ghana and Nigeria, have less developed regulatory frameworks for SEA. In these countries, organisations may be required to report on their environmental performance, but there are no specific requirements for reporting on social and economic performance.

The strength of the South African reporting environment is reflected in the country's regulatory framework, which requires companies to disclose information on their social and environmental impacts. Not only are there a multitude of compliance requirements, but also there are numerous agencies that have different mandates and reporting obligations. The results? A complex landscape where it can take time for companies to keep track of this information.

In South Africa, the Companies Act of 2008 and King Report on Governance for South Africa (Institute of Directors in South Africa, 2016) provide guidance on sustainability reporting for organisations and require them to develop integrated reports (Haji & Anifowose, 2016). King IV recommends that organisations report on their social and environmental performance using the Global Reporting Initiative (GRI) framework. In addition to King IV and the GRI, the South African Integrated Reporting Framework (SA-IR) is also widely used in the country. The SA-IR is a comprehensive framework that integrates financial and non-financial information to provide a more holistic view of an organisation's performance. It encourages organisations to consider the long-term sustainability of their business and its impact on society and the environment. The Department of Environmental Affairs has issued guidelines on environmental reporting, which outline the information companies should include in their environmental reports. The South African government also encourages companies to use integrated reporting, which enables stakeholders to assess the organisation's progress towards sustainability goals.

All companies must prepare financial statements following Generally Accepted Accounting Principles (GAAP) and the International Financial Reporting Standards (IFRS). These financial statements must be audited by an independent external auditor and submitted to the Companies and Intellectual Property Commission (CIPC). Companies on the Johannesburg Stock Exchange (JSE) comply with its Listings Requirements, involving the submission of quarterly, half-yearly, and annual reports. These reports consist of detailed financial statements, social and environmental accounting, sustainability reporting, and a report from an independent auditor (Marx & van Dyk, 2011). The sustainability report must include information on the company's corporate governance, environmental performance, social and community initiatives, human rights, and other relevant topics. The report also includes a description of the company's environmental, social, and governance performance targets; progress made towards achieving these targets; a description of the company's policies, processes, and performance indicators related to ESG issues; and any material sustainability risks associated with these issues. To ensure that companies meet their ESG obligations, they must develop and implement sustainability policies and strategies. Companies must regularly monitor and report on their progress in achieving their sustainability goals and strive to create a culture of sustainability in the workplace by encouraging and rewarding employees who demonstrate an obligation to sustainability. Finally, companies must engage with key stakeholders, such as investors, suppliers, customers, and other relevant parties, to meet their sustainability objectives. Generally, listed companies are expected to adhere to the core sustainability principles, such as environmental protection, social responsibility, economic development, and good governance, to ensure long-term financial stability and sustainable growth.

Despite these regulatory requirements, the social and environmental reporting level in South Africa varies widely among companies. Some companies, particularly those in the mining and manufacturing sectors, have robust social and environmental reporting practices, while others have less comprehensive reporting. This can make it difficult for stakeholders, including investors and consumers, to obtain reliable and consistent information on the social and environmental impacts of companies operating in South Africa.

Companies such as Richemont, Anglo-American, Shoprite, Sanlam, and Sasol engage in sustainability practices and reporting. Richemont (2022), for example, has implemented a sustainability framework that includes measures to reduce its environmental impact, create jobs, and build stronger communities. Anglo-American (2021) has developed a strategy to reduce its ecological footprint and ensure its operations are resilient to climate change. Shoprite (2022) has established a sustainability programme focusing on reducing its carbon footprint, investing in renewable energy sources, and creating sustainable jobs. Sanlam (2021) has also set up a sustainability fund to support projects that promote economic growth and development in South Africa. Sasol (2022) has developed a sustainability strategy that includes reducing its operations' environmental impacts, improving its employees' and contractors' safety and health, and investing in renewable energy and energy efficiency initiatives. They have also developed internal sustainability targets and indicators, including external reporting frameworks such as the GRI to provide transparency to stakeholders. These companies are just a few examples of South African businesses leading sustainability reporting.

The South African reporting environment is characterised by unique features that can impact the quality and reliability of social and environmental accounting reports. Some of the key characteristics of the South African reporting environment include:

* A diverse range of stakeholders with varied interests and expectations, including shareholders, employees, customers, regulators, NGOs, and community groups
* A highly regulated reporting environment, with several legal and regulatory requirements for organisations to report on their social and environmental performance
* A growing demand for greater transparency and accountability from organisations, particularly in the areas of corporate governance and sustainability

- A relatively developed infrastructure for reporting, with established reporting frameworks and guidelines available for organisations to follow

Overall, the sustainability reporting environment in South Africa is relatively strong, but there is still room for improvement. In particular, there is a need for greater standardisation and consistency in reporting practices including increased transparency and accountability.

Future of Social and Environmental Accounting

The future of social and environmental accounting in Africa is an important and timely topic, as it has the potential to shape the economic and social development of the region. Looking ahead can help ensure that investments and policies are made with a long-term view of the social and environmental consequences and that resources are directed to maximise sustainable development.

Trends and Emerging Issues

Some trends and issues are emerging, for instance, the increasing adoption of international reporting standards, such as the Global Reporting Initiative (GRI) and the International Integrated Reporting Council (IIRC), as well as the growing use of technology and digital tools to collect, analyse, and report data. Other trends include the increasing use of sustainability reporting to measure and communicate organisations' social and environmental performance and the growing recognition of the importance of stakeholder engagement in decision-making processes.

Environmental accounting researchers such as Bebbington and Unerman (2018) have begun to investigate the roles academic accounting can play in supporting the attainment of the SDGs through improved understanding, accounting policy and practice.

In addition to increased reporting, there has also been a trend towards greater integration of ESG considerations into business decision-making, e.g., investment choices.

Challenges and Opportunities for Growth and Innovation

Despite the numerous benefits of sustainability accounting, there are challenges in implementing them in African countries. One of the most significant challenges is measuring and reporting responsible financial accounting strategies. There is also a need for more awareness and understanding among businesses and policymakers about the benefits of sustainability and the implications of not taking action. The resources and infrastructure in place to support the development of SEA are limited, as well as capacity and expertise in the field. Also, access to data and information needs to be improved, and resources and capacity for data collection and analysis are often inadequate. There is also a need for more standardisation, strong regulatory frameworks, and enforcement to support the development of SEA. Finally, cultural and societal barriers can also impede progress in this area.

Despite these challenges, significant opportunities exist for promoting sustainable and responsible business practices. This includes the potential to contribute to regional economic growth and development, addressing social and environmental issues such as poverty, inequality, and climate change. The shift towards sustainability in Africa has created tremendous opportunities for businesses to innovate and develop new products, services, and processes that focus on a triple bottom line of people, profit, and the planet.

There is a unique opportunity to use SEA to optimise operations and reduce environmental impacts. Companies can use data more effectively to identify areas of opportunity, such as methods to reduce waste and increase efficiency. They can also leverage new technologies such as solutions for data gathering, analysis and reporting processes, artificial intelligence, and blockchain to create more efficient and transparent processes. This could include leveraging AI to develop more accurate forecasts and predictions or using blockchain to ensure data integrity and transactions. Companies can also capitalise on the growing demand for sustainable products and services by developing innovative strategies to meet customer needs and capture new markets. Finally, businesses can participate in initiatives to create new standards and frameworks for social and environmental accounting to increase transparency and trust. This could include setting new accounting and reporting standards or creating guidelines to ensure that companies adhere to best practices. By taking advantage of these opportunities, African businesses can unlock more significant growth and innovation in social and environmental accounting.

African businesses can differentiate themselves from their global competitors by adopting social and environmental accounting practices, which can help to build trust and credibility with stakeholders. There are opportunities for partnerships and collaborations with international organisations. These can be particularly important in a globalised business environment where consumers and investors are increasingly concerned about companies' environmental and social impacts.

Overall, while there are challenges to implementing social and environmental accounting in Africa, there are also many opportunities for promoting sustainable business practices and addressing important social and environmental issues in the region.

Future Directions

One key expectation for the future of social and environmental accounting in Africa is increased adoption and implementation. Thirteen sub-Saharan African countries have signed the Sustainable Stock Exchange (SSE) Initiative. Still, only four (including South Africa, Namibia, Nigeria, and Zimbabwe) have mandatory reporting as a listing condition (Tilt et al., 2020). As awareness of the importance of sustainability grows, more organisations are likely to adopt social and environmental accounting practices. There may be increased pressure for mandatory reporting requirements for companies in certain sectors. In addition, there is likely to be an improvement in reporting standards practices as organisations seek to provide more accurate and comprehensive information about their social and environmental impacts.

Another prediction is that social and environmental accounting will become more integrated with traditional financial reporting using triple-bottom-line accounting. This could involve incorporating non-financial information, such as environmental and social data, into formal financial statements, and developing integrated reporting frameworks that combine financial and non-financial information. This integration could help organisations better understand and communicate the risks and opportunities associated with their sustainability performance and provide stakeholders with a more holistic view of their operations.

More businesses may increasingly adopt sustainable financial accounting strategies depending on the specific needs and goals of the business in question. These strategies may include:

1. Impact investing: There is growing interest in impact investing in Africa, which involves businesses using their financial resources to support sustainable development projects, such as renewable energy, clean water, and sustainable agriculture. It allows businesses to contribute to sustainable development while potentially generating a financial return. By using accounting techniques to measure and report on the impact of these investments, investors can better understand the sustainability of their portfolios.
2. Sustainable finance: African financial institutions are increasingly offering sustainable finance products, such as green bonds or loans for renewable energy projects. Accountants may be involved in developing and monitoring these products to ensure they meet sustainability criteria.
3. Social accounting: Businesses can also use social accounting to report their social impacts and contributions to sustainable development. This can include reporting on employment practices, community engagement, and social investments.
4. Green accounting: This involves accounting for the economic value of natural resources and ecosystem services, such as water, soil, and biodiversity. This can help ensure that the actual cost of resource use is reflected in financial statements, which can inform more sustainable

business practices. It also involves investing in green accounting software and systems to help reduce carbon footprint and renewable energy sources to reduce emissions.
5. Support for sustainable supply chain management: Accountants can help organisations understand and use accounting practices to support the development of sustainable supply chains. This can involve tracking and reporting on the sustainability of the company's suppliers and implementing programmes to reduce waste and increase resource efficiency throughout the supply chain. MNCs are under increasing pressure from civil society organisations to follow globally accepted best practices to avoid harming their African supply networks (Lauwo et al., 2019; Ruggie, 2013).
6. External assurance: This includes external assurance, in which independent third parties verify the accuracy and reliability of an organisation's sustainability reports.

There is also potential for African companies to lead the way in sustainable business practices and use social and environmental accounting to demonstrate their duty to sustainability. This could help to boost the reputation and credibility of African companies and make them more attractive to investors and other stakeholders within and outside the region.

Factors Influencing the Future of SEA in Africa

Several factors will influence the future of social and environmental accounting in Africa. Economic development and globalisation are likely to play a role as more organisations seek to adopt sustainable practices to stay competitive in an increasingly globalised economy. Government policies and regulations will also be important, as they can provide incentives or penalties for companies that adopt sustainable practices or require certain levels of sustainability reporting. The growing demand for transparency from stakeholders, including investors, customers, and employees, is also likely to drive the adoption of social and environmental accounting practices. Finally, technological advancements, such as using digital tools to collect and analyse data, are likely to make it easier for organisations to measure and report on their social and environmental impacts.

In conclusion, the future of social and environmental accounting in Africa is promising, with increasing opportunities for growth and improvement. African countries must prioritise and invest in social and environmental accounting to address pressing issues and contribute to sustainable development. By adopting sustainable business practices and using social and environmental accounting to communicate their performance, African companies can help to drive change and positively impact the continent.

Key Recommendations

To help ensure long-term financial success, responsible financial accounting practices must be adopted and implemented in sub-Saharan Africa. The following key recommendations are provided in this chapter to ensure the region's economic and financial stability.

First, stakeholders must develop a comprehensive sustainability strategy aligning with the United Nations Sustainable Development Goals (SDGs) and the African Union's Agenda 2063.

Second, businesses, accounting professionals, and regulators need greater environmental accounting awareness and understanding. This can be achieved through education, training programmes, and the promotion of best practices.

Third, there must be greater political will and support for environmental accounting. Governments need to recognise the importance of environmental accounting and the potential benefits it can bring. They must create policies and incentives to promote and support environmental accounting initiatives.

Also, there needs to be greater access to resources and infrastructure to support environmental accounting. This includes data, technology, and expertise. Governments can play an important role by funding and supporting research, development, and implementation of environmental accounting systems.

Furthermore, environmental accounting initiatives need to be integrated into existing accounting systems, such as financial accounting. This will ensure that environmental accounting data is collected and tracked systematically and consistently. The Global Reporting Initiative (GRI) and the Sustainability Accounting Standards Board (SASB) are two examples of standardised sustainability reporting systems that can be integrated.

Finally, stakeholders must prioritise partnerships and investments in sustainable projects and technologies to drive innovation and long-term sustainability.

Conclusion

Social and environmental accounting (SEA) practices in sub-Saharan Africa have undergone a process of development and evolution over the past several decades, with increasing interest in how businesses in the region engage with and disclose their commitment to sustainable development. However, more scholarly attention is still needed, and the adoption and implementation of these practices vary across the region. Despite this, it is clear that accounting practices and sustainable development have intersected significantly over time, and there has been a push towards mandating more sophisticated forms of SEA, such as sustainability reporting and integrated reporting.

South Africa has a notable history of mandating integrated reporting. It will be necessary for other countries in the region to consider similar measures to promote more transparent and sustainable business practices. However, it is worth noting that implementing SEA practices is not just the responsibility of businesses themselves but also the accounting profession, governments, and other relevant organisations. All of these stakeholders have a role to play in supporting and promoting the adoption of SEA practices in the region.

Looking towards the future, sub-Saharan African businesses must continue prioritising social and environmental considerations in their accounting practices. This not only demonstrates responsibility for sustainable development, but it also helps to build trust with stakeholders and can contribute to long-term organisational success. By continuing to focus on SEA practices, businesses in the region can contribute to the well-being of their communities and the environment. Still, they can position themselves for long-term success in a rapidly changing world.

References

Ackers, B. (2009). Corporate social responsibility assurance: How do South African publicly listed companies compare? *Meditari Accountancy Research, 17*(2), 1–17.

African Development Bank Group. (2015). *Environmental and Social Assessment Procedures (ESAP)*. Retrieved January 10, 2023, from https://www.afdb.org/fileadmin/uploads/afdb/Documents/Publications/SSS_%E2%80%93vol1_%E2%80%93_Issue4_-_EN_-_Environmental_and_Social_Assessment_Procedures__ESAP_.pdf

African Union. (2015). *Agenda 2063: The Africa We Want*. Retrieved January 10, 2023, from https://au.int/sites/default/files/documents/33126-doc-framework_document_book.pdf

Agyemang, G., O'Dwyer, B., Unerman, J., & Awumbila, M. (2017). Seeking "conversations for accountability" mediating the impact of upward accountability processes of non-governmental organisations (NGOs). *Accounting, Auditing and Accountability Journal, 30*(5), 982–1007.

Anglo-American. (2021). *Sustainability report*. Retrieved January 10, 2023, from https://www.angloamerican.com/~/media/Files/A/Anglo-American-Group-v5/PLC/investors/annual-reporting/2022/aa-sustainability-report-full-2021.pdf

Bebbington, J., & Unerman, J. (2018). Achieving the United Nations Sustainable Development Goals: An enabling role for accounting research. *Accounting, Auditing and Accountability Journal, 31*(1), 2–24.

Denedo, M., & Egbon, O. (2021). Africa, from the past to the present: Moving the critical environmental accounting research on Africa forward. In J. Bebbington, C. Larrinaga, B. O'Dwyer, & I. Thomson (Eds.), *Handbook of environmental accounting* (pp. 265–275). Routledge.

Denedo, M., Thomson, I., & Yonekura, A. (2017). International advocacy NGOs, counter accounting, accountability and engagement. *Accounting, Auditing and Accountability Journal, 30*(6), 1309–1343.

Federica, D., Andrea, G., & Pasquale, P. (2016). Early adopters of integrated reporting: The case of the mining industry in South Africa. *African Journal of Business Management, 10*(9), 187–208.

Ghana. (2017). *The sustainable development goals (SDGs) in Ghana. Why they matter & how we can help*. Retrieved January 10, 2023, from https://ghana.un.org/en/download/3407/19077

Grey-Johnson, C. (1992). The African informal sector at the crossroads: Emerging policy options. *Africa Development/Afrique et Développement*, 65–91.

Haji, A. A., & Anifowose, M. (2016). The trend of integrated reporting practice in South Africa: Ceremonial or substantive? *Sustainability Accounting, Management and Policy Journal, 7*(2), 190–224.

Hamann, R., Muthuri, J. N., Nwagwu, I., Pariag-Maraye, N., Chamberlin, W., Ghai, S., et al. (2020). COVID-19 in Africa: Contextualizing impacts, responses, and prospects. *Environment: Science and Policy for Sustainable Development, 62*(6), 8–18.

Institute of Directors in South Africa. (2016). *King IV: Report on corporate governance for South Africa 2016*. Retrieved January 10, 2023, from https://www.iodsa.co.za/page/king_iv_report

International Finance Corporation. (2016). *IFC, ACCA promote sustainable businesses to strengthen Ghana's economy*. https://pressroom.ifc.org/all/pages/PressDetail.aspx?ID=18056

International Monetary Fund. (2022). *Africa (region)*. Retrieved January 10, 2023, from https://www.imf.org/external/datamapper/profile/AFQ

Kenya. (2017). Implementation of the Agenda 2030 for sustainable development in Kenya. *Ministry of Devolution and Planning*. Retrieved January 10, 2023, from https://sustainabledevelopment.un.org/content/documents/15689Kenya.pdf

KPMG International. (2017). *The KPMG survey of corporate responsibility reporting*. Retrieved January 10, 2023, from https://home.kpmg/be/en/home/insights/2017/10/the-kpmg-survey-of-corporate-responsibilityreporting-2017.html

Lauwo, S., Kyriacou, O., & Otusanya, O. J. (2019). When sorry is not an option: CSR reporting and "face work" in a stigmatised industry – A case study of Barrick (Acacia) goldmine in Tanzania. *Critical Perspectives on Accounting, 71*, 102099.

Marx, B., & van Dyk, V. (2011). Sustainability reporting and assurance: An analysis of assurance practices in South Africa. *Meditari Accountancy Research, 19*(1/2), 39–55.

Mugano, G. (2020). The economic nexus of the COVID-19 pandemic. *Социолошки преглед, 54*(3), 737–760.

Negash, M., Lemma, T. T., & Samkin, G. (2019). Factors impacting accounting research output in developing countries: An exploratory study. *The British Accounting Review, 51*(2), 170–192.

Nigeria. (2017). *Nigeria: Sustainable development goals (SDGs) indicators baseline report 2016.* Retrieved January 10, 2023, from https://www.undp.org/sites/g/files/zskgke326/files/migration/ng/Nigeria-SDGs-Indicators-Baseline-Report-2016.pdf

Okaro, S. C., & Okafor, G. O. (2021). Corporate social responsibility in Nigeria. In S. O. Idowu (Ed.), *Current global practices of corporate social responsibility* (pp. 525–541). Springer.

Richemont. (2022). *Sustainability report.* Retrieved January 10, 2023, from https://www.richemont.com/media/agondiwh/richemont-sustainability-report-2022-1.pdf

Ruggie, J. G. (2013). *Just business: Multinational corporations and human rights.* W.W. Norton & Company.

Sanlam. (2021). *Resilience report.* Retrieved January 10, 2023, from https://www.sanlam.com/downloads/reporting-suite/2021/Sanlam-Resilience-Report-2021.pdf

Sasol. (2022). *Sustainability report.* Retrieved January 10, 2023, from https://www.sasol.com/sites/default/files/2022-08/2022%20Sasol%20Sustainability%20Report_0.pdf

Shoprite. (2022). *Sustainability report.* Retrieved January 10, 2023, from https://www.shopriteholdings.co.za/content/dam/shp/docs/shp-sr-2022.pdf

The Economist. (2020, March 28). Africa's population will double by 2050. Africa, *Special Report: The African Century.* Retrieved January 10, 2023, from https://www.economist.com/special-report/2020/03/26/africas-population-will-double-by-2050

The World Bank. (2021). *Unemployment, total (% of total labor force) (modeled ILO estimate) - Sub-Saharan Africa | Data.* Retrieved January 10, 2023, from https://data.worldbank.org/indicator/SL.UEM.TOTL.ZS?locations=ZG

Tilt, C. A. (2018). Making social and environmental accounting research relevant in developing countries: A matter of context? *Social and Environmental Accounting Journal, 38*(2), 145–150.

Tilt, C. A., Qian, W., Kuruppu, S., & Dissanayake, D. (2020). The state of business sustainability reporting in sub-Saharan Africa: An agenda for policy and practice. *Sustainability Accounting, Management and Policy Journal, 12*, 1–30.

Uganda Investment Authority. (2021). *Green economy: UIA spearheading investments in green products*. Retrieved January 10, 2023, from https://www.ugandainvest.go.ug/green-economy-uia-spearheading-investments-in-green-products/

Wise, I. (2021). A review of accounting developments in Africa. *The Business & Management Review, 12*(1), 32–40.

Zulkifli, N. (2008). Understanding social and environmental accounting: Social and environmental accounting. *Asian Journal of Accounting Perspectives, 1*(1), 26–42.

9

Understanding, Developing and Supporting Desirable Workplace Behaviour and Careers

Adeola Yetunde Ekpe

Introduction

It is universally accepted that employers seeking to build sustainable businesses must pay attention to fundamental issues such as strategy, structure and processes governing their workplaces. They must also pay attention to the human resources executing the strategy to build their businesses. However, work is where humans get defined as where humans display their individual skills and abilities and garner experience that facilitates their movements between teams and organisations. Therefore, understanding human behaviour at individual, group and organisational levels is a critical need that helps evaluate workplace dynamics and make appropriate decisions to improve organisational performance and effectiveness. This understanding has become even more important as global workplace environments undergo rapid change (e.g. the recent COVID-19 pandemic illustrated in stark detail how the workplace has

A. Y. Ekpe (✉)
Lagos Business School, Pan Atlantic University, Lekki, Nigeria
e-mail: tekpe@lbs.edu.ng

fundamentally and radically changed and necessitated new ways of thinking and behaving) and, with the associated volatile and uncertain shifts in global conditions, organisations. By implication, their employees need to be more agile to adapt, respond and cope.

Human behaviour is thus a fundamental feature of the global workplace, and extensive research posits that all human behaviour is tied to underlying values and beliefs of the individuals of interest. Ingram and Choi (2022) stress the importance of values defined as goals viewed as fundamentally important to the individual, and beliefs which are individual perspectives on the steps required to attain those goals, steps necessary to achieve defined by what is important to them. Thus, two individuals may have similar values but act differently if their beliefs differ. For example, two people may have an equal underlying value of prosperity. Their goal to have a prosperous lifestyle is an underlying value. However, one may decide to work hard and be ethical, whilst the other may decide to defraud others. These differing actions or plans would be dependent on their beliefs. Fundamentally, one individual believes the end justifies the means, while the other believes the justify justifies the end. Ingram and Choi (2022) state unequivocally that values are critical and should always be viewed as goals, and organisational and individual values must be aligned to organisational performance. This essential link between individuals and organisations is acknowledged by the vast number of annual reports worldwide that typically state that 'our employees are our greatest assets' and also mention' shared values' and 'diversity, equality and inclusion'.

Similarly, researchers and consultants across the western world focus on the war for Talent' and the foregoing indicates that organisations recognise a need to recruit the most talented employees and maximise their contributions.

Ideally, by applying organisational behaviour principles, rigorous research and practical interventions, employers should always seek to build processes that enhance employee engagement and contributions in the workplace.

In this chapter, given that employees are regarded universally as key stakeholders in organisational success, we review some of the works promulgated to examine workplace human behaviour. We then question if these frameworks are universally applicable and efficacious in Africa and why not. We explore crucial issues and social challenges that affect African employees and may influence their behaviours in Africa. We raise some useful insights towards practical, culturally sensitive solutions and strategies that employers may wish to consider for business success in Africa.

Frameworks for Exploring the Roots of Workplace Behaviour

Human behaviour in the workplace is best understood by observable actions and comprehension, not only of the underlying drivers of perceived activities but awareness of and sensitivity to the environments within which the behaviour is enacted. Observable actions include evident changes in behaviour as generations change in the workplace and the nature of the workplace itself changes. For example, technological advances have been very rapid in recent times, and employees described as Gen Z (born between 1997 and 2002) or Millennials (those who turned 21 at the dawn of the year 2000) have been quicker to adapt to those changes than workers of the preceding generations. Such differences have had to be considered when allocating jobs or managing people. They may have, for example, resulted in the need to upskill or retire older workers whilst selecting and placing younger tech-savvy individuals into technical positions.

Apart from direct observation, our understanding of workplace behaviour is aided by organisational behaviour literature that is a source of useful frameworks such as the resource-based view of the firm (Barney, 1991) and strategic human resource management linkages to organisational outcomes (Becker, Huselid, Pickus & Spratt, 1997). A recent analysis of organisational behaviour research by Kalwani and Mahesh (2020) was conducted to facilitate an understanding of emergent trends. They carried out a systematic literature review of published research between 1990 and 2019 and categorised behavioural areas into Individual (workplace emotions, personality, motivation), Group (leadership, communication, group effectiveness, competition and performance) and Organisation (organisational citizenship behaviour, technology and virtual organisations, demographics and gender roles, work stress and workplace deviance, organisational culture, organisational politics and conflict management).

Their analysis positions our understanding of human behaviour as one which helps to devise the solutions to the workplace challenges that employers face at all levels and reveals the optimal or good behaviour required and the way employees should interact, collaborate and communicate for the best organisational results.

A simple emergent model thus treats employees as internal stakeholders whose fortunes are bound up with the organisation's and whose actions are aimed at mutual benefit. Human behaviour is inextricably linked to organisational behaviour because, at the Individual, Group and Organisational structural levels, humans behave in ways that will affect organisational outcomes. Research also suggests that ideally, individuals behave in ways that are congruent with organisational goals, collaborate with their teams and groups to get optimal results and seek ways at the organisational level to drive strategies and processes that maximise outputs.

To further understand the drivers of behaviour, examining the underlying factors that induce or incite people to act is generally considered useful. These factors can be labelled as motivators and can be extrinsic or situational (e.g. when the employer provides stimulus such as high pay) or can be intrinsic (i.e. the stimulus is internally derived and personal) to the employee who wants to give their energy to achieving corporate goals in exchange for satisfaction that goes beyond financial or another reward.

An example of behaviour that can be attributed to intrinsic motivation is when someone with commendable qualifications works in a position for which they are overqualified simply because they enjoy that job, despite the fact they could move into a higher role with higher pay if they chose to.

Drawing from currently observable trends in the world of work and borrowing from the behavioural disciplines of Psychology, Sociology and Anthropology, it is evident that universally desired behaviours in the organisation include employees being engaged and directing their energy and passion to working better, being more safety conscious and avoiding workplace accidents or sabotage, using their time more effectively as evidenced by their outputs, and being more efficient in terms of their outputs relative to their time spent.

Additional desirable behaviours that can be clustered as organisational citizen behaviour include employees making positive statements about their organisation, performing beyond expectations, delivering quality outputs and supporting others.

Counterproductive or undesirable work behaviours include consistent failure to deliver expected outputs, drug or alcohol abuse, stealing, absenteeism, lack of respect for deadlines and tardiness.

Desirable behaviours are tied to values. According to Ingram and Choi (2022), organisational values should not be imposed on employees but serve as indicators that should be proactively considered when attracting, recruiting and managing talent and building employee careers. Thus, according to Ingram and Choi, if a company wishes to get the best from its employees, such employees should be recruited because they have values already aligned with the organisation. The underlying logic is that values tend to be ingrained; thus, having upfront alignment is easier than recruiting based on other criteria and then trying to get employees to change their values to those imposed by the organisations.

The previously mentioned study by Kalwani and Mahesh (2020) was beneficial in defining the types of behaviours expected at the individual, group and levels national level. However, of the eighty-one relevant research papers appropriate for the study, only one paper was related to Africa (Egypt), whilst more than half originated in the USA (42) and the UK (12). Thus, most of the research was conducted in the Western world. This interesting fact calls into question the universality of the results of western research. However, in the absence of published research in other contexts, the western frameworks may prove helpful as a guide. Still, the practitioner would be wise to remain open to the possibility that such frameworks might not be fully operable in places such as Africa, China or India, where typically there is a dearth of published organisational behaviour resear*ch. Universal frameworks may not work in Africa.*

Universal theories of organisational behaviour acknowledge that to thrive and succeed sustainably, organisations need to focus on strategy and planning, organisational structure, formulating execution processes and evaluating risks, opportunities, failures and achievement of plans and strategies. Still, increasingly, *they must also heed their operating environments and adapt to prevailing political, economic, geographical and social external forces*. Employers, therefore, need to guard against sweeping generalisations of what is desired or not. By adopting a culturally flexible lens, balance the needs of those who desire certain behaviours and those from whom the behaviours are expected. Employers in Africa, as elsewhere, want workers who have relevant knowledge, skills and abilities appropriate to the jobs they are being recruited for. They also want employees with the right attitude, self-motivation, conscientiousness, initiative-taking, helpful, honest, amiable and, most importantly, for Africa, to have a learning mindset. Such effective behaviours and attributes are deemed universally desired. Still, when examined in specific contexts, they may be alien to those from which the models of behaviour are demanded, and the way they manifest may be different.

Multinationals and African employers trained in the Western world typically apply models of human interaction, motivation and reward that neither takes into account the peculiar features of the context of the African environment nor the global evolution of the workplace that is unearthing a greater need for cultural sensitivity and adaptability, recognition and management of diversity, managing social media impact and increased ethical dilemmas. In the author's experience, organisations are often surprised at the differences in comparative outcomes and how difficult it can be to manage a situation deemed unacceptable in one culture within a more permissive culture. At the individual level, they are also surprised when their star performers in other countries are relocated to Africa and fail to perform. Similarly, relatively low performers in the African context are relocated abroad and may thrive in their new environment. The foregoing indicates that values, motivation and reward and the work environment comprising geographic, economic, social and political facets are fundamental factors in the manifestation of workplace behaviours which should be considered extensively. Simply put, when approaching the understanding of human behaviour in any context, it is advisable, if not essential, to adopt cultural humility. This approach encourages continuous reflection and observation, resulting in a greater appreciation of the need for understanding whilst building up intercultural/intergenerational knowledge and skills.

This concept was originally formulated to incorporate multiculturalism in healthcare and reduce diagnostic errors and misunderstandings (Tervalon & Murray-Garcia, 1998). However, it is a useful approach for employers to adopt if they wish to operate in Africa, as a continent with 54 countries cannot ever be deemed monocultural. The wise operator will seek to understand the peculiarities of each country within which they wish to operate successfully. Cultural humility is a useful approach for understanding and interpreting human behaviour not only in African organisations but across generations as well as different subgroups which may otherwise be excluded. It encourages people to be critically aware of their biases rooted in their own traditional or cultural norms and to adopt a neutral yet empathic stance when viewing others in alien cultural contexts or evolving environments. Being open-minded and humble encourages learning about other cultures or generations and improves the interpersonal effectiveness and agility of thinking of the parties concerned.

Human behaviour is a central theme crucial for success in all global organisations. These include those operating in Africa, a continent comprised of 54 countries but typically clustered and described as part of the developing world. In the business context, in line with the universal frameworks discussed before, employees should be treated as stakeholders, and all employee behaviours are goal-oriented and aligned with organisational goals. However, there could be a disconnect between the organisational culture rooted in western models and employee behaviours rooted in the country's local culture and practices. A foreign organisation operating in Africa may view its employees as stakeholders, but this may not necessarily give rise to reciprocity or mean that employees consider themselves stakeholders or need to be engaged or loyal to the organisation. For example, tardiness may be regarded as undesirable in many parts of the world. Still, unfortunately, there is the adage of 'African Time', which is a cultural norm that permits people to ignore appointment times, deadlines and so forth and to view time as a fluid construct that does not merit strict adherence.

If employers hold punctuality dear, their employees need to be 'trained' and have it ingrained in them that timing is important, meetings should be held as scheduled and the ramifications of not keeping time is a sign of disrespect with consequences. More specifically, the employees need to understand that tardiness is a symptom of poor priority setting and leads to lower productivity, poor decision making and inefficiency. Employees also need to be trained on specific skills such as time management and prioritising the most critical tasks necessary to achieve organisational goals. Organisational behaviours must be communicated to the employees if changes in their behaviour are desired.

Adopting a cultural humility approach, any desired change must be communicated sensitively. Many in Africa still feel a sense of condescension and patronisation being perpetrated by 'old colonial masters' or western expatriates. Therefore, desired behaviours must be explained in a win-win situation for all involved at individual, group and organisational levels. In summary, employees must be advised that complying with desired change will make them more productive, help them contribute better to their teams and achieve higher-level results. This is a departure from the traditional models, which posit that employee organisation fit is important. After recruitment, employees must be engaged and loyal to the organisation for optimal organisational outcomes. In the prevailing post-pandemic world, the nature of engagement has changed. There is more fluidity of movement with the advent of working from home (WFH), and there is a rising number of digital nomads and secondary employment; with the plethora of choices, engagement has also evolved. Thus, employees may be engaged in the jobs they do but are only sometimes loyal to their primary employer organisations.

Workplace Environment and Motivation

The traditional desirable workplace model built on western (developed world) studies is where employees with appropriate qualifications develop their careers and strive to achieve organisational goals. Individuals work with others in groups or teams with leaders who show inclusiveness, fairness and equity. In return for observable and measurable behaviours that demonstrate intrinsic motivation, challenging work, ethics and initiative, the workers are rewarded, and the organisation thrives. If, or when, employees are let go, there are alternate employment opportunities and redundancy benefits from the employer. As a last resort,

9 Understanding, Developing and Supporting Desirable...

government-backed social security and pension systems support and prevent total obliteration of their lives.

The scenario in Africa is different. As with the West, a workplace is a place where people go to build careers and achieve organisational goals. However, underlying motivational factors at play can create huge distinctions between motivational factors in the developed and developing world, and the traditional models no longer exist in the pure sense. To make behaviours goal-oriented, goals have to be clear, and employee contributions to plans must be made clear in feedback, emotional intelligence and awareness of individual's needs. From the psychology field, Maslow's (1943) hierarchy of needs is a valuable framework for examining the drivers or motivations for behaviours. Maslow theorised that people are motivated to fulfil their needs in a certain order starting with the most basic needs of shelter, food and safety (the physiological needs). Once those are met, people go on to fulfil their needs for affiliation and belonging to a social group or community, followed by esteem needs. The highest level of attainment is self-actualisation, where personal potential has been achieved, and in the workplace, this is considered the area where employees put service above self (see Fig. 9.1).

The model has its critics, especially since it suggests that lower levels of the pyramid must be completely achieved and satisfied before individuals pursue higher levels of attainment.

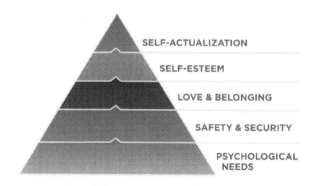

Fig. 9.1 Maslow's hierarchy of needs (after Maslow, 1943)

In Africa, the basic levels of Maslow's hierarchy of needs (physiological and security conditions about food, water, health, clothing, shelter, sleep, personal resources, security and safety) are even more critical to motivation than in the West, where the social and economic system assures a basic level of living. In sharp contrast, many African governments provide few or none of these necessities. Thus any employer needs to understand that basic needs need to be covered by them before they can expect any employees to be motivated. Depending on the level of the employee, the amenities provided will vary in size and amounts. For example, in a typical private bank in Nigeria, tier 3 employees will respond well to a salary package that covers the essential cost of their living (rent, food, data and transportation) and also provides health cover, life insurance and pension purse.

Tier 2 employees or middle management may expect additional benefits such as official cars and help with further education and training.

At the top tier 1, in the C suite, additional amenities may include paid for superior housing, security guards, domestic help, chauffeurs, fees paid for children, business class tickets and hotel expenses for official trips abroad and other perks that the organisation may decide such as overseas private health care, evacuation in the event of illness and holiday allowances for the employee's family.

Many employers wonder why they may have to pay salaries with more perks than would be available in the West. They need to understand that usually, to get the best; employers have to pay for the best packages possible. Once their basic needs are covered, employees are more likely to give more energy to performing well and to pay attention to the following levels of Maslow's pyramid, i.e. affiliation, esteem and status and ultimately self-actualisation.

Skills Shortages, Economic and Social Pressures

Anyone doing business in Africa knows that there are significant disparities between the Western and the developing world and the local employed and the unemployed. On the one hand, many job seekers are chasing the few jobs available, which suggest that jobs should be easy to fill. On the other hand, according to recruiters, jobs are hard to fill in Africa due to limited talent and a seeming lack of motivation for work beyond survival.

Jobs are hard to find in Africa, according to employment statistics. The unemployment rates in Africa vary from country to country, but compared to the rest of the developed world, they are relatively high. According to June 2022 data from the International Labour Organisation and Statista.com, in South Africa, there are 34.5% of the labour workforce actively looking for jobs, Nigeria which has a bigger economy registers 12.5% unemployment and smaller economies such as Niger and Benin register 8% unemployment. If the job market is full of people seeking work, why do recruiters across Africa decry their inability to find the right people to fill many jobs?

Firstly, there needs to be a match between the wants of employers and what knowledge, skills and abilities job seekers can provide. Secondly, once employees are recruited, they are more motivated and engaged than employers would like. Thirdly, far from being a collectivist culture where all work for the common good, there seems to be a culture of 'everyone for themselves'. In the following section, the available knowledge and skills and emergent attitudes to work are explored, and the impact on the workplace is examined.

Knowledge, Skills and Attitudes: There is a need for more talent in Africa. There are many graduates in Nigeria, for example. Still, many local graduates are deemed unemployable due to a steady decline in educational standards, intermittent strikes by university lecturers and many substandard or outdated qualifications that have yet to keep pace with the new demands of the workplace.

By the time they come to the job market, they are disillusioned and unmotivated, having been worn down by the travails of getting their qualifications. They are also more likely to be passed over in favour of graduates from abroad who have quickly finished their academic journeys in record time. Suppose they are lucky enough to get employed. In that case, they need further intensive training, way beyond what might be required in the USA or the UK, to achieve the minimum performance required by the employer. They also constantly fear being terminated, and their basic physiological needs for survival are not met. The most pressing reason for fear of termination is that many African countries do not have social security programmes. Some countries have pension fund systems, but they need to be adjusted for galloping inflation and be well managed and paid out enough for people to live on. Thus, anyone with a job ends up being the social security provider for many family members, and anyone employed lives from pay cheque to pay cheque and needs to earn a living, not just for him/herself, but for the extended family. So often, to the outsider, this is deemed a manifestation of Ubuntu, a collectivist mindset emanating from South Africa that posits the notion of sharing and a belief in humanity towards others. The behaviour would seem to support the notion, but upon investigation, the real underlying reason is revealed; sometimes collectivism is not altruistic or culturally ingrained but borne out of necessity.

An empathetic understanding of the burden of employment on employees helps employers to understand not only how critical jobs are for employees' survival but also realise the increased possibility of fatigue and burnout which a worker in the West might also face, but not for the same reasons as their counterparts in Africa. In the West, burnout typically occurs due to stress within the workplace; in Africa, many stressors arise from family, cultural and social expectations. The more proactive graduates do not wait to be offered employment but become forced entrepreneurs, many of whom earn a living. The cycle of poverty is real, and entrepreneurs take care of their personal and extended family needs. Thus, any employers seeking employees in Africa should be aware that many of their employees may need to operate a 'side hustle' to make up for what they need.

Reports of too many graduates in forced entrepreneurship and fighting for too few jobs have resulted in advocates for more job creation. Recruiters, however, insist that graduates' skills are not appropriate for workplace demands, and this mismatch needs to be addressed to make people more employable. Employers also lament the dearth of critical thinking skills, which would enhance effectiveness. The foregoing points to a need for the educational systems to be overhauled and more fitting for workplace demands. Knowledge and skills can be gained through internships and experience from industrial training sessions.

Africa has a youthful population who are tech-savvy. With increasing awareness of the opportunities that globalisation and the World Wide

Web afford, they are already making significant transitions into foreign employment with or without physical relocation. At the time of writing, giant organisations such as Amazon, Microsoft, Google and Meta have made Africa a recruiting ground but are also laying off swathes of employees worldwide. This suggests that Africa is a cheap recruitment pool. In response to this, many graduates are taking inexpensive online tech-related courses to meet the expectations of their online recruiters, who remunerate them in dollars rather than the rapidly falling purchasing power of the local currency.

This compounds the difficulties associated with building a sustainable business in Africa. The talent pool shrinks as employees defect to the competing foreign online companies, and local companies are forced to share resources as best as possible.

The impact on employee behaviour is significant. Engagement, defined in the traditional sense, is challenging because there are so many opportunities for employees that talent is increasingly transient. What used to be a predictable environment in terms of engaging employees has now become one in which, due to the economic climate, employees in Africa increasingly hold down up to three jobs with a mix of local and foreign remuneration and are less connected to their organisations; at the lowest levels, their primary driver and motivation is money.

Bills must be paid; not all employers can produce enough to cover employee needs. Once employees' basic needs are satisfied, however, most are likely to be motivated by the nature of the job. If jobs are challenging and exciting, employees are engaged till they find something more exciting and challenging. Thus, employees are seemingly involved in projects, not organisations. At the top end of the employee pyramid, executive pay soars and many perks are being paid as 'golden handcuffs' to secure the long-term stay of the executives. However, what lures those at the bottom of the employment pyramid may also affect the top. Higher paid executives may be tempted by the allure of foreign-based organisations or the challenges of new technological positions that do not require relocation.

Apart from rewards and motivation, other factors that have an impact on behaviour are personality types. Media attempts have been made to categorise Africans as cheerful, resilient and optimistic in the face of adversity. Images in the western press typically illustrate the hardships of

African countries. One could be forgiven for thinking the continent only deals with war, poverty, starvation and pestilence. More rigorous studies have been carried out by NERIS Limited using a 16PF tool to map personality types across Africa and document measures of how clear people of different nationalities are about their preferences on other dimensions. Thus, for example, there is the introversion/extraversion dimension, or the extent to which people prefer to reflect and glean ideas from within or look to external sources for their inspiration. The intuitive or observant dimension compares how people view things in the abstract/realm of possibilities or a definite observable sense and how they communicate and behave in interpersonal situations. Such data is important as personality influences behaviour, and different personality types are likely to behave in certain ways.

For example, assertive individuals tend to be more self-assured, emotionally balanced, less worrying and resilient under pressure. The flip side is that they may need to be more confident, over-optimistic and pay attention to detail. In the African context, an employer may wish to hire some employees based on their personality and how they are likely to behave, but across the continent, there are variations.

Recently, studies carried out on African populations by Neris analytics limited shared on the web, aggregated and anonymised results gathered over three years from a population of 40 million respondents, and various personality profiles were indicated for countries across Africa. From the data, comparisons were possible. For example, Nigerians were compared with Kenyans. Nigerians are more extroverted than introverted and are more observant than intuitive compared to Kenyans. They have also been found to be more emotional (feeling) than analytical (thinking) and are significantly more comfortable with defined routines (and rigid) than Kenyans, who are more likely to go with the flow. Though it's just an indicative profile that shouldn't be generalised to avoid stereotyping, these findings align with my observations over the past 30 years of working in Africa and with Africans.

Where skills could be improved, employers may rely on attitude and personality when recruiting. If employees are trainable, employers will do well to employ workers who can carry out specific aspects of desired projects well. Thus recruitment may be for lower skills than traditionally done in the West with more emphasis on attitude. Personality findings can be used to get some idea of possible behaviours, using the big five personality traits, which are deemed to be the five basic components of personality (Conscientiousness, Extraversion, Agreeableness, Openness to experience and low Neuroticism). The five-factor model is borrowed from psychological research.

Individuals who are highly open to experience will be more innovative and creative. Those high in conscientiousness will be more likely to execute as they pay attention to detail and follow through. Those high on extraversion and agreeableness would likely adopt a relational approach to others and be assertive and sociable. Such employees would be highly likely to be very useful in interpersonally related jobs such as customer service,

Whilst employers may have to recruit based on attitudes and personality traits for sustainable business in Africa, a pipeline of talent (based on skills) must be built. There is a mismatch between available talent and the skillset required for the organisation's success; the wise operator will invest in perpetual training for those that matter.

Values

Values are basic convictions that govern how humans see certain actions' desirability. Such convictions typically stem from cultural, tribal, social and religious influences and are set against the individual's background. African values are complex and difficult to generalise. There are threads of similarities, however, that run across cultures. For example, across the continent, there is respect for elders that can have a significant impact on workplace behaviours. There is also a general preoccupation with hierarchy and titles. In research carried out across an organisation operating in eleven African countries, the author found vehement employee resistance to a flat organisational structure. In Francophone and Anglophone Africa, many believe their job title is important and can be linked with self-esteem and resultant behaviours. However, according to a recent report by Mercer consultants in South Africa, with the younger generation, there is less focus on titles and status and more on social issues such as climate change and other environmental factors. Younger people across Africa may be more concerned about the impact of organisational practices on the planet. With the digital age and rapid sharing of information from around the world, the youths of Africa and other dispersed countries can come together online to share their experiences and matters of mutual concern.

Traditionally, names are significant in the African context, and to address anyone by their first name is a privilege given to those with whom one is familiar. Many western organisations seeking to operate in Africa constantly introduce the notion of calling colleagues by their first name. Most older employees express difficulty with this idea, particularly evident across West African countries such as Ghana, Sierra Leone and Nigeria. Younger employees are much more flexible though they tend to comply with the prevailing organisational culture.

Formal modes of address are more likely to be used in the workplace when there is an interaction between younger and older workers. Where an organisation insists on people being addressed by their first names, many youth prefer to use the preface Mr., Mrs. or even Chief or to use the title of the person they are addressing. One will often find people calling another 'MD' or' FC' when addressing a Managing Director or Financial Controller, for example, and they might expect to be called by their title. Thus, someone who wants to be addressed as Jimi may end up being addressed as Mr. Jimi because the norms emanating from National culture are deeply ingrained.

Religious values are also important. Anyone working in Africa has to heed and have respect for religious practices. Fridays are half days for observant Muslims who may attend their Mosque around lunchtime and not return to the office. This could be labelled absenteeism in the Western sense, but it is a behaviour that tends to be accommodated across the Continent once understood. In Muslim countries, Friday is a non-working day. Similarly, employees believe in taking off religious public holidays irrespective of their faiths. For business practices to be sustainable, accommodating public holidays is desirable. It is also desirable to be aware that in Africa, public holiday pronouncements can be spontaneous and declared for activities deemed of national significance, such as supporting national football teams in global tournaments.

Key Takeaways

Humans are the essential workforce that execute strategy and help to deliver organisational goals. Understanding human behaviour is therefore critical to ascertaining what will help rive the behaviours that will enhance the chance of achieving those goals.

There are 'universal' models of behaviour expected to work globally. Still, these models have been researched and developed in the western world and may not operate the same way in Africa.

Cultural humility has to be adopted by anyone seeking to build a sustainable business in Africa. The first consideration should be that fifty-four countries on the continent and what works in one might not work in another. The effective employer must constantly observe and reflect on exceptions regarding how so-called universal models work in the African context.

There are severe pay gaps between Africa and the rest of the world, and perceived hopelessness and lack of social support have led to a flood of emigration, especially of professionals such as doctors, nurses and accountants with transferable skills. The world, which once was hostile to African migrants, is seeking young, qualified talent; thus, Africa's brain drain is the world's brain gain. The pay disparities may eventually even out, but some more significant technology companies are already cutting costs by shedding global workers whilst recruiting Africans. At the time of writing, Meta has announced a layoff of 11,000 staff, and Tesla has cut 66% of its workforce.

The 'brain drain' has become more severe in the post-pandemic world as millennials and *Gen Z* pursue better lives and comfort. The young hope to attain more than a basic standard of living and believe they may have to work even harder in developed economies but have a better chance of achieving their potential and securing their future and their children's futures. There is also active recruitment from Canada, the USA and the UK, with teachers and carers being the most recent targets.

Those who stay may be planning to emigrate, distracted by side hustle and not be as engaged as the employer would like.

Recommendations

From the author's practitioner perspective, it is recommended that new models should be tried in the African workplace in the currently evolving situation. Employers need to be cognizant of socio-economic and cultural factors and constantly driven to understand what motivates employees and how best behaviours can be optimised. Organisational and employee values might not be aligned, so employers may have to adopt a transactional stance to get what they need. They may have to reconcile themselves to their employees being distracted by thoughts of emigration and not having the desired level of engagement or commitment. They will have to use compensation as a reward for transactions delivered without expectations of long-term employment or careers.

There are skills shortages due to an inadequately educated workforce and the brain drain. Therefore, employers should recruit for attitude and personality and prepare to upskill or train recruits in a never-ending cycle. Pipelines of succession will still be built, but multiple individuals should be considered for roles where typically only one individual would previously have been identified as a successor. Leaders must be continuously developed and adequately compensated, and institutional goals and past glories are constantly shared to ensure some level of engagement and sustainability.

In view of the brain drain, especially amongst the youth, employer organisations need to accept that training is perpetual and employees pass through a revolving door. Organisations, therefore, need to build a culture of continuous learning and encourage employees to build up their skills proactively through supportive interventions such as paying for certifications on the completion of online courses. Employers also need to recognise that the workplace has changed, and employees are likely to be a heterogeneous workforce, capable of multi-tasking and moving across different organisational roles. This approach will help to build agile teams and a core skilled leadership team.

More importantly, employers need to heed data evidence and proactively predict skills shortages and prepare for the replacement of such skills. As in many western countries, African employers can encourage retirees to upskill and return to work. Retirees are usually less likely to need the compensation that younger people require to build their lives and careers. Their foundational knowledge can be passed on to the younger entrants in the workforce.

Where possible, businesses need to be involved in advocacy with Government to help facilitate the allocation of more government funding to health, education and social support.

Conclusion

It cannot be overemphasised that human behaviour in the workplace is best understood by observable actions and comprehension, not only of the underlying drivers of perceived activities but awareness of and sensitivity to the environments within which the behaviour is enacted. Workforce development requires skills, and many in Africa need to gain the right skills for the future workforce; however, with technology, many young Africans are upskilling and using their newly acquired education to leave for greener pastures abroad. Their basic motivation is a better life ', and they want to maximise their potential in the future.

As companies collaborate more and develop talent, there is the possibility that fewer youths will emigrate as their needs are met locally, and they start to feel more secure. However, the workplace realities at the time of writing suggest that emigration will continue so long as governments do not initiate attractive programmes for health, education, housing, social security and pensions.

Despite its environmental, social and geographic challenges, Africa, with its large youthful population, is resilient, has many opportunities for sustainable businesses and its countries are making progress in different ways. Employees remain key stakeholders, and with sensitivity to their issues and tenacity in overcoming challenges, employers should, by and large, achieve the successes they seek.

References

Barney, J. (1991). Firm resources and sustained competitive advantage. *Journal of Management, 17*, 99–120.

Becker, B., Huselid, M., Pickus, P., & Spratt, M. (1997). HR as a source of shareholder value; research and recommendations. *Human Resource Management Journal, 31*(1), 1–8.

Ingram, P., & Choi, Y. (2022, November–December). What does your company really stand for? *Harvard Business Review*.

Kalwani, S., & Mahesh, J. (2020, March). Trends in organizational behaviour: A systematic review and research directions. *Journal of Business and Management, 26*(1), 40–78. https://doi.org/10.6347/JBM.202003_26(1).0003.

Maslow, A. H. (1943). A theory of human motivation. *Psychological Review, 50*(4), 370–396.

Mercer LLC. (n.d.). *Mercer global talent trends* 2020–2021.

NERIS Analytics Limited 16PF. (n.d.). Personalities.com

Tervalon, M., & Murray-Garcia, J. (1998, May). Cultural humility versus cultural competence; a critical distinction in defining physician training outcomes in multi-cultural education. *Journal of Healthcare for the Poor and Underserved, 9*(2), 117–125.

10

Ethical Leadership

Rose Ogbechie

Ethics

The word "ethos," which means custom or character in Greek, is the root of the philosophical concept known as ethics. It is focused on defining and recommending moral standards and conduct, which implies that there are appropriate and improper acts that are determined by philosophical precepts (Minkes et al., 1999)—being ethical means acting in a way that is morally regarded as "good" and "right," as opposed to "bad" or "wrong," in a particular circumstance (Sims, 1992). The moral code that establishes what is right and wrong for a person or a group of people is known as ethics. The study of ethics generally examines questions about right and wrong, virtue, duty, justice, fairness, and responsibility towards others. Various authors have defined ethics differently, so one could find as many definitions of ethics as there are writers. This chapter will not dwell on the definitions of ethics but more on what ethical leadership is

R. Ogbechie (✉)
Lagos Business School, Pan-Atlantic University, Lekki, Nigeria
e-mail: rogbechie@lbs.edu.ng

about, the benefits, particularly for African countries, and how managers can become ethical leaders.

Ethics was emphasised during the time of the ancient Greek philosophers such as Aristotle and Plato, who understood that man, as a social being, needs to know how to live and interact with other people to have a better outcome for all (Kraut, 2001; Parry & Thorsrud, 2004; Huppes-Cluysenaer & Coelho, 2013). It is descriptive and prescribes how we ought to behave not how we behave (Metz, 2007). Therefore, ethical behaviour reflects the common good against actions that are done for selfish interests (Baker & Connaughton, 2022).

Good behaviour is important because bad behaviour has dire consequences, which can be far-reaching. In recent times there have been many corporate scandals due to the unethical actions of top executives who ought to know better and should only take actions that achieve corporate and personal goals responsibly. The management of any organisation is expected to direct the organisation's affairs and drive the culture there. They are to take charge and are accountable to the Board of Directors. If the very people expected to lead the way are not ethical, then an unethical culture would arise in the organisations. Organisations such as Enron, WorldCom, News of the World, Volkswagen, and many others have collapsed or had scandals that seriously affected their reputation (Barreveld, 2002). Man, as a social being, has different relationships, such as work, family, and others. These relationships can only make sense if everyone in the team recognises that everyone has intrinsic value and dignity and deserves respect. The human being is endowed with emotion, intellect, and will and can reason and react to external and internal stimuli. This implies that the actions of leaders and colleagues can impact employees and other stakeholders of the organisation and can help bring out the best or the worst in them. However, ethics is about improving people, not making them worse. This requires that leaders do everything to value and help their people. It is about realising that human beings have the potential and capacity to grow if they are not limited by illness or any other limiting factor.

Business Ethics

One of the proponents of the idea that there is no such thing as business ethics is the well-known business-management theorist Peter Drucker; he claimed that the only thing that existed was ethics in business. He was criticised for his view by Hoffman and Moore (1962) though his thoughts were long before the field was developed. Both ethics and business have a long history, as does business ethics.

Before business ethics became a distinct profession, there were sporadic studies on moral concerns in business and talks and essays concerning ethics in business. The earlier literature used the phrase "ethics in business" to refer to the definition of the term as it relates to business ethics. Business ethics have also gone global due to business globalisation, and literature focused on business ethics in each country or region has improved.

A person's actions and behaviour within a business organisation are governed by relevant organisational values, principles, standards, and practices referred to as business ethics (Ferrell & Fraedrich, 2021). In many respects, the same rules people employ to behave appropriately in personal and professional contexts also apply to organisations. Business ethics applies to the commonly believed notion that morality holds in all spheres of life, including business. The public typically links commercial misconduct, more specifically, the inability of firms to operate ethically, with stories about Enron, Arthur Andersen, WorldCom, News of the World, and Bernard Madoff's Ponzi scheme. These scandals involve deception, manipulation of accounts, conflict of interest, bribery, insider trading, and other business-related issues. All facets of society are affected by the transgression of moral standards. In business ethics discussions, one would often hear different tales of company or business leaders' acts of irresponsible business behaviours. To achieve sustainability in business, leaders must believe in the importance of business ethics. They must decide to give voice to their values and behave responsibly despite the many challenges that could be facing the organisation. Knowing about business ethics is not enough; leaders must have the willpower to act responsibly in the moment of truth.

Ethical Leadership

Ethical leadership has become crucial in the world and particularly in Africa due to the ever-increasing rate of irresponsible behaviour of leaders acting out of selfish interests. Some of their actions have brought about the collapse of the organic organisation in Nigeria, and some banks and organisations have collapsed due to unethical leadership. Velasquez (1992) proposed that managers cultivate qualities such as perseverance, public-spiritedness, honesty, truthfulness, fidelity, compassion, and humility to apply ethics to leadership and management. Brown et al. (2005) summarised that ethical leadership entails a just, fair, altruistic, empowering, honest, and empathetic leader. Mahsud et al. (2010) argued that these behaviours result in confidence and faith in leaders as they are observed to be fair and have high integrity. Brown et al. (2005) outlined that subordinates are more likely to trust an ethical leader and have confidence that they are acting in the subordinate's best interest. As a result, ethical leaders are highly effective and can achieve superior results.

Ethical leaders would treat each person with respect and care and with dignity and value. This requires reflection on the decisions before actions are taken and an analysis of the impact of decisions on the subordinates and all other stakeholders. Respecting people in the organisation is very important, as a lack of respect could lead to a toxic climate and culture. Employees' benefits from a conducive work environment cannot be quantified. When employees are respected and treated with dignity, they are more likely to go the extra mile for the organisation, make more sacrifices and be more productive. Ethical leaders would ensure that their actions do not convey anything that can mean a lack of respect. Leaders set the tone by watching their behaviours and the impact on their people as they realise the effects could be good or damaging. Leaders who respect their followers show empathy and often can tolerate opposing points of view. This view from leaders is emphasised by Grover (2014) as "a behavioural manifestation of believing another person has value." Ethical leadership's characteristics are altruism and a willingness to serve the followers and the organisation. Altruism supposes that the leader must first attend to the needs of the followers, not be egocentric. True leadership requires seeking the most humane way to solve challenges. When difficulty arises, leaders must find the most humane and fair way to solve the problem.

Human beings like to be respected; when they are not, they could suffer in silence especially at work when they are afraid of losing their jobs. This could give rise to counterproductive attitudes and actions by the employees. Actions that could cause emotional distress include but are not limited to the following: bullying, the use of condescending or abusive words, shouting or shouting people down, and not listening to others, especially one's subordinates. The implications of these actions are enormous. When employees suffer from emotional harm, they cannot give their best to the organisation. Sometimes, people are forced to leave the organisation even when they do not have other jobs because of the unconducive environment. Suppose an employee is forced to do that without much reflection; that employee could suffer from financial distress, as it may be difficult for the person to get another job immediately. This is particularly true of some African countries like Nigeria, where jobs are limited and large, and extended family members depend on the worker. Ethical leadership implies that leaders must act not out of selfish interests but for the common good of all. Human beings, by nature, tend to think of themselves first (Roughley 2021). However, care must be taken to ensure that the leaders look at other courses of action that benefit others.

Ethical leadership entails acting with fairness and justice (Eisenbeiss, 2012). Being fair means that leaders must be clear about the standards they use for their people. They must be seen to be fair in their dealings with all people. The leaders must apply the same standards so that everyone sees that they are fair in their treatment of the different people in the organisation. It is essential to have policies in place in the organisation to ensure that people are given fair treatment. When employees perceive that they are not fairly treated, they would either react negatively or become demotivated and no longer challenge themselves. Without policies and standards in place, employees could easily feel that they are not fairly treated. When policies are implemented, it becomes easier for employees to compare actions and policies and to see more clearly if the actions are in line with fairness.

If different standards are used for different people, it is easy for people to perceive some form of injustice in the workplace. The results of this perception can be enormous and could lead to negative behaviour from employees. Negative employee behaviour includes but is not limited to sabotaging the organisation's efforts, not showing any improvement, low productivity, and self-dealing. Ethical leadership implies that leaders must show that they are just to all people. Justice means giving people their fair due, giving all stakeholders what they are entitled to, and keeping to the contract agreements. In addition, when necessary, go beyond it by looking at the implicit expectations of employees and other stakeholders. This includes paying employees just wages, paying bonuses when they have worked hard, ensuring that employees participate in the profit sharing of the organisation, and generally rewarding employees for their contributions to the organisation. Justice also includes running the organisation profitably in line with the ethical principle of efficiency so that shareholders can get their dividends. It would constitute a form of injustice when leaders delay the payment of salaries due to flimsy excuses without considering the impact on the employees. Paying wages that are not commensurate to the work done could constitute an injustice, and so ethical leaders would be concerned to ensure that they give people what is due to them (Bakotic & Babic, 2013). Another example is paying suppliers as and when due and awarding contracts to the right people.

Apart from wages and salaries, ethical leaders should show concern for employees' well-being to obtain favourable outcomes from them. Showing empathy, understanding the employees, and seeing things from their points of view are good ways of showing them they are valued (Fu et al., 2020). Empowering employees, giving them room to use their initiatives, and helping them to be more creative not only help them recognise that they are valued but also give them a sense of belonging. Recognising their capacity to contribute to the organisation and challenging them to do more without humiliating them often improve their self-worth. All these would contribute to their general well-being and perception of the leaders. Ethical leaders would also listen to the employees as listening has tremendous benefits to the organisation and the individuals. People feel ignored and frustrated when they are not listened to. Listening shows employees that they are valued; it helps them feel a sense of worth. They are more ready to contribute to the organisation's success and growth. Ethical leaders would communicate clearly to ensure issues are well understood.

This helps employees avoid making mistakes and feeling inadequate when errors arise due to a misunderstanding. Ethical leaders would listen to feedback, work on the feedback, and direct employees properly. They strive to make employees' and other stakeholders' appraisals objective so that they understand their weak points and where they need to improve. Such leaders would desire all the stakeholders to grow and flourish and endeavour to do everything to fill the gaps identified. Hiring employees and awarding contracts to vendors are done on merit. This ensures that the right people get the jobs and the organisation remains sustainable. Policies, processes, systems, and procedures are streamlined, so stakeholders have seamless encounters.

Ethical leadership entails also always keeping in mind the responsibilities the organisation owes to all stakeholders. Ensuring that those responsibilities are met would be given priority, and the realisation of the ethical implications of not doing so would be kept in mind. Running the organisation professionally and putting ethical policies, systems, and processes in place to deliver good results would be the focus because failing to do so would not be responsible, as the stakeholders could suffer some harmful effects. Ethical leadership also includes ensuring employees find meaning in their work. Employees that find meaning in their work are more likely to challenge themselves and to give of themselves to the organisation. They are more likely to look forward to coming to work and contributing to the organisation's growth. This was evident from participants' responses in the various executive programmes at the Lagos Business School. Ethical leadership also includes ensuring employee engagement which is also paramount and it leads to positive organizational outcomes (Chandrasekar, 2011). Meaningful employees engagements help boost the morale of employees. In addition, it can lead to improved productivity and a more relaxed working environment which is important to employee well-being. Employees are more open to learning and growing if they find their work meaningful (Coplan & Goldie, 2011).

Ethical leadership is concerned not only with profit maximisation but rather with profit optimisation. This means that leaders understand that to live up to their ethical responsibilities to the organisation, the focus must not only be on maximising shareholder returns but on living up to their responsibilities to the other stakeholders of the organisation as well. Increasing shareholder value can be negatively impacted if the leaders fail to consider the needs of the other parties in making decisions (Hillman & Keim, 2001). This is in line with the stakeholder's theory of corporate governance.

This means that leaders would ensure that the legal and ethical duties owed to others are met (Bakotic & Babic, 2013). Ethical leaders are also concerned with the social well-being of employees. This means that the leaders consider the effects of their decisions on employees' well-being and social life. Using employees round the clock could impact not only the employees but their families as well. Organisations operate in communities and also have social responsibilities. They are expected to engage in activities that would have a social impact on their communities and, subsequently, the economy.

Ethical leadership includes ensuring that the organisation treats the environment responsibly, that waste is responsibly disposed of, taxes are correctly paid, and that products that do not cause harm to customers and their environment are sold. Ethical leaders are aware of the impact of climate change on the planet and make conscious efforts to make profits responsibly while taking care of the people. They also show concern with carrying out corporate social responsibilities (CSR) in communities. The organisation, as a good corporate citizen, should be in a position to give back to the society where they operate as CSR initiatives benefit not just the communities but the organisations as well. Communities expect good behaviours from operators; they expect them to show concern for their affairs, which would help create stability. Many organisations in Nigeria, including banks, now incorporate CSR in their corporate strategies. They appreciate the goodwill and brand equity that comes with such actions.

Ethical leadership entails being more reflective in decision-making. The leaders study the situation and reflect on the impact of their decisions on employees and other stakeholders before deciding what course of action to take. In line with their moral beliefs, they try to go with the alternative that would not be harmful to people but rather add value to them. They avoid making hasty decisions as they are aware of the problems that could cause. Such leaders are more likely to lead according to their values. If they are people of integrity, their decisions and actions would exhibit that since they realise that doing otherwise would be a lack of integrity. They would integrate ethics into their decisions rather than make decisions without considering the ethical dimension of the issue. This is due to the realisation that doing otherwise would show that they have no integrity. Additional values that ethical leaders would exhibit in decisions and actions would include but are not limited to honesty, accountability, professionalism, and hard work. Living such core values would undoubtedly show the employees that the leader leads by example and can be relied on always to take the right course of action, even when difficult decisions are to be made.

Leading by example is crucial for organisational success as it is an excellent way to build trust. Some organisations in Nigeria and Africa practise this approach to leadership. Making difficult decisions is a way to assess whether leaders value ethics. Many times, leaders are faced with having to make very difficult decisions: decisions about whether to retrench employees or not. How do the leaders go about this? Do they see employees as just other costs that could be retrenched without a thought, as in some organisations in Nigeria? Do they reflect on the implications and impact of such a decision on the employees and their families, the morale of the remaining employees and the impact on the larger society? Has the leader taken time to find out if the issue in the organisation is about people or processes and systems that need to be taken care of? Even when retrenchment appears necessary, how do the leaders go about it? Do they show any form of empathy at all? Ethical leadership requires that leaders show some form of concern and empathy, failing which they may not be viewed as ethical.

Perception is very important as it can lead to an increase or a decrease in trust. When employees perceive that their leaders are not trustworthy, whether that perception is real or not, it could create some problems. Ethical leaders would ensure that this perception is managed such that a wrong impression is not created. Ethical leadership is also about running a professional and efficient organisation in line with the ethical principle of efficiency. Much as the leader would want to show empathy, it is equally important that the leader is courageous enough sometimes to make seemingly unpopular decisions that are beneficial to the organisation and other stakeholders, ensuring that the organisation remains profitable. Aristotle, one of the ancient Greek philosophers, states the need for managers to have 4 cardinal virtues pivotal to leadership success. They are to be like the blocks on which the foundation of good leadership hinges. Courage, one of the virtues, is not making hasty and fearless decisions but rather making right and appropriate decisions. This is also linked to Prudence, another cardinal virtue, that requires that leaders make a rational decision, ensuring that the short- and long-term impacts of such decisions are considered before making them. This implies that leaders would necessarily ensure that they get all the facts required beforehand and analyse the situation before drawing. As role models, leaders must act as beacons to others. Leadership is about service and a key attribute of an ethical leader entails ensuring that they render service instead of expecting others to serve them. Leaders must be service oriented and place their ethical responsibilities at the top of their priorities.

Ethical leaders are honest, inspire confidence, and encourage their followers to take responsibility. They take responsibility for their actions and are always concerned about anything that could be damaging or misleading. Honesty is a fundamental ethical principle, as dishonesty has a lot of negative consequences. Dishonesty is a form of lying and a way of misrepresenting reality (Northouse, 2013). For example, a finance company that is trying to raise capital has a twenty-one-story building on the front cover of its brochure but only rents a quarter of a floor in that building. This could be misleading as it could indicate that organisation owns the building and therefore is financially stable. Honesty means telling the truth, keeping promises, presenting the facts as they are, and not feigning ignorance. It engenders dependability and reliability. Leaders can give the wrong impression of persuading others while manipulating or lying to them. When leaders are dishonest, trust is eroded in the organisation, and they lose the ability to inspire and influence and could lose stakeholders' commitment to the organisation. This is not being responsible.

There should be a balance between being truthful and leaving out unnecessary details that could harm the organisation. The leaders must decide which information should be kept secret. To maintain honesty, leaders must avoid making excessive promises they cannot deliver. Ethical leaders build communities by taking into consideration the needs of others and creating shared value. They try to engage in projects that have a social impact and act in the interest of the organisation and the community; that way, they are trusted and respected. Nestle Nigeria PLC created shared value by training farmers across Nigeria and helping them achieve higher yields. That way, both the farmers and the organisation benefited immensely.

In all, ethical leadership is about helping the organisation achieve its corporate objective, and communities are essential to do this. Ethical leaders build effective teams and partnerships. They guide, nurture, and compensate them. They create win-win situations such that the partners and communities are happy. Their main priority is to act responsibly for the good of all stakeholders.

Why Ethical Leadership Is Important in Africa

African countries have many human and natural resources and yet have remained underdeveloped and poor. Corruption has become systematic in Nigeria as it seems to cut across every aspect of society. Over half of the population lives below the poverty line (less than a dollar a day). While many people cannot afford two meals daily, others are excessively rich. Some top executives and government officials pay their employee's unfair wages, subjecting them to hardships. Many indigenous organisations in Nigeria collapse before the second or third generation because of unethical leadership. Employees are not treated with respect or fairness (Rogers & Ashforth, 2017), so many do not trust their employers. They are ready to sabotage the organisation at any opportunity that they have. However, organisations that imbibed ethical leadership by integrating ethics into their decisions have shown that ethical leadership has benefited the organisation. For example, Nestle Nigeria PLC, has remained consistently profitable with very low staff turnover and happy customers and employees. Their stock price has remained consistently very high as a result of ethical leadership. In the case study on Nestle Nigeria by Ogbechie (2021), different employees and stakeholders were interviewed, and they attested to the ethical culture of Nestle Nigeria. The MD had great respect for the dignity of each person and operated an open-door policy which made employees gain access to him. They pointed out how the management led with the values such as integrity, respect for all, spirit of service, professionalism, and empathy. These made employees and all stakeholders feel committed to the organisation.

Another example is Pharma Nigeria Plc (PNP), in a case study by Adewale (2020). It was found that PNP was distinguished by its "family-like" workplace culture. The organisational structure was friendly and respectful, allowing employees a high degree of autonomy. There was an informal structure, and the culture was amicable with less emphasis on hierarchies, which allowed for better interactions. The MD and his management team exhibited ethical leadership skills, which endeared the employees to the organisation. Values such as truthfulness, humility, courage, and humanity were demonstrated in the organisation to the employees and other stakeholders.

Unethical Practices in Business in Africa

Unethical practices in organisations abound and include maltreatment of employees, corporate scandals, deceptive sales, unfair pricing, bribery and corruption, misleading advertising, manipulations of financial accounts, irresponsible behaviour towards the environment (climate change conditions), and many others. In Africa, corruption is on the rise, and according to the corruption perception index (CPI), countries in Africa rank the highest in corruption, with countries like Nigeria ranking 150/180 countries and Kenya ranking 123/180 countries in the 2022 index. Some corporate executive leaders, in a bid to meet shareholders' demands, make irresponsible business decisions. Examples from class discussions in the Lagos Business School show that many leaders find living up to their values challenging due to the very difficult business environment in Nigeria and some other African countries. They seem to find it easier to give bribes to get contract awards rather than stay the course. Some find it easier to shout at employees to get results rather than showing empathy and being firm at the same time. They forget that being ethical comes with a cost and requires courage and discipline. Short-term gains may appear attractive, but they are not sustainable. This was evident in the cases of the liquidated Nigerian banks in 2006 due to unethical practices by their managers. Some Nigerian and African organisations collapsed or had serious scandals due to unethical behaviours by their management.

Importance of Ethical Leadership

The importance of ethical leadership cannot be over-emphasised due to the huge impact unethical leadership could have on the organisation.

Leaders are expected to help their organisations achieve their corporate goals; to do this, they need to inspire employees to be productive. This cannot happen if leaders do not value their employees and other stakeholders. Valuing people and recognising their dignity help them contribute to the organisation's growth. Leadership is about effectively managing resources, and ethical leaders strive to manage the organisation's resources responsibly. Due to their desire to act ethically, they put policies and processes that help avoid the wastage of human and other resources. Organisations that do so achieve growth as processes are more efficient and resources are better utilised. This helps build a more positive image and a good brand. Leading ethically enhances trust as communication is open and respectful. Effective communication makes employees and stakeholders feel valued and take ownership of the organisation.

Employees who take ownership of the organisation show more commitment, loyalty, and zeal to see the organisation succeed. They are more willing to take on more responsibilities and initiative. When customers feel valued, they remain with the organisation rather than move to competing brands. Ethical leadership is crucial to achieving the long-term sustainability of the organisation. The failures and scandals witnessed in the corporate world have all pointed to the unethical actions of top management. These unethical actions negatively impacted several organisations, including seemingly hitherto profitable ones and those that have been in operation for many years.

Ethics is about making choices and looking at different alternatives. It is, therefore, important that leaders refrain from copying and pasting. They must not take a particular course of action just because the management of another organisation has taken that route. This is important because ethical leaders are meant to analyse situations and reflect on their responsibilities to the various parties before taking action. Leaders' choices and how they respond in different situations are informed and directed by their ethics (Trevino, 1986; Northouse, 2013).

Key Recommendations

Given the explanations and discussions around the positive impact of ethical leadership in sustainable and responsible business, it is evident that its practice is most advisable to businesses, especially in Africa. Thus, it is recommended that

1. Leaders must endeavour to integrate ethics into their decision-making.
2. They must ensure that in making decisions, they bear in mind their responsibilities to the business' various stakeholders, as ignoring any of them could have serious repercussions.
3. They must ensure that the actions taken would not deliberately cause harm to any of the stakeholders.
4. In pursuing profit, the focus must not be only on making gains for the organisation alone but also on creating a win-win situation for all.
5. Leaders must also anticipate any side effects resulting from their operations and develop strategies to eliminate and minimise them.
6. Running a responsible and sustainable business should be the motive for all leaders, which means that they must always strive to take responsible actions.

Conclusion

Ethical leadership is essential for business sustainability, especially now that the world is a global village and leaders are held accountable for their actions. Customers and, indeed, all other stakeholders are more complex and demanding. Customers are ready to boycott unethically sourced products. Employees are more ready to move to other organisations when not well treated. The world is suffering tremendously due to the impact of climate change. Leaders cannot henceforth take their customers, employees, and stakeholders for granted but must ensure that they treat them respectfully and fairly and create value for them. They must ensure that they act responsibly towards the planet and its people to remain profitable and sustainable.

References

Bakar, H. A., & Connaughton, S. L. (2022). Ethical leadership, perceived leader–member ethical communication and organisational citizenship behaviour: Developing and validating a multilevel model. *Leadership & Organization Development Journal, 43*(1), 96–110.

Bakotic, D., & Babic, T. (2013). Relationship between working conditions and job satisfaction: The case of a Croatian shipbuilding company. *International Journal of Business and Social Science, 4*(2).

Barreveld, D. (2002). *The Enron collapse.* iUniverse.

Brown, M. E., Treviño, L. K., & Harrison, D. A. (2005). Ethical leadership: A social learning perspective for construct development and testing. *Organisational Behaviour and Human Decision Processes, 97*(2), 117–134.

Chandrasekar, K. (2011). Workplace environment and its impact on organisational performance in public sector organisations. *International Journal of Enterprise Computing and Business Systems, 1*(1), 1–19.

Coplan, A., & Goldie, P. (Eds.). (2011). *Empathy: Philosophical and psychological perspectives.* Oxford University Press.

Eisenbeiss, S. A. (2012). Re-thinking ethical leadership: An interdisciplinary integrative approach. *The Leadership Quarterly, 23*(5), 791–808.

Ferrell, O. C., & Fraedrich, J. (2021). *Business ethics: Ethical decision making and cases.* Cengage Learning.

Fu, J., Long, Y., He, Q., & Liu, Y. (2020). Can ethical leadership improve employees' well-being at work? Another side of ethical leadership is based on organisational citizenship anxiety. *Frontiers in Psychology, 11*, 1478.

Grover, S. L. (2014). Unraveling respect in organisation studies. *Human Relations, 67*(1), 27–51.

Hillman, A. J., & Keim, G. D. (2001). Shareholder value, stakeholder management, and social issues: what's the bottom line? *Strategic Management Journal, 22*(2), 125–139.

Huppes-Cluysenaer, L., & Coelho, N. M. (Eds.). (2013). *Aristotle and the philosophy of law: Theory, practice and justice.* Springer Science & Business Media.

Kraut, R. (2001). *Aristotle's ethics.*

Mahsud, R., Yukl, G., & Prussia, G. (2010). Leader empathy, ethical leadership, and relations-oriented behaviours as antecedents of leader-member exchange quality. *Journal of Managerial Psychology, 25*(6), 561.

Metz, T. (2007). Toward an African moral theory. *Journal of Political Philosophy, 15*(3), 321.

Minkes, A. L., Small, M. W., & Chatterjee, S. R. (1999). Leadership and business ethics: Does it matter? Implications for management. *Journal of Business Ethics, 20*(4), 327–335.

Northouse, P. G. (2013). *Leadership: Theory and practice.* Sage Publications.

Ogbechie, R. (2021). Nestlé Nigeria Plc: Doing business the right way. Case Ref No. 721-0013-1. https://casecent.re/p/175498

Parry, R., & Thorsrud, H. (2004). Ancient ethical theory.

Rogers, K. M., & Ashforth, B. E. (2017). Respect in organisations: Feeling valued as "we" and "me". *Journal of Management, 43*(5), 1578–1608.

Sims, R. R. (1992). The challenge of ethical behaviour in organisations. *Journal of Business Ethics, 11*(7), 505–513.

Trevino, L. K. (1986). Ethical decision making in organisations: A person-situation interactionist model. *Academy of Management Review, 11*(3), 601–617.

Velasquez, M. (1992). International business, morality, and the common good. *Business Ethics Quarterly,* 27–40.

11

Waste Management Issues for Today's African Businesses (Circular Economy)

Marvel Ogah

Introduction

According to a report by the world bank, the need for a global efficient waste management system stems from the consequent increase in population, massive migration to urban cities, enhanced economic development and heightened consumption patterns; by 2050, waste production is estimated to be 73% higher than it was in 2020 (World Bank, 2021). Management of waste has become more complicated and a major source of concern in recent times, unlike the pre-historic era when the population was quite small, and there was sufficient land available to the population for waste disposal, as the environment quickly absorbed the volume of waste produced without degradation (Tchobanoglous et al., 1993). A substantial increase in the volume of waste produced globally was noticed in the wake of the sixteenth century, which marked the beginning of the industrial revolution; people migrated from rural settlements to urban

M. Ogah (✉)
Lagos Business School, Pan-Atlantic University, Lekki, Nigeria
e-mail: mogah@lbs.edu.ng

cities, causing a population explosion and a surge in the volume and variety of waste generated within the cities (Wilson, 2007). Waste started gaining attention in the nineteenth century as the unhealthy practice of waste management led to several outbreaks of epidemics with high death tolls (Tchobanoglous et al., 1993).

What exactly is waste? This has recently emerged as an essential question as we seek new ways of managing waste in the twenty-first century. White et al. (1995) defined waste as a by-product from human activities that are not useful and physically contain the same substance that is available in the useful product. Waste was also defined as materials that owners willingly dispose of even when it requires payment for their disposal (Dijkema et al., 2000). The concept of waste is entirely subjective, as a material can only be regarded as waste when labelled as such by the owner because what constitutes waste to an individual, a resource to another (Dijkema et al. 2000; Amasuomo & Baird, 2016). What constitutes waste has to be clear despite the subjective nature of its definition because the proper classification of material as waste will determine its adequate management. Classifying waste is essential because waste exists in different forms, and effective management will necessitate disposal in an environmentally friendly manner. Some standard classifications from previous literature (Demirbas, 2011; Dixon & Jones, 2005; White et al., 1995) include physical states, reusable potentials, biodegradable potentials, source of production and the degree of environmental impact. The most used classification of waste:

Physical state

- Solid waste
- Liquid waste
- Gaseous waste

Source

- Household/Domestic waste
- Industrial waste
- Agricultural waste
- Commercial waste

- Demolition and construction waste
- Mining waste

Environmental impact

- Hazardous waste
- Non-hazardous waste

Due to the increase in the volume of waste over the years, continuous disposal of waste using a conventional method such as landfills could be more sustainable (Basu, 2009). Hence, subjecting waste to adequate processing is necessary to protect the environment and safeguard public health. Waste management involves gathering and transporting the waste efficiently to a site where it is processed and securing the remaining residues' disposal. Tchobanoglous et al. (1993) posit that to safeguard the environment and the public, waste management will include the following: supervision and handling, keeping, collection, conveying, treatment and effective disposal. He also emphasised that efficient waste management is a systemic operation that will utilise the skills and knowledge of various stakeholders in its daily management, such as legal and policy, finance and administration, among others. New methods have emerged recently for efficient waste management, such as reuse, recycling, composting and energy generation from incineration. According to the World Bank, in a business-as-usual scenario, the gap between the current generated and the appropriately managed waste will widen further based on the projected growth in waste generation (World Bank, 2021).

Waste Management Flow

The waste flow is a flow diagram that explains the municipal waste management process from the point of generation to the point of final disposal. Municipal solid waste includes discharged wastes from homes, offices, shops and waste generated when public spaces are cleaned. While some generated wastes are discharged, others are recycled, and some are used as a livestock feed or compost source. Understanding waste flow and

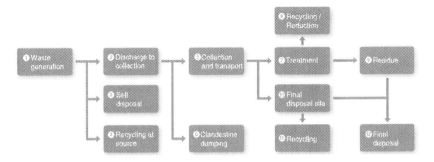

Fig. 11.1 Waste management service flow. Source: African Clean Cities Platform (ACCF) (2019). Africa Solid Waste Management Data Book 2019

the amount of waste generated is essential for determining the type and capacity of the collection containers and vehicles, intermediate treatment methods and other measures.

The waste management flow starts with the waste generation process, either self-disposed or sent as inputs to recycling plants or collected as discharge from the waste generation unit. Discharged wastes are either dumped at an off-site disposal location or collected and transported for further treatment, with the residue sent for final disposal. In several African cities, a vast amount of waste must be captured within the waste management service flow. This waste may end up being burned in the open air, collected as valuable goods by the informal sector or just dumped illegally (Fig. 11.1).

Waste Management in Africa

Africa is facing a growing waste management crisis. Projected waste generation is expected to reach 244 m tonnes per year by 2025, almost double 2012, according to the Africa Waste Management Outlook (African Business, 2019). The continent must adopt effective ways of managing its waste. Africa was undergoing a social and economic transformation with its population explosion, urbanisation and increased purchasing habits for imported items (The Point, 2021). This situation may lead to exponential growth in waste generation, which will put considerable strain on already constrained public and private sector waste services and infrastructure and further exacerbate the current state of waste management (The Point, 2021). In their growth process, some developed countries have witnessed periods when they have improved environmentally; however, they have been able to contain their waste generation effectively and address their health and environmental implications. Unfortunately, most African countries are yet to develop and adapt their waste management processes to the increasing rate of urbanisation and development happening at an unprecedented pace. According to Wilson (2007), these emerging countries are now repeating the same historical problems developed countries have had to address.

While the volumes of waste generated in Africa are insignificant compared to developed regions, the mismanagement of waste in Africa is a source of concern. Inefficient waste management in the continent is already impacting human and environmental health. Current reasons for poor waste management in Africa include, amongst others, weak organisational structures, lack of appropriate skills, inadequate budgets, weak legislation, lack of enforcement, low public awareness, corruption, conflict, political instability and lack of political will. At the heart of the problem is a failure in governance (The Point, 2021). Despite global awareness drive and emerging consequences, several African countries still need to contend with these reasons and gaps regarding their waste management policies. A situation that might breed a waste management crisis if checked or solved later.

The main reason ambitions expressed in national strategies or international commitments still need to be fulfilled is that a gap exists between aspirations described in the mid-level waste policy and the ability to implement processes that meet those aspirations (World Bank, 2021). Thus a 'gap between intent and actual performance usually points to a failure in institutional frameworks and the enabling environment' (World Bank, 2021). Setting the institutional, policy and legislative framework for municipal waste management is the primary responsibility of the central government, while providing on-the-ground services and ensuring the controlled administration of solid waste is the responsibility of the local authorities (World Bank, 2021).

Waste Management Issues in Sub-Saharan Africa: Nigeria, South Africa, Ghana, Kenya and Tanzania

Nigeria Waste Management System

Nigeria is one of the largest economies in Africa, with a GDP of US $440.00 billion (in 2021), with over 210 million people making it the most populous country in Africa. About 49.5% of this population resides in urban areas. The country is in the West Africa region of the continent and borders Benin in the west, Chad and Cameroon in the east and Niger in the north. Nigeria covers an area of 923,770 square kilometres. The Nigerian economy relies heavily on oil as its primary foreign exchange earnings and government revenue source. The country's waste management system is the Department of Pollution Control, Solid Waste Management and Technology's primary responsibility under the Ministry of Environment. Other institutions involved in solid waste management include the Ministry of Health (responsible for medical waste), the Ministry of Agriculture and Rural Development (responsible for agricultural waste) and the Abuja Environmental Protection Board (in charge of trash within the federal capital territory). However, informal operators collect recyclable materials in the streets or at disposal sites. Nigeria's policy plan for waste management is the National Policy on Solid Waste Management 2017, and no basic law currently exists on solid waste management.

The financial system currently in place for waste management in Nigeria includes a budget between NGN 150,000,000 and 500,000,000 for solid waste management, no tax related to solid waste and a subsidy for intervention projects on waste management. Nigeria is strongly supported by the United Nations Industrial Development Organization (UNIDO) in the development of a policy and institutional framework for sustainable integration for municipal solid waste management and the Japan International Cooperation Agency (JICA) in the development of human capital through training. Areas in Nigerian waste management for improvement are Institutional reform and the development of fundamental laws and policies on solid waste management. Although in some states like Lagos and Abuja (the federal capital), the government systematically seeks to manage waste via incipient processes and legislations; however, much more is yet to be done regarding waste management.

South Africa Waste Management System

South Africa is the southernmost country in Africa. It is bordered by Namibia, Botswana, Zimbabwe, Mozambique and Swaziland, and it surrounds Lesotho. It is around 1.2 million square kilometres and has a population of about 56.72 million. The country has three capitals; the legislative capital is Cape Town, the administrative capital is Pretoria and Bloemfontein is the judicial capital. The government has nine provinces which are in turn divided into 52 districts: 8 metropolitan and 44 district municipalities, with Johannesburg being the largest city. The district municipalities are further subdivided into 226 local municipalities.

The development of waste policies and strategies is the responsibility of the National Department of Environmental Affairs, as well as the collection, verification and management of waste data nationally. The department works with several ministries, such as the Ministry of Trade and Industry (Which oversee the import and export of waste) Ministry of Health (In charge of medical waste), amongst others, through the Intergovernmental Forum to cover hazardous, non-hazardous and medical waste. They implement laws/regulations by conveying them and providing technical assistance. They monitor the implementation of laws/regulations in cities based on reports received from local governments. The information obtained is used to give the provincial government instructions, prepare plans, etc.

The legal system in place to manage waste in South Africa is the National Environmental Management: Waste Act (NEMWA), Act 59 of 2008, the fundamental national law on municipal waste management. This act clearly states what municipal waste is and the responsibilities of stakeholders. The following are regulations under NEMWA; Plastic Carrier Bags and Plastic Flat Bags Regulations, Waste Tyre Regulations, Regulations for the prohibition of the use, manufacturing, import and export of asbestos and asbestos-containing materials, list of waste management activities that have or are likely to have a detrimental effect on the environment, Waste Information Regulations, Waste Classification and Management Regulations.

The financial system for waste management in South Africa involves solid waste management for local government is subsidised with funds from the National Treasury; at the local government level, solid waste service charges are set in several cities; and there is no specific tax on waste. Policies and plans under NEMWA include the National Policy on thermal treatment of general and hazardous waste, the National Policy for the provision of basic refuse removal services to indigent households, the National Organic Waste Composting Strategy, the National Waste Management Strategy, Municipal Solid Waste Tariff Strategy and National Pricing Strategy for Waste Management. South Africa's waste management is supported by German Corporation for International Cooperation (GIZ). Waste management in South Africa will require improvements in compliance and enforcement of laws/regulations, informal sector inclusion, full management cost recovery and administrative and technical capacity development.

Ghana Waste Management System

The Republic of Ghana is in the subregion of West Africa, located along the Gulf of Guinea and the Atlantic Ocean; the Côte d'Ivoire borders Ghana in the west, Burkina Faso in the north, Togo in the east and the Gulf of Guinea and the Atlantic Ocean in the south. Ghana has ten administrative regions subdivided into two hundred and sixteen districts. The Environmental Health and Sanitation Directorate under the Ministry of Sanitation and Water Resources (MSWR) takes responsibility for the municipal solid waste management in Ghana. MSWR is saddled with the responsibility of developing a Policy on Environmental Sanitation, which includes waste management, providing technical backstopping and regulation monitoring and evaluation.

The legal structure for managing waste in Ghana is as follows: Environmental Protection Agency, Environmental Assessment

Regulation, Environmental Assessment (Amendment) Regulation, Pesticides Control and Management Act, Management of Ozone Depleting Substances and Products Regulations, Governance Act—regulates the use of plastic bags. The financial system put in place by the Ghana government in managing waste includes a budget of US $45,000 allocated within the national budget for solid waste management, no tax is paid for waste disposal and there are no subsidies related to waste management from the central government to local government. Ghana currently needs a donor to assist its waste management sector. The policies and plans initiated to drive waste management in Ghana are the Environmental Sanitation Policy, which commenced in June 2010; National Environmental Sanitation Strategy and Action Plan (NESSAP), which began in 2010; and Health Care Waste Management Guidelines in 2006. Areas the Ghanaian government must improve to see a considerable change in how waste is managed include establishing statutory funding for waste management, the General capacity of waste management staff at all levels should be developed and an independent institution should be saddled with the responsibility of managing waste.

Tanzania Waste Management System

Tanzania is in eastern Africa within the African Great Lakes region, officially known as the United Republic of Tanzania. Tanzania has a population of about 54 million at an annual growth rate of 3.1%. The following countries share a boundary with Tanzania, Kenya and Uganda to the north; Rwanda, Burundi and the Democratic Republic of the Congo to the west; Zambia, Malawi and Mozambique to the south; and the Indian Ocean to the east. Africa's highest mountain, Mount Kilimanjaro, is in north-eastern Tanzania. * Mainland Tanzania is divided into twenty-six regions (Mikoa in Swahili). Each region is subdivided into districts (Wilaya) and local government authorities (called Councils). The districts and councils are subdivided into divisions (Tarafa) and further into local wards (Kata). Tanzania has brought under control the dumping of garbage on roadsides and in drains; the following are several initiatives by the government and particularly local government authorities on environmental cleanliness, heavy investments in country-wide urban infrastructure services and intense public awareness and inclusion, the sanitary environment of most parts of urban areas has improved. Right from the highest levels of government, Tanzania has a strong political will for every Tanzanian to adhere to the basics of environmental sanitation. Although there is no national basic law on municipal solid waste management, related laws and regulations are as follows: Environmental Management Act (EMA) 2004: Environmental and Social Impact Assessment (ESIA) is stipulated in the EMA. Local Government (Urban Authorities) Act of 1982 (revised in 2002). Public Health and Sewerage Act 2007: covers sanitation issues. Laws and programmes support the informal sector as follows: Business Activities Registration Act 2007: SWM is a part of this Act; Property and Business Formalization Program, 2004 to date: deals with social inclusion of informal sectors; the Local Government (Urban Authorities) Development Control Regulations No. 242 of 2008. Policies established to manage waste in Tanzania are as follows: National Environmental Management Policy, 1997; and National Solid Waste Management and Action Plan, 2010.

The financial system for waste management in Tanzania is as follows: Ratio of SWM budget allocated. Within the national budget, a ratio is given to solid waste management: less than 5% (recurring funding); local government authorities charge a fee for each incoming truck (tax on waste disposal); local government authorities charge a fixed rate for waste from low-income areas, but a higher rate of higher-income regions; subsidies from central government to local government are provided for the operation of the waste management services and the procurement of collection vehicles; and VAT is exempted for all SWM. The following donors support waste management in Tanzania; Danish International Development Agency (DANIDA) provides a capacity enhancement for solid waste management, institutional setup in national, regional and local government, 2010–2016. JICA: conducted intensive studies on urban SWM. UN-Habitat: conducted several participatory studies in solid waste management in the 1990s and early 2000s and the World Bank. The following are areas for improvement in Tanzania's waste management system; social issues: Tanzanian community needs more awareness of the value of handling solid waste sustainably. Policy issues: solid waste management should be given priority at the policy level. Institutional issues: basic solid waste management law should be prepared to define stakeholders' roles and responsibilities more clearly. Technical issues: provide skills and knowledge on solid waste management at the grassroots level.

Challenges of Waste Management in Africa

While governments of several African countries strive to meet their citizens' basic needs for food, health and education, addressing waste issues has veered down the policy agenda and deprived them of budgetary allocation (African Business, 2019). The management of waste in developing countries is more complicated than they appear on the surface; this makes the issue a daunting task for the government to manage. The factors that have led to poor waste management in Africa are rooted in diverse cultures, backgrounds, unique histories and socio-economic systems. Waste management problems in Africa, amongst other factors, are caused by; weak organisational structures, poor skills levels, inadequate budgetary support, weak legislation, lack of enforcement of the rule of law; low public awareness, corruption, conflict and political instability; and lack of political will (The Point, 2021).

As earlier highlighted, handling waste in Africa is complex and overwhelming for governments and institutions. Still, a closer look at the factors that constitute these complexities will give strategic insights into what can be done to address these gaps.

1. *High population growth in Africa*

    Africa's population is growing at an unprecedented pace; it is said to be the fastest-growing continent in the world in recent years. From 2000 to 2015, it increased by over 150% and is predicted to keep growing. The African population is expected to double from 2015 to 2050 (UN, 2014). As the human population grows, urban settlement is increasingly getting congested as individuals migrate from rural to urban settlements for economic reasons. The urban population in Africa is expected to triple from 2015 to 2050 (World Bank, 2018), and the amount of generated waste is also expected to triple, from 174 million tons in 2016 to 516 million tons in 2050 (World Bank, 2018). This growth in population and urban settlement will inevitably require municipal waste management. But Governments of several African countries are still unable to keep up with the greater demand for waste collection and disposal services.

2. *Damage to the sanitary and aesthetic condition of the cities*

    Poor waste management in Africa damages African cities' sanitary and aesthetic beauty. In several cities, regardless of the size, it is customary to see indiscriminate disposal of waste scattered around areas such as back alleys and vacant land not covered by public services. This wrongly disposed waste attracts insects and pests, especially organic waste. They eventually become breeding grounds for flies and gastrointestinal pathogens that can trigger the spread of diseases such as hepatitis, gastroenteritis and cholera. And also, water contained in plastic waste breeds mosquitoes and causes the spread of dengue, malaria and yellow fever.

3. *Environmental degradation from improper waste disposal*

    The impact of poor waste management on the environment transcends beyond being a breeding ground for insects and pests; other problems, such as the contamination of surface and groundwater from leachate, offensive odours and fires, are commonly observed. Methane gas is often released from decomposed organic waste into the atmosphere at open dumpsites, contributing to climate change. And recently, we have witnessed the incessant collapse of pilled waste at open dumpsites in cities due to improper waste disposal management claiming the lives of many. Amongst others is the March 2017 pilled waste collapse at Addis Ababa in Ethiopia, claiming over 115 victims.

4. *Presence of difficult-to-dispose waste due to lifestyle changes and increased importation*

    Industrialisation and change in lifestyle have led to increased importation in Africa. Whereas organic waste was the composition of waste generated in Africa before this time, lifestyle changes due to increased economic activities have increased the volume of waste requiring special disposal measures such as electrical and electronic products, plastics and tyres. Wilson et al. (2013) explain that harmful metals and chemical substances such as lead and dioxin from improper disposal of electrical and electronic waste cause health problems. Many African countries import large volumes of used electrical and electronic products from developed countries, which are no longer helpful or helpful on the continent's shores as waste. Only a tiny fraction of this accumulated waste is collected for recycling, most of which becomes mere waste. No organised techniques and legal systems for properly disposing of this waste require special treatment.

5. *Weak leadership will and poor waste management legislative systems*

    A critical common denominator across most African countries regarding waste management is weak leadership will and poor legislative systems. A fallout of poor economic processes that have bedevilled most African countries in sub-Saharan Africa is the twin challenge of poor waste management.

Opportunities for Waste Management in Africa

1. *Secondary resource materials*: Waste recycling allows us to generate secondary resource materials; Africa is still the most miniature continent in waste recycling, with only about a 4% recycling rate, and unexplored opportunities still abound in African waste recycling (Godfrey et al., 2019). Current practice in waste management overlooks the value that waste can provide local economies. As a result, valuable materials that could have been reused to support manufacturing to reduce the economic burden on imported products are being lost through waste disposal to dumpsites and landfills. Examples of secondary resource materials are viable polymers (from plastic), fibre (from paper), metals and nutrients (from organic waste), amongst others (Godfrey et al., 2019).

2. *Economic opportunities*

    There are economic rewards from proper waste management, but traditional practice only sees waste as a problem to the environment, not an opportunity. While developing economies like Africa are yet to yield economic benefits from waste, developed economies maximally utilise the economic potential of waste. Waste can provide considerable opportunity for the continent if only it could be safely collected and directed towards reuse, recycling and recovery. Informal reclaimers have played an active role in managing and diversifying reusable and recyclable waste away from landfills in Africa (Godfrey et al., 2019). And so, it is very strategic to integrate the informal sector into the waste management activities of the future as this will unlock significant opportunities for Africa while also ensuring their improved livelihoods (Godfrey et al., 2019). Informal reclaimers engage in labour-intensive collection, sorting and processing of secondary resources, which create direct jobs for many and even more indirect and induced employment opportunities at higher pay levels (Godfrey et al., 2019). There is little dependence on raw material import as local markets support using secondary resources developed from waste materials.

3. *Social and technological innovations*: In an effective society, any societal pain point becomes an opportunity for innovation; waste is an obvious problem to society, but until Africa starts seeing an option, the inadequacies of current waste management processes offer real innovation value that will not be created. Due to the gaps in current waste collection and disposal systems and the waste reuse, recycling and recovery model, social and technological innovations have emerged in the continent over the past decade (Godfrey et al., 2019). These social and technological innovations in Africa's waste collection models are "Wecyclers" in Nigeria or "Packag-ching" in South Africa. In Nigeria, Wecyclers is changing the waste collection process by using low-cost, environmentally friendly cargo bicycles called "cycles" to provide households and businesses in Lagos with convenient collection services for recyclable waste by using an SMS-based incentives system (Iwuoha, 2015). The Wecyclers and Packag-ching collection programmes reward residents for their recyclables through convenient collection systems.

4. *Production of valuable goods from waste*

    Only some innovative end-users are rethinking the use of waste in Africa. Such as the "Repurpose Schoolbags initiative" founded by Thato and Rea to help hundreds of school children in their local community in South Africa. They aim to collect and recycle plastic waste into low-cost school bags for disadvantaged local students. These "upcycled" plastic bags have solar panels attached to the flap, thus charging as the children walk to and back from school. The bag also comes with an added safety design that makes kids having them visible to traffic in the early hours. Another innovative end-user product is "YELI," Uganda's first paper bag production company founded by Andrew Mupuya. He got the idea to start this business when the government of Uganda banned plastic bags from reducing the environmental damage they caused. Today YELI employs over 20 people, with over 20,000 paper bags in production each week. Andrew still produces these bags by hand as he cannot yet afford a machine with a list of customers across restaurants, retail stores, supermarkets, medical centres and multinational companies like Samsung.

5. *Increased foreign direct investment in waste management*

Recently, we have witnessed increased investment in Africa's waste management. These investments have contributed to the 4% recycling rate we currently experience as a continent with many opportunities for more investment. We recently saw investments on a large scale for traditional waste treatment technologies, such as the first waste PET plastic food-grade bottle-to-bottle recycling plant, an Extrupet project in South Africa established in 2015. Extrupet can recycle over 2.5 million PET bottles daily; the PET bottles are converted into the fibre, thermoforming, food-grade and strapping-grade material (Yonli & Godfrey, 2018). This has produced high-quality, reliable end-products for packaging and other applications. And in Addis Ababa, the Reppie 50 MW waste-to-energy plant at the Koshe dump is a significant sign of investments in Africa's waste management (Yonli & Godfrey, 2018).

Key Recommendations for Business Leaders in Sub-Saharan Africa

1. Creating the right institutional framework for effective waste management is crucial to generate a seamless flow across the entire process. There is an imperative need for African business leaders to work and

collaborate with their governments at various levels towards creating and fostering suitable institutional structures for effective waste management; this is a crucial step that would help generate seamless flows across the entire process architecture in their respective home countries.
2. Policy, planning and legal frameworks to achieve urban and national solid-waste goals are essential to enforcing compliance. This is another area that should warrant attention from the governments and leadership in sub-Saharan Africa; there is also an urgent need for efficient policy and legal frameworks that would help to institutionalise urban and rural solid-waste goals geared towards achieving regional compliance in these countries.
3. Financing to ensure investments and sustained operational funds and to provide incentives for change. Some countries in sub-Saharan Africa need adequate funding to actualise investment and sustained operational drive investments and sustainable operational support for cohesive waste management. Thus, there is a need for the leaders in these countries to warehouse the inherent support for adequate fund mobilisation for national and regional waste management.
4. A strong political will is required from leaders, and there is a need to drive waste management with an encompassing and enabling political will. This drive will engender organisational models in the African continent for waste management and foster appropriate value mechanisms.
5. Inclusive stakeholders' engagement to integrate relevant stakeholders and the informal sector from the onset during waste management planning is essential for developing countries in sub-Saharan Africa.

Conclusion

In conclusion, Africa's waste management system is still in its early stage. Therefore low-technology (and low-cost) solutions such as cargo bicycles, motor tricycles or donkey carts are still perfect substitutes for waste collection across African cities. Although, in recent times, we are witnessing some exceptional social and technologically innovative breakthroughs emerging in the waste sector of the continent, conventional waste treatment technologies will remain challenging to implement at scale in Africa due to inefficient waste separation processes at the source. Uncontrolled dumping and open burning will remain the dominant "technology" choices for managing waste on the African continent. Including the informal sector in the waste management system will be very strategic for developing countries in handling waste. It provides opportunities for improved livelihoods, income generation for informal actors and increased economic activity within the country. And a chance to scale waste management in Africa by developing and strengthening local and regional end-use markets. The primary scale strategy is reusing end-of-life goods and recycling technologies. At the same time, the former is currently driven informally across Africa; recycling technologies are being implemented for wastes such as plastic, paper, glass, metal, oil, e-waste and organic waste.

References

African Business. (2019, January 22). *Rethinking waste: Africa's challenges and opportunities.* Retrieved March 17, 2022, from https://african.business/2019/01/economy/rethinking-waste-africas-challenge%EF%BB%BFs-and-opportunities/

African Clean Cities Platform (ACCF). (2019). *Africa solid waste management data book 2019.* Retrieved April 1, 2022, from https://africancleancities.org/data/JICA_databook_EN_web_20191218.pdf

Amasuomo, E., & Baird, J. (2016). The concept of waste and waste management. *Journal of Management and Sustainability, 6,* 88.

Basu, R. (2009). Solid waste management-a model study. *Sies Journal of Management, 6,* 20–24.

Demirbas, A. (2011). Waste management, waste resource facilities and waste conversion processes. *Energy Conversion and Management, 52*(2), 1280–1287. https://doi.org/10.1016/j.enconman.2010.09.025

Dijkema, G. P. J., Reuter, M. A., & Verhoef, E. V. (2000). A new paradigm for waste management. *Waste Management, 20*(8), 633–638. https://doi.org/10.1016/S0956-053X(00)00052-0

Dixon, N., & Jones, D. R. V. (2005). Engineering properties of municipal solid waste. *Geotextiles and Geomembranes, 23*(3), 205–233. https://doi.org/10.1016/j.geotexmem.2004.11.002

Godfrey, L., Ahmed, M. T., Gebremedhin, K. G., Katima, J. H., Oelofse, S., Osibanjo, O., et al. (2019). Solid waste management in Africa: Governance failure or development opportunity. In *Regional development in Africa* (p. 235). IntechOpen.

Iwuoha, J. P. (2015, February 15). *Business ideas, environment and green, get inspired!* Retrieved April 13, 2022, from http//www.smallstarter.com/category/browse-ideas/environmental-businesses/

Tchobanoglous, G., Theisen, H., & Vigil, S. (1993). Integrated solid waste management: Engineering principles and management issues. *Water Science and Technology Library, 8*(1), 63–90.

The Point. (2021, February 16). *Africa: Solid waste management in Africa - Governance failure or development opportunity?* Retrieved March 17, 2022, from https://thepoint.gm/africa/gambia/editorial/solid-waste-management-in-africa-governance-failure-or-development-opportunity

UN. (2014). *World urbanization prospects.* Retrieved April 5, 2019, from https://population.un.org/wup/

White, P. R., Franke, M., & Hindle, P. (1995). *Integrated solid waste management: A lifecycle inventory.* Springer.

Wilson, D. C. (2007). Development drivers for waste management. *Waste Management & Research, 25*(3), 198–207. https://doi.org/10.1177/0734242X07079149

Wilson, D. C., Velis, C. A., & Rodic, L. (2013). Integrated sustainable waste management in developing countries. *Proceedings of the Institution of Civil Engineers: Waste and Resource Management, 166*(2), 56–58.

World Bank. (2018). *What a waste 2.0: A global snapshot of solid waste management to 2050,* p. 2.

World Bank. (2021, October 29). *Bridging the gap in solid waste management.* Retrieved March 17, 2022, from https://www.worldbank.org/en/topic/urbandevelopment/publication/bridging-the-gap-in-solid-waste-management

Yonli, A. H., & Godfrey, L. (2018). *Appropriate solutions for Africa. Africa waste management outlook* (pp. 119–150). UNEP. Retrieved April 13, 2022, from https://www.unep.org/ietc/resources/publication/africa-waste-management-outlook

12

Enhancing Corporate Social Responsibilities in Emerging Business Environments in Africa: Challenges and Opportunities

Silk Ugwu Ogbu

Introduction

In the last three decades, the conception and practice of Corporate Social Responsibility (CSR) have changed significantly worldwide. Corporate investments in CSR have been increasing consistently over the years, pointing to the growing recognition of its impact on business performance and organisational reputation, especially by the top global brands. In 2020, the companies that made the top ten list of international brands with the best CSR reputation were Lego, The Walt Disney Company, Rolex, Ferrari, Microsoft, Levi's, Netflix, Adidas, Bosch and Intel (Gonçalves, 2020). The companies were selected from a study that involved over 230,000 participants in 15 major economies. The findings confirmed that reputation is tied to CSR performance regarding how

S. U. Ogbu (✉)
Lagos Business School, Pan-Atlantic University, Lekki, Nigeria
e-mail: sogbu@lbs.edu.ng

organisations manage issues around products and services, corporate governance, citizenship, financial performance, innovation, executive leadership and workplace quality (Gonçalves, 2020).

The increasing significance of CSR as a measure of corporate reputation and performance underscores the need for businesses to periodically interrogate their assumptions and practices and, where necessary, modify their approach to optimise their value. In Africa, the trend of corporate investments in social responsibility projects has changed only marginally in the last decade. Some big companies, such as MTN, Dangote, Zenith Bank, United Bank of Africa and Access Bank, have made remarkable contributions to social causes, especially during the COVID-19 Pandemic. However, such contributions appear to be drops of water in an ocean. As the continent with the highest prevalence of humanitarian and social disasters, many of which are caused by the operations of corporate entities, Africa deserves and needs every form of social investment it can get. Unfortunately, the uptake and application of CSR as a strategic business tool for the benefit of society and businesses have continued to suffer setbacks in the continent because of several factors.

First, the conception and practice of CSR are still primarily guided by the philosophy of philanthropy rather than business strategy and corporate citizenship (Amaeshi et al., 2006). Several organisations in emerging economies grapple with high operational costs and must understand how additional CSR spending could contribute to their bottom line. Interestingly, such organisations constitute the majority, who still see CSR as mere philanthropic gestures or voluntary donations to social causes that become necessary or justifiable if a company makes a sufficient profit. However, several studies indicate that CSR is not just an add-on but a core element in the determination of brand reputation, brand equity, brand awareness, consumer buying behaviour and the social licence to operate (Porter & Kramer, 2006; Daubry, 2020; Mamudu et al., 2021; Ogbu, 2022). Therefore, African corporate entities must interrogate the philosophy behind their CSR activities or social investments and develop metrics for measuring impact and value additions to make well-informed decisions on CSR interventions.

Second, the regulatory environment in Africa needs to be stronger and more effective. As a result, corporate entities that should account for the impact of their operations on the social, economic and environmental well-being of society continue to avoid such responsibilities. In the Niger Delta region, for example, the pollution and denigration of the environment by the Multinational Oil Companies (MOCs) have continued over the years because of the weakness of regulatory and enforcement mechanisms. Similarly, in the banking and telecommunication sectors, malfeasance and abuse of corporate ethics have refused to abate despite the preponderance of regulators and extant laws. The inability of regulators to curb corporate malpractices in Africa is compounded by the problems of corruption and systemic failures. Over time, the CSR landscape has degenerated considerably, making it possible for companies perpetrating fraud and unethical behaviours to hide behind some voluntary but deceptive CSR projects. Against this background, whether CSR should be voluntary or compulsory continues to attract scholarly interest and attention.

Third, the field of CSR practice is becoming specialised and requires expertise to harness its enormous potential. However, many African companies that should leverage CSR to drive their financial performance are Medium, Small and Micro Enterprises (MSMs). Unfortunately, most companies require support to afford professionals to manage such specialised functions. Many of them are run by owners with limited or no experience in PR or individuals who need assistance to understand the relevance of applying CSR as a strategic business tool. As a result, many MSMEs and start-ups with only huge potentials do not survive the first three years of operations—either because of the inability to manage the challenges arising from their operating environment or because of the incapacity to leverage the immeasurable benefits of a robust CSR strategy.

The COVID-19 Pandemic has disrupted the world around us like nothing else in the past 100 years. As people battle with unexpected dislocations that have affected their lives and livelihoods, they need all the help they can get. As corporate citizens, organisations are expected to support society at a time like this by championing social responsibility. However, the pandemic also allowed corporate entities to reinvent their brands and explore strategic ways of applying CSR to foster sustainable growth. Against that backdrop, this chapter re-examines existing approaches and practices of CSR in Africa. It attempts to identify actionable ways of enhancing responsible business practices for the benefit of all stakeholders.

The chapter is divided into sections. The first section provides a background to the ideas espoused in this study. The second section is a conceptual review of the existing and emerging thoughts on CSR, while the third section provides a theoretical anchorage for the study's postulations. In the fourth section, the chapter takes a deep dive into the challenges and opportunities for enhancing CSR in emerging business environments across Africa. In the last quarter, the chapter takes its position, concludes and offers some recommendations.

Conceptual Framework

The notion that corporate entities have responsibilities to shareholders and stakeholders in the economic, social, environmental, legal, ethical and philanthropic contexts of their existence gave rise to CSR. Corporate Social Responsibility as a concept has generated enormous scholarly interest and debates. Over the last six decades, the debates have metamorphosed into a body of knowledge and insights guiding business operations and performances.

On one side of the aisle are the scholars who argue that corporate entities have only one corporate responsibility—profit-making! As long as corporations obey the laws and pay their taxes, these scholars insist that it is the responsibility of the government to manage society's needs since managers are unelected, unaccountable and poorly educated decision-makers concerning public goods and wealth redistribution (Friedman, 1970; Wishloff, 2009; Knippenberg & De Jong, 2010; Smith, 2013). On the other side of the aisle are scholars who contend that business operations impact the environment and various stakeholders, and to that extent, organisations must ensure that all stakeholders' interests are protected, especially as they make or increase profits (Freeman & Dmytriyev, 2017; Freeman et al., Tensions in Stakeholder Theory, 2020; Porter & Kramer, 2011).

Against that background, it is essential to note that scholars and practitioners describe CSR in various ways based on their interests, which compounds the concept's definitional problem. James (2012) identifies five dimensions of CSR definitions in literature: environmental, social, economic, stakeholder and voluntariness based on their bias or emphasis. For instance, the definitions of those interested in the environment express concerns about environmental protection or stewardship in business operations. On the other hand, the definitions of those concerned about social issues stress the relationship between business and society or the consideration of the social impact of businesses on people and communities. Still, some definitions address multiple dimensions of interests, while others attempt to incorporate a holistic view of the issues in their conception of CSR (Fig. 12.1).

One of the most cited definitions refers to CSR as the continuing commitment by businesses to behave ethically and contribute to economic development while improving the quality of life of the workforce and their families as well as the local community and society at large (World Business Council for Sustainable Development, 2000). The acceptability

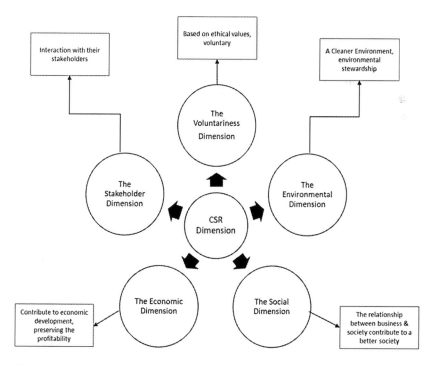

Fig. 12.1 Dimensions of CSR definitions. *Source:* James (2012)

of the definition is because it attempted to include all the dimensions of interests espoused by scholars and practitioners on the subject matter. Similarly, Carroll's (1979) description of the concept as encompassing four fundamental business responsibilities: economic, legal, ethical and philanthropic, has remained relevant in the discourse because it did not define CSR as one thing or another. However, the effort to classify or categorise those responsibilities using a pyramid (Carroll, 1991) received much less acceptance from scholars and practitioners because of their bias (Fig. 12.2).

Carroll's (1991) hierarchical classification of corporate responsibilities suggests that economic responsibilities are the most important, followed by legal, ethical and philanthropic. In that sense, business entities must strive to make a profit first, but in the process, they should obey the laws and remain ethical and responsive to social needs. In other words, profit-making is the primary responsibility of business, upon which other responsibilities rest because unprofitable organisations cannot support social or environmental causes (Gudjonsdottir & Jusubova, 2015). Likewise, the philanthropic responsibilities of businesses are the least important because they are desirable but discretionary.

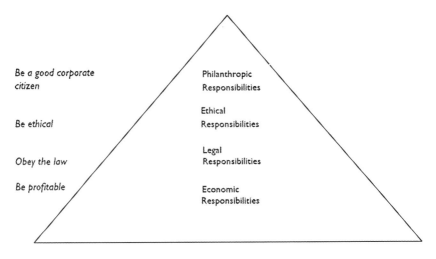

Fig. 12.2 Pyramid of Corporate Social Responsibilities. *Source:* Helg (2007)

Although 'Caroll's Pyramid' offers a detailed categorisation of the responsibilities of business, it does not provide sufficient information or explanation about the components of each category and where the boundaries should be drawn in the field of practice. While there is less controversy on the economic and legal dimensions of the framework, the debate over the ethical and philanthropic or discretionary aspects has raged on over the years (Okoye, 2009; Ormiston & Wong, 2013). At the heart of the contentions is the lack of clarity or understanding about what constitutes ethical and philanthropic obligations of corporate entities and whether CSR practice should remain voluntary or regulated by the state (Chaudhry & Ramakrishnan, 2019; Daubry, 2020).

Understandably, corporations have pushed back on the idea of making CSR compulsory. However, its promoters insist that discretionary CSR allows firms to hide unethical practices behind deceitful CSR projects (Sheehy, 2015). For example, some banks that donated money to the COVID-19 Relief Fund in Nigeria at the height of the pandemic were later found guilty of illegal deductions from customers' accounts (Wodu, 2021).

Since the emergence of Carroll's (1991) Pyramid, several scholars have theorised CSR responsibilities from different perspectives and offered alternative models, either as explanatory tools for understanding the phenomenon or for practice direction (Ketola, 2008; Aguinis & Glavas, 2012; Hamidu et al., 2015; Mamudu et al., 2021). However, for this chapter's purpose, especially in strategically leveraging CSR to enhance society's progress and achieve corporate objectives in Africa, Porter and Kramer's (2006) work provides tremendous insights and guidance.

In making a case for a new approach to CSR practice, the authors contend that most efforts of corporate entities in this essential area end in futility or even become counterproductive because of two reasons—they are generic rather than strategic and they pit business against society when the two are interdependent and can create shared value (Porter & Kramer, 2006; Porter & Kramer, 2011). Therefore, approached strategically, CSR can be much more than costs, constraints, philanthropic gestures or PR gimmicks. It can open the doors of opportunity, innovation and competitive advantage for companies while solving crucial social problems. The big question is how companies in emerging economies, including Africa, can strategise CSR.

Porter and Kramer (2006) propose an interesting way of looking at the relationship between business and society that does not treat corporate success and social welfare as a zero-sum game. It entails identifying the intersection between business activities and society from two dimensions—*inside-out and outside-in*. Inside-out linkages encompass all the activities of the business that affect society. In contrast, outside-in linkages refer to the external social conditions influencing a corporation's competitive contexts, either positively or negatively. For example, for an oil-producing company in the Niger Delta, the *inside-out* intersection points of its activities with society may include issues of pollution, environmental degradation and safe working conditions for its staff. On the other hand, the *outside-in* intersections may include vandalism of pipelines, oil theft, inability to source specialised human resources from local communities and several other issues associated with the ease of business.

Having identified the intersections, a company must carefully prioritise and select its social projects to optimise CSR spending. Organisations can choose from three categories of social issues: first, generic social issues that are not significantly affected by a company's operations nor materially affect its long-term competitiveness; second, value chain social impact issues that arise from a company's day-to-day activities; and third, issues emerging from the social dimensions of the competitive context that significantly affect the organisation's competitiveness in the locations where it operates (Fig. 12.3).

In choosing CSR projects to mount, Porter and Kramer (2006) suggest that companies should focus mainly on a small number of initiatives that simultaneously generate significant and distinctive benefits for the firm and society. In that regard, they can adopt either the responsive or the strategic approach to CSR.

Responsive CSR is predicated on ethics and moral values. Businesses have obligations as corporate citizens to obey the laws and ensure that ethical principles in the workplace, marketplace and community guide their conduct. Therefore, CSR projects must aim to demonstrate good corporate citizenship in addressing stakeholders' social concerns or seek

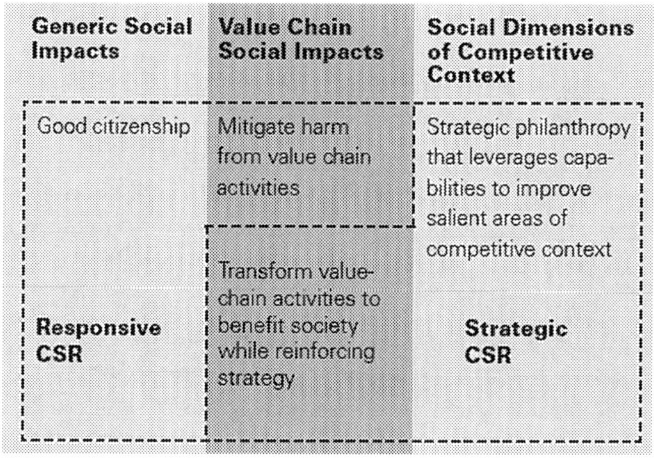

Generic Social Impacts	Value Chain Social Impacts	Social Dimensions of Competitive Context
Good citizenship	Mitigate harm from value chain activities	Strategic philanthropy that leverages capabilities to improve salient areas of competitive context
Responsive CSR	Transform value-chain activities to benefit society while reinforcing strategy	Strategic CSR

Fig. 12.3 Corporate involvement in CSR: a strategic approach. *Source:* Porter and Kramer (2006)

to mitigate existing and anticipated harm to society from a company's value-chain activities.

On the other hand, strategic CSR goes beyond responsive CSR in that it integrates both the *inside-out* and *outside-in* dimensions of the social context. It does that by strategically leveraging philanthropy to improve the salient areas of the competitive context or transforming value-chain activities to benefit society while reinforcing the firm's competitive strategy. For example, the high prevalence of malaria in Nigeria may be a generic social issue for a US-based company like Apple but a value-chain impact issue for a pharmaceutical company like Pfizer. At the same time, it could be a competitive context issue for a telecommunications firm like Globacom, which depends heavily on local labour for its operations. In this regard, it would be strategic CSR for Globacom to fund malaria elimination programmes in Nigeria. Although such philanthropic projects address society's needs, they also protect the health of the company's workforce and its productivity. Typically, the closer social projects are to an organisation's strategic goals, the more excellent the opportunity to simultaneously leverage the firm's resources and benefit society.

Indeed, business operating environments are changing rapidly worldwide. Globalisation and technological advancements are introducing new dimensions to business social and competitive contexts and increasing social performance and responsiveness demands. As businesses grapple with unending demands from society, especially in poverty or disaster-laden environments such as Africa, it is vital to remember that corporations are not responsible for all humanity's problems. The vehemence of social activists or stakeholder groups does not necessarily signify the importance of an issue—either to the company or to the world (Porter & Kramer, 2006). Even if they wish to, they may never have the resources to solve all of society's problems. Therefore, companies interested in gaining a competitive advantage must strategically enhance CSR by moving from a fragmented, defensive mindset to an integrated, affirmative way of creating shared value for business and society (Porter & Kramer, 2011).

Theoretical Framework

Stakeholder Theory

The notion popularised by Professor Milton Friedman that CSR is essentially an immoral idea which violates the rights of business 'owners' was hinged on the premise that using corporate resources to solve non-corporate 'social' problems amounts to stealing from shareholders (Friedman, 1970). Although the core assumptions underlying Friedman's (1970) arguments have been extensively challenged, managers' prioritisation of shareholder interests has neither diminished in practice nor disappeared from the teachings of some business schools since the 1970s. Easily traced to Professor Edward Freeman's seminal work, *Strategic Management: A Stakeholder Approach* (1984), Stakeholder Theory (ST) represents a radical departure from Friedman's controversial postulations on corporate responsibilities. Freeman's (1984) primary contention is that businesses have multiple and interdependent stakeholders whose interests are intertwined in a complex web of relationships, obligations and reciprocities. If both agree to balance their interests and work collaboratively, the shareholder's interest to maximise profit does not necessarily contradict that of the employee to earn a decent wage. Likewise, spending money on safeguarding the environment or providing social amenities for a host community does not reduce the profit-making potential of the shareholders of an oil-producing company in Angola. On the contrary, the investment in social causes protects and even increases the profit-making potential of the shareholder in the long run, who otherwise could have lost money in the event of social unrest or environmental disaster. Thus, the expression 'from Friedman to Freeman' is often used to illustrate the shift in the debate on the role of business in society (António, 2007).

Stakeholder Theory affirms the centrality of an organisation's relationship with multiple actors, such as customers, suppliers, employees and local communities, to its performance and survival. It argues that organisations must provide value for all stakeholders and questions the thesis that the fundamental objective of the firm is to create wealth for its shareholders. According to (Freeman, n.d.),

> *The 21st Century is one of "Managing for Stakeholders". The task of executives is to create as much value as possible for stakeholders without resorting to trade-offs. Great companies endure because they align stakeholder interests in the same direction.*

However, among the scholars who subscribe to the stakeholder's approach, one issue that has remained contentious is the definition of a stakeholder. Freeman's (1984, p. 8) definition of stakeholders as '*any group or individual who can affect or is affected by the achievement of the organisation's objectives*' appears encompassing (Crane, 2020) but hardly useful for CSR practice. The definition leaves the notion of stake and the field of possible stakeholders ambiguously open to include virtually everyone. From that perspective, the basis for stakeholder identification could be unidirectional, bi-directional or multi-directional.

To provide more specific guidance to managers and CSR practitioners, Clarkson (1995) argues that stakeholders can be categorised into two major groups: primary and secondary. The primary actors directly relate to the organisation and are vital to its survival and growth. This group includes shareholders, employees, customers, suppliers, government and host communities. On the other hand, secondary actors may significantly influence the organisation's performance but are not central to its operations or survival. Examples include media organisations, interest or pressure groups, influencers and opinion leaders. Classifying stakeholders is relevant because it provides a framework for prioritisation, especially when managers with limited resources cannot meet all stakeholders' demands. In that case, Clarkson (1995) suggests that the needs of the primary actors must be prioritised since the organisation depends on them to survive. However, Mitchell et al. (1997) recommend that the prioritisation of stakeholders should be guided by salience with respect to three attributes: the legitimacy of their relationship with the organisation, the power to influence the firm's objectives and the urgency of their demands. The analysis of these attributes enables the business manager to determine the stakeholder with the greatest salience (Jhunior et al., 2021). Thus, the most important actor is the one who possesses all three attributes (Menezes et al., 2022).

Over the years, the advancements in ST have moved in three specific directions: descriptive, instrumental and normative (Donaldson & Preston, 1995; Rose et al., 2018). According to Menezes et al. (2022), these dimensions of ST are still relevant and have continued to underpin the various ways business managers can use the theory for CSR interventions. The descriptive or empirical dimension refers to the use of the theory to describe or explain organisational characteristics and behaviours in terms of how stakeholders relate or act in furthering their interests. The instrumental use of the ST is characterised by its application with empirical data to identify and harness the nexus between stakeholder management and the achievement of organisational goals, such as enhancing reputation, brand equity, sales and profit-making. On the other hand, the normative dimension refers to the theory's usage for interpreting organisational functions, including identifying moral guidelines for a firm's operations and behaviours.

Although ST and CSR are deeply interconnected, it is important to stress that there are fundamental differences in scope and focus. While ST posits that the primary essence of business is to create value for *all* its stakeholders, CSR is mainly concerned with the social responsibilities of business that affect people, communities and the wider society. From ST's perspective, *all* stakeholders—employees, suppliers, government, communities and shareholders—are important and should be treated fairly, without trade-offs. On the other hand, CSR is an umbrella concept for a company's activities oriented towards society at large that includes charity, volunteering, environmental efforts and ethical labour practices (Freeman & Dmytriyev, 2017). Thus, ST is concerned about '*corporate responsibilities*' as a whole, while CSR is focused on '*corporate social responsibilities*', as illustrated in Fig. 12.4.

Notwithstanding the differences in the orientation and scope of ST and CSR, both speak the same language. ST offers a comprehensive framework for guiding business executives in mitigating risks and managing responsibilities to all stakeholders, including communities, customers, employees and society at large. According to Freeman and Dmytriyev (2017), three common elements—*purpose, value creation and stakeholder interdependence*—make corporate responsibilities overall and Corporate Social Responsibilities in particular unified and inseparable.

Without a doubt, Stakeholder Theory has inspired enormous conversations around how corporate entities should manage their responsibilities and reimagine a future where profit maximisation and social

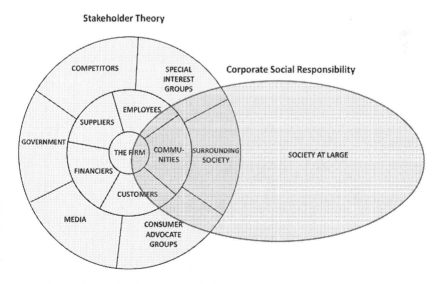

Fig. 12.4 Relationship between Stakeholder Theory and CSR. *Source:* Freeman and Dmytriyev (2017)

performance are not mutually exclusive. However, some criticisms have trailed ST's postulations, mainly because of its prescriptive imprecision. The definition of stakeholders by the theory has been criticised as too broad (Sheehy, 2015; Crane, 2020), while the *balancing* of interests or the *equal* treatment of *all* stakeholders has been described as impractical (Pesqueux & Damak-Ayadi, 2005; Dorobantu, 2019; Menezes et al., 2022). Nevertheless, it is difficult to diminish the theory's massive contribution to a deeper understanding of the relationship between business and society. Given ST's descriptive, instrumental, normative and other emerging attributes, it is easy to predict that the theory will remain relevant in the foreseeable future—as a tool for enhancing the conceptualisation and practice of CSR in emerging economies.

Enhancing CSR Practice in Africa: A Way Forward

The business climate in Africa presents immense opportunities as well as challenges. However, the COVID-19 Pandemic introduced businesses' additional complications and success requirements, forcing managers to rethink their extant strategies. Creating agile and resilient business models anchored on ethical corporate cultures and mutually beneficial relationships with stakeholders could be the sensible way forward. However, to successfully navigate the turbulence ahead, organisations must be prepared to deal with volatility, uncertainty, complexity and ambiguity (VUCA) creatively and creatively.

One tool that businesses can strategise in a VUCA world is CSR. Unfortunately, most companies operating in the continent have migrated from *Responsive* to *Strategic* CSR. The conception and practice of CSR as philanthropy rather than strategy have remained the dominant approach in Africa, with implications for social transformation and corporate performance.

In Ghana, for instance, the economic landscape is changing with the increasing diversification of activities across various sectors, including mining, agriculture, oil production, manufacturing and services.

However, CSR practice generally has remained largely discretionary and philanthropic. The big spenders on CSR, such as ABL SABMiller, Barclays Bank of Ghana, Ghana Commercial Bank, Multichoice Africa, Goldfields Ghana Limited and Unilever, have one thing in common—social projects are focused on issues of health, education, sports, community development and other morally inspired causes. The story is more or less the same for Nigeria. The big companies, including MTN, Dangote, Airtel, Zenith Bank, United Bank of Africa and Nigerian Breweries, have 'Foundations' created to manage their social investments as philanthropic gestures.

Similarly, CSR projects in Cameroon by large corporations such as SGBC, Nestlé, Cam Iron, Alucam, MTN, Diageo, Rodeo, Perenco and Orange Cameroon are charity-oriented and mostly *responsive*. For Kenya, there is no significant departure from the trend. The prominent players in the CSR space include Bamburi Cement Ltd., Unilever Kenya, OSRAM, Henkel Kenya and Tata Chemical Ltd. Again, most of these companies invest in social projects such as education, sports and HIV/AIDS prevention from a philanthropic perspective. In South Africa, however, the story is slightly different. The practice of CSR reflects a diversified portfolio of social investments and a deeper understanding of the need for a strategic approach. Companies such as ABSA, Anglo American Plc, Anglo Gold Ashanti, Merafe Resources, Gold Field Ltd., Group Five, Standard Bank, Tongaat Hulett, Nedbank, SABMiller and MTN are the game changers. They seem to be investing more in improving the salient areas of their competitive contexts instead of spending on generic social projects in the health, education, sports or entertainment sectors (Rampersad & Skinner, 2014).

Understandably, the high prevalence of poverty, disease and insurgencies in the continent and the failure of governments to address social needs are escalating expectations and the request for philanthropic assistance from corporate entities. The volatile, uncertain, complex and ambiguous business environments in Africa also exacerbate the challenges organisations face in managing the demands of the triple bottom line (profits, people and planet). However, beyond the challenges are immense opportunities for organisations to create tremendous value for *all* of their stakeholders by leveraging strategic CSR and the recommendations of the Stakeholder theorists. As Porter and Kramer (2006) posit, there are two ways it can be done—by transforming regular value-chain activities to benefit society and by enhancing a company's competitive edge through strategic social investments and realistic *inside-out/outside-in* intersection analysis.

Another area where significant challenges lie in enhancing the relationship between business and society through CSR is regulatory failures. Many African countries suffer from poor governance structures, weak institutions/regulatory mechanisms and corruption. As a result, several organisations need to be held accountable for the impact of their operations on society and stakeholders. In resource-rich countries such as Nigeria, Congo, Angola, South Africa and Ghana, multinational oil-producing or mining companies denigrate their host communities' lives, livelihoods and environments without consequences. This situation stems from the absence of necessary laws/policies, weak regulatory and enforcement institutions/personnel and systemic corruption to poor governance and ethical standards in corporate entities.

A good example is the case of Shell Petroleum Development Company (SPDC) and the Ogoni community in the Niger Delta region of Nigeria. The United Nations Environmental Programme's (UNDP) report on investigating the oil exploration and producing activities of SPDC in Ogoni affirmed that the company disregarded global best practices and national and international laws. According to Vidal (2011), the UNEP's three-year investigation found:

- Heavy contamination of land and underground water courses, sometimes more than 40 years after oil was spilt
- Community drinking water with dangerous concentrations of benzene and other pollutants
- Soil contamination more than five metres deep in many areas studied
- Most of the spill sites oil firms claimed to have been cleaned were still highly contaminated
- Evidence of oil firms dumping contaminated soil in unlined pits
- Water coated with hydrocarbons more than 1000 times the level Nigerian drinking water standards allow

- Failure by Shell and others to meet minimum Nigerian or own standards.

The report, released in 2011, estimated that it would cost over $ 1 billion and require between 25–30 years of diligent work to clean up the oil spill and pollution in Ogoni perpetrated by SPDC's 50 years of negligence (Vidal, 2011). Eleven years later, it appears that very little progress has been made towards cleaning up the mess in Ogoni as new concerns continue to emerge regarding the commitment of both the government and the company to the exercise (Stakeholder Democracy Network, 2022).

The case of SPDC and the Ogoni Community is not an isolated incident. It reflects what is happening across many African countries and communities where regulatory agencies and large multinationals have failed to do the right thing, sometimes because of financial or selfish reasons. The result is usually a breakdown in the relationship between business and society, leading to massive losses for shareholders and stakeholders. For example, the forced exit of SPDC from Ogoni in 1993 as a result of the attacks on its operations and other conflicts arising from the oil spills is estimated to have cost Nigeria over $178 billion in revenue loss so far (Yafugborhi, 2022).

Unscrupulous managers and corrupt government officials are found everywhere in the world. However, where there are few or no consequences for wrongdoing or some powerful actors are above the law, as is in many African countries, CSR is unlikely to have any meaningful impact on society or business performance. Therefore, it makes sense to re-examine the call by some scholars to jettison discretionary CSR and go for mandatory CSR in the African context (Ihugba, 2012; Amodu, 2017). South Africa seems to be moving in this direction, albeit strategically, by embedding CSR into the law designed to address the unequal distribution of wealth and encouraging businesses to go beyond the law to create this necessary balance in society. One example is the government's formalisation of the Broad-Based Black Economic Empowerment (B-BBEE) scorecard to measure and enforce companies' compliance with the transformation initiatives of the programme (Juggernath et al., 2011). The scorecard contains seven elements: ownership, management, employment equity, skills development, preferential procurement, enterprise development and socio-economic development (Rampersad & Skinner, 2014). Although these elements reflect the desire of the government to correct some of the apartheid era's ills, the 'mandatory' role assigned to CSR in this context indicates a departure from the traditional cap-in-hand approach.

Also, South Africa's 1994 King's Committee Report, which enunciated the principles of corporate responsibility, is the first global corporate governance code to formally outline companies' commitment to shareholders and stakeholders (Kabir et al., 2015). Since then, the ideas espoused by King 1 have been expanded by King II, King III and many other subsequent reports to the extent that adherence to those principles has now become a requirement for listing on the Johannesburg Securities Exchange (Rampersad & Skinner, 2014). Similarly, the demand for compulsory CSR has been growing in Nigeria as the government continues to introduce new legislations to hold corporate entities more accountable for the impact of their operations on society. From the NEITI Act of 2007 to the Petroleum Industry Act of 2021, the country is probably moving slowly towards a more compulsory CSR regime.

Nevertheless, companies need to go beyond the legal or mandatory obligations being proposed to an ethical higher ground to optimise the opportunities inherent in CSR. Although Carroll's (1991) pyramid categorises the legal obligations above ethical considerations for CSR, some scholars argue that ethical principles propel organisations to behave well in *all* circumstances, regardless of the legal boundaries, which may be subject to varied interpretations or manipulations (Aguinis & Glavas, 2012; Ogbu, 2022). Lantos (2003) recategorised Carroll's (1991) pyramid of CSR responsibilities into three: *Ethical* CSR, *Altruistic* CSR and *Strategic* CSR, but recommends that CSR should be focused on two significant aspects:

* preventing injuries and harm that could result from business activities;
* accomplishing strategic business goals.

From the above perspective, integrating ethical and strategic CSR is the best chance of delivering optimal value to African society and businesses. The infusion of ethics in CSR will guarantee that corporate entities conduct themselves as responsible citizens who obey the laws and respect fairness, equity and justice in the workplace, marketplace and community. This idea aligns with the postulations of the Stakeholder Theory and the position of Porter and Kramer (2006).

Furthermore, enhancing CSR in the twenty-first-century internet-driven economy requires professionalism and a clear understanding of the dynamics of an increasingly interconnected world. Several organisations deploy CSR merely as a PR gimmick or a moral cleansing tool because it enables them to pursue a seemingly 'good cause' in society, perhaps, as atonement for previous destructive behaviours or maltreating other stakeholders (Ogbu, 2022). When applied correctly, studies have shown that CSR can enhance brand perception, brand image, brand equity, brand loyalty and brand trust—all of which contribute to an improved bottom line and organisational performance (Aaker, 1991; Hoeffler & Keller, 2002; Akhigbe & Olokoyo, 2019; Daubry, 2020) (Fig. 12.5).

However, a majority of the businesses in Africa are Micro, Small and Medium Enterprises (MSMEs)—owned and managed by individuals who may need more expertise or the resources to hire professionals to

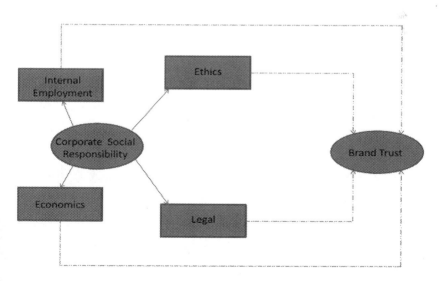

Fig. 12.5 CSR effects on brand trust. *Source:* Aimie-Jade (2011)

handle CSR functions. For example, Nigeria has over 41.5 million MSMEs (National Bureau of Statistics, 2019), accounting for 80% of employment and more than 50% of its GDP (PwC, 2020). All over the world, MSMEs are recognised as the engine of economic growth and social transformation because of their volume of activity and the value-chain effects of their operations. Therefore, empowering them to perform better through effective CSR is in the interest of African countries and the businesses concerned. The COVID-19 Pandemic allowed corporate entities to reinvent their brands, either by transforming value-chain activities to serve corporate and social interests simultaneously or by leveraging extant capacities to improve the salient aspects of their competitive contexts. Unfortunately, several MSMEs did not decode that opportunity either because they need access to professional advice and guidance or are run by individuals who still consider CSR a waste of scarce resources. In any case, the metrics for measuring the contribution of CSR to the bottom line are available and easily accessible on the internet. What is necessary is more education and awareness creation so that small and medium business owners can begin to adopt strategic CSR initiatives from the early stages of their business. Given the number of MSMEs across Africa, the impact of their CSR involvement on the continent's social and economic transformation will be unprecedented.

Conclusion

Corporate entities can contribute a lot to the development of Africa through CSR. On the other hand, the continent has enormous potential and opportunities for business growth that are untapped and still need to be explored. By strategising CSR and enhancing the competencies of managers to create and implement innovative solutions to social issues, it is possible to balance the interests of shareholders and all stakeholders without trade-offs. That is the fundamental position of the Stakeholder Theory, and this chapter aligns with that viewpoint. However, the critical question is how businesses struggling to make ends meet in Africa's volatile, uncertain, complex and ambiguous business environments can carry the additional burden of social investments, especially where governments are negligent, incompetent, corrupt and derelict. In that regard, the chapter offers a few recommendations:

- Organisations should rethink the underlying philosophy guiding their social investments. There is nothing wrong with philanthropic gestures or giving back to society, but as a basis for CSR, it can hardly deliver optimal value for shareholders or stakeholders. As Porter and Kramer (2006) suggest, organisations operating in Africa should migrate from 'responsive' CSR to 'strategic' CSR by carefully transforming their value-chain activities or improving their competitive contexts to benefit society and business. For example, it makes more sense for a bread-making factory in Nairobi to provide funding or assistance to wheat-growing farmers in nearby communities and offer scholarships to encourage breakthroughs in wheat processing than investing in HIV prevention programmes.
- Although the regulatory environment in Africa is weak and easy to manipulate, organisations that intend to remain in business over the long term must resist the temptation to take advantage of the situation. While African governments are encouraged to improve regulatory and enforcement mechanisms to prevent harm to society and hold businesses more accountable, the conduct of corporate entities must be ethical! Being ethical implies that organisations should respect the laws/policies governing their operations, promote fairness, justice, trustworthiness, citizenship and care for *all* stakeholders in their day-to-day activities. As one can see from the experiences of several oil-producing companies in the Niger Delta, businesses that ignore ethical principles will fail eventually, sooner or later.
- The gateway to scaling the impact of CSR in the continent is expanding the net to include MSMEs, especially in the post-COVID-19 Pandemic era. CSR is still conceived as only the responsibility of large corporations with deep pockets. That fallacy has prevented the cascading of the benefits of CSR—especially concerning brand value, brand loyalty, brand trust, brand equity and brand patronage—to MSMEs. Perhaps, a lot more education is required to help small and medium business owners understand how CSR can contribute to the growth of their business and how to approach it strategically. This

chapter suggests that governments and other relevant organisations should sponsor more workshops and seminars on the subject matter to create the necessary awareness across the continent to support MSMEs. It also recommends that MSMEs seek professional guidance for CSR activities to optimise value creation for shareholders and stakeholders with limited resources. Where they cannot afford one, it is possible to pull funds together and engage the service of professionals or consultants on CSR. Some small and medium enterprises are currently doing that to access the services of other professionals, such as lawyers, accountants and financial consultants.

Africa is of great interest to the world as the next frontier of economic revolution. Enhancing CSR to create sustainable value for business and society will reposition the continent for investments, stability and growth in the years ahead. It is not just the right thing to do; it is the smart thing to do now!

References

Aaker, D. A. (1991). *Managing brand equity: Capitalising on the value of a brand name.* Free Press.

Aguinis, H., & Glavas, A. (2012). What we know and don't know about corporate social responsibility: A review and research agenda. *Journal of Management, 38*(4), 932–968.

Aimie-Jade, B. (2011, July). *Corporate social responsibility and its effects on Brand Trust.* AUT Business School, Auckland University of Technology.

Akhigbe, J. O., & Olokoyo, F. O. (2019). Corporate Social Responsibility & Brand loyalty in the Nigerian telecommunication industry. *Earth and Environmental Science, 3*(31), 1–16.

Amaeshi, K., Adi, B., Ogbechie, C., & Amao, O. (2006). *Corporate social responsibility in Nigeria: Western mimicry or indigenous influences?* International Centre for Corporate Social Responsibility. Nottingham University Business School.

Amodu, N. (2017). Regulation and enforcement of corporate social responsibility in corporate Nigeria. *Journal of African Law, 61*(1), 105–130.

António, N. S. (2007). Stakeholders' theory and corporate social responsibility in China. *Euro Asia Journal of Management, 17*(34), 109–121.

Carroll, A. B. (1979). A three-dimensional model of corporate social performance. *Academy of Management Review, 4*(4), 497–505.

Carroll, A. B. (1991). The pyramid of corporate social responsibility: Toward the moral management of organisational stakeholders. *Business Horizons, 4*(1), 39–48.

Chaudhry, A. A., & Ramakrishnan, S. A. (2019). Corporate social responsibility, brand equity, and shareholder value: Theoretical and conceptual perspectives. *International Journal of Recent Technology and Engineering, 8*(2), 22–31.

Clarkson, M. B. (1995). A stakeholder framework for analysing and evaluating corporate social performance. *Academy of Management Review, 20*(1), 92–117.

Crane, B. (2020). Revisiting who, when and why stakeholders matter: Trust and stakeholder connectedness. *Business & Society, 59*(2), 263–286.

Daubry, P. M. (2020). *Corporate social responsibility and Organisational performance of oil companies in southern Nigeria*. Walden University. Walden Dissertations and Doctoral Studies. https://scholarworks.waldenu.edu/dissertations

Donaldson, T., & Preston, L. (1995). The stakeholder theory of the corporation: Concepts, evidence and implications. *Academy of Management Review, 20*(1), 65–91.

Dorobantu, S. (2019). Sketches of new and future research on stakeholder management. In J. S. Harrison, J. B. Barney, R. E. Freeman, & R. A. Phillips (Eds.), *The Cambridge handbook of stakeholder theory* (pp. 256–263). Cambridge University Press.

Freeman, R. E. (n.d.). *Stakeholder theory*. Retrieved October 1, 2022, from about the stakeholder theory http://stakeholdertheory.org/about

Freeman, R. (1984). *Strategic management: A stakeholder approach*. Boston, MA: Pitman Publishing.

Freeman, R. E., & Dmytriyev, S. (2017). Corporate social responsibility and stakeholder theory: Learning from each other. *Emerging Issues in Management, 2*(1), 7–15.

Freeman, R. E., Phillips, R., & Sisodia, R. (2020). Tensions in stakeholder theory. *Business & Society, 59*(2), 213–231.

Friedman, M. (1970, September 13). The social responsibility of a business is to increase its profits. *The New York Times Magazine*.

Gonçalves, A. (2020, March 4). *Top 10 companies with the best corporate (CSR) reputation in 2020*. Retrieved August 12, 2022, from Youmatter: https://youmatter.world/en/top-10-companies-reputation-csr-2020/

Gudjonsdottir, E., & Jusubova, A. (2015). *CSR's effect on brand image*. Kristianstad University.

Hamidu, A. A., Haron, H. M., & Amran, A. (2015). Corporate social responsibility: A review on definitions, core characteristics and theoretical perspectives. *Mediterranean Journal of Social Sciences, 6*(4), 83–95.

Helg, Å. (2007). *Corporate social responsibility from a Nigerian perspective*. Handelshögskolan vid Göteborgs Universitet.

Hoeffler, S., & Keller, K. (2002). Building brand equity through corporate societal marketing. *Journal of Public Policy & Marketing, 12*(2), 78–89.

Ihugba, B. U. (2012). Compulsory regulation of CSR: A case study of Nigeria. *Journal of Politics and Law, 5*(2), 68–81.

James, L. (2012). Sustainable corporate social responsibility: An analysis of 50 definitions from 2000–2011. *International Journal of Multidisciplinary Research, 2*(10), 169–193.

Jhunior, R. O., Johnston, N. G., Boaventura, J. M., & Barbero, E. R. (2021). Value cocreation within the stakeholder theory: Taking stock and moving forward. *Revista de Administração da UNIMEP, 19*(1), 26–50.

Juggernath, S., Rampersad, R., & Reddy, K. (2011). Corporate responsibility for socio-economic transformation: A focus on broad-based black economic empowerment and its implementation in South Africa. *African Journal of Business Management, 5*(20), 8224–8234.

Kabir, M. H., Mukuddem-Petersen, J., & Petersen, M. A. (2015). Corporate social responsibility evolution in South Africa. *Problems and Perspectives in Management, 13*(4), 281–289.

Ketola, T. (2008). A holistic corporate responsibility model: Integrating values, discourses, and actions. *Journal of Business Ethics, 80*(3), 419–435.

Knippenberg, L., & De Jong, E. D. (2010). Moralising the market by moralising the firm. *Journal of Business Ethics, 96*(1), 17–31.

Lantos, G. P. (2003). Corporate socialism masquerades as "CSR": The difference between being ethical, altruistic and strategic in business. *Strategic Direction, 19*(6), 31–35.

Mamudu, A., Mamudu, A., Elehinafe, F., & Akinneye, D. (2021). Recent trends in corporate social responsibilities in Nigeria—A case study of major oil firms in the Niger Delta region. *Scientific African, 13*(1), 1–16.

Menezes, D. C., Vieira, D. M., & Oliveira, J. E. (2022). Stakeholder theory: Its evolution and research agenda. *Iberoamerican Journal of Strategic Management, 21*(1), 1–34.

Mitchell, R. K., Agle, B. R., & Wood, D. J. (1997). Toward a theory of stakeholder identification and salience: Defining the principle of the who and what really counts. *Academy of Management Review, 22*(1), 853–886.

National Bureau of Statistics. (2019). *Micro, small, and medium enterprises (MSME) National Survey 2017 report*. National Bureau of Statistics.

Ogbu, S. U. (2022). Corporate social responsibility and brand development in emerging markets: Lessons from the COVID-19 interventions in Nigeria. In O. Adeola, R. E. Hinson, & A. M. Sakkthivel (Eds.), *Marketing communications and brand development in emerging economies* (pp. 157–179). Palgrave Macmillan.

Okoye, A. (2009). Theorising corporate social responsibility as an essentially contested concept: Is a definition necessary. *Journal of Business Ethics, 89*(1), 613–627.

Ormiston, M. E., & Wong, E. M. (2013). License to ill: The effects of corporate social responsibility and CEO moral identity on corporate social irresponsibility. *Personal Psychology, 66*(4), 861–893.

Pesqueux, Y., & Damak-Ayadi, S. (2005). Stakeholder theory in perspective. *Corporate Governance, 5*(2), 5–21.

Porter, M., & Kramer, M. R. (2011). Creating shared value. *Harvard Business Review, 2*(1), 62–77.

Porter, M. E., & Kramer, M. R. (2006). Strategy and society: The link between competitive advantage and corporate social responsibility. *Harvard Business Review, 84*(12), 78–92.

PwC. (2020, June 1). *PwC's MSME survey 2020*. Retrieved from www.pwc.com; https://www.pwc.com/ng/en/assets/pdf/pwc-msme-survey-2020-final.pdf

Rampersad, R., & Skinner, C. (2014). Examining the practice of corporate social responsibility (CSR) in sub-Saharan Africa. *Corporate Ownership & Control, 12*(1), 723–732.

Rose, J., Flak, L. S., & Saebo, O. (2018). Stakeholder theory for the e-government context: Framing a value-oriented normative core. *Government Information Quarterly, 35*(1), 362–374.

Sheehy, B. (2015). Defining CSR: Problems and solution. *Journal of Business Ethics, 1*(31), 625–648.

Smith, G. H. (2013). *The system of liberty - themes in the history of classical liberalism*. Cambridge University Press.
Stakeholder Democracy Network. (2022, August 31). *Amid new concerns over the Ogoniland clean-up*. Retrieved October 6, 2022, from SDN: https://www.stakeholderdemocracy.org/press-release-amid-new-concerns-over-the-ogoniland-clean-up-uneps-departure-will-worsen-the-situation-and-the-people-of-ogoniland-deserve-better/
Vidal, J. (2011, August 4). *Niger delta oil spill clean-up will take 30 years, says UN*. Retrieved October 6, 2022, from The Guardian: https://www.theguardian.com/environment/2011/aug/04/niger-delta-oil-spill-clean-up-un
Wishloff, J. (2009). The land of realism and the shipwreck of idea-ism: Thomas Aquinas and Milton Friedman on the social responsibilities of business. *Journal of Business Ethics, 85*(2), 137–155.
Wodu, A. (2021, August 6). *Illegal deductions: Bank customers lodge 23,526 complaints, recover N89.2bn*. Retrieved August 27, 2022, from Punch: https://punchng.com/illegal-deductions-bank-customers-lodge-23526-complaints-recover-n89-2bn/
World Business Council for Sustainable Development. (2000). *Corporate social responsibility: Making good business sense*. World Business Council for Sustainable Development.
Yafugborhi, E. (2022, January 20). *Ogoni oil: Shell's exit has cost Nigeria $178bn loss—MOSOP*. Retrieved October 6, 2022, from Vanguard: https://www.vanguardngr.com/2022/01/ogoni-oil-shells-exit-has-cost-nigeria-178bn-loss-mosop/

13

Enhancing Responsible Logistics and Supply Chain Effectiveness: Navigating Current Challenges

Marvel Ogah

Introduction

The international markets have been liberalised and deregulated, as the production and consumption in several markets are strongly shaped by firms operating a globalised supply chain. Most businesses, especially multinational brands based in the developed worlds, focus on activities on the high end of the value chain, such as product design, marketing, and brand management within their countries, but tend to outsource their operations to developing and transitioning countries to reduce their production and distribution costs (Camilleri, 2017). As a result, low-income countries' suppliers are often accused of their social and environmental deficits as they are pressured to enhance their productivity levels without the proper ethical considerations. There may be perceived shortcomings in the companies' procurement of materials and products and their supply chain's regulatory capacity, and unfair employment

M. Ogah (✉)
Lagos Business School, Pan-Atlantic University, Lekki, Nigeria
e-mail: mogah@lbs.edu.ng

conditions and unethical work practices are very likely to occur. Where labour is mainly intensive and automation is minimal, production activities tend to neglect social responsibility.

Irresponsible behaviours towards employees and the surrounding environment could negatively affect a company's competitiveness in the long term (Camilleri, 2017), as stakeholders, including consumers, are holding companies responsible for unethical practices within their supply chain (Camilleri, 2017). According to a report by Gartner, supply chain professionals tend to see an increase in their financial performance, decreased investment in waste reduction, ethical sourcing, water-efficiency improvements, and carbon emission reduction as they imbibe a sustainable supply chain (Vakil, 2021). Another study by EY shows that sustainable supply chain investments can add 12–23% to supply chain revenue. To achieve high monetary, reputational, and competitive advantages, organisations must operate their supply chain and logistics to be sustainable and ethical, prioritising visibility and transparency (Vakil, 2021).

Concepts of Responsible Logistics and Supply Chain Management

Supply chain management (SCM) coordinates the flow of goods, services, and information from the point of supply to the point of consumption; it also helps to manage complex relationships among manufacturers, intermediaries, and end users. SCM also provides companies means of developing competitive advantage and strategic positioning (Gurzawska, 2020). While organisations carry out activities within their supply chain, they tend to undertake unethical practices that harm social well-being and society's environmental or economic activities. For example, big brands in developed countries have their companies' suppliers, manufacturers, or distributors in third-world countries where their workplace environment is inhumane and hazardous.

Responsible logistics and supply chain tend to hold organisations accountable for every practice within the supply chain to ensure no social or environmental impact. Non-governmental organisations (NGOs) and customers constantly demand an increased focus on corporate responsibility practices in the value chain (Camilleri, 2017). It takes account of the issues in the supply chain, like ethical sourcing, workers' rights, fair wages, intellectual property rights, and carbon and water footprints. Inadequate monitoring of corporate social responsibility (CSR), environmental and social governance (ESG), and sustainability risk can lead to losses, a bad reputation, and legal troubles for the company (Vakil, 2021). Some organisations have contended with the challenges of how to elicit responsible development in their operational imperatives; thus, it is becoming apparent that organisations must adapt their process architecture to comply with applicable regulations, economic cum environment performance, implementing and improving logistics and supply chain while balancing the need to meet the interests of stakeholders and generate competitive advantage for their business.

According to Vakil (2021), organisations must insist on high transparency and visibility within the supply chain to ensure safe practices and responsible management along the value chain. The activities and processes of the partners down to the third-tier supplier in the supply chain must be appropriately mapped and evaluated. This depth of visibility and transparency provides a vivid picture of the entire supply chain, including the countries and factories you source commodities, parts, and materials. Take cocoa, for example: Long before it reaches a retail shelf like chocolate in Europe, the raw material used to make it (cocoa) is harvested in Africa by individual or cooperative collectors. From this initial touch point, there will likely be three to four additional touch points (processing plant, packaging facility, distributor, etc.). Supply chain mapping helps organisations stay informed on how their suppliers are connected across tiers and also understand what's happening at these touchpoints; this is vital for sustainable sourcing and responsible management.

The responsible supply chain is quickly gaining attention amongst stakeholders for the following reasons. Firstly, the flow of information amongst stakeholders is becoming faster, and therefore incidents of environmental misconduct, human rights violations, or unethical business behaviour are immediately reflected in the market (Gurzawska, 2020). As the supply chain network grows and becomes complex and unclear, management becomes increasingly difficult. These challenges are tied to identifying resource scarcity, population growth, massive urbanisation, shifting consumption patterns, market developments and internationalisation, technological advances, and disruption risks (Gurzawska, 2020). Secondly, as consumers, our beliefs, attitudes, and buying behaviour are biased due to societal and environmental concerns; therefore, we evaluate organisations according to their reputation Gurzawska, 2020. And thirdly, as corporations grow, their importance becomes an essential factor and plays a crucial role in attracting employees (both current and future) as well as investors (Gurzawska, 2020). This forces them to ensure that they are perceived rightly by talents and investors. The visibility and transparency of the supply chain are the foundation for mitigating sustainability, CSR, and ESG risks. The proper knowledge of what's happening and where it is happening across your supplier network allows a deeper understanding of potential issues and the ability to offset any brand, legal, or logistical trouble. At the same time, lack of it results in production halts, investigations, lawsuits, and regulatory action (Vakil, 2021).

Hence, the firms' proactive stance on responsible supply chain management (in conjunction with their stakeholders) will help them enhance their reputation by promoting fair practices in the labour market. At the same time, it is in their interest to protect the natural environment throughout their distributive value chain (Camilleri, 2017).

Challenges of Responsible Logistics and Supply Effectiveness in Sub-Saharan Africa: Nigeria, Ghana, Kenya, Tanzania, and South Africa

Nigeria

Nigeria is home to over 70% of the West African population, with 853 km of the Atlantic Ocean coastline spanning seven states; Nigerian market presents a vast economic opportunity for other countries, but the nation's logistics operations and seaports management is bedevilled with lots of setbacks (Kuteyi & Winkler, 2022) ranging from bottlenecks from traffic gridlock to massive trucking activity, multiple checkpoints to corruption and poor customs performance. Other critical issues affecting logistics in the region include insecurity and militancy, information asymmetry, dysfunctional road network, inadequate rail systems infrastructure, corruption, and inconsistent fiscal policies.

South Africa

In the World Bank's 2018 Logistics Performance Index, South Africa is ranked highest in Africa and 33rd globally (Kuteyi & Winkler, 2022). Its well-integrated intermodal transportation system enhances efficiency and significantly reduces the hitches experienced in logistics operations. This makes it the most favourable gateway to the rest of the African continent (Kuteyi & Winkler, 2022). However, there are some pressing issues of concern in the logistics system of South Africa, amongst others are rising costs of transportation and the increasing cost of operational infrastructure and personnel. Barloworld Logistics reported in 2014 that the highest constraint experienced in the South African supply chain is a shortage of skills—particularly in the supply chain, communications, and engineering (Kuteyi & Winkler, 2022). Despite the fact that reasoning portends improvement in environmental and overall supply chain performance, the contributions and impact on the economic growth of South Africa as occasioned by responsible supply architecture have been hindered by a plethora of challenges (Cant & Wiid, 2013; Kengne, 2016; Pretorius, 2009). These include lack of access to financing, lack of supply chain-enabled skills, lack of systems for attracting and retaining experienced managerial talents, and lack of formalised organisational structures.

Kenya

The logistic infrastructures in East Africa, especially Kenya, have improved tremendously. For instance, Kenya's infrastructure has contributed 0.5 percentage points to annual per capita GDP growth over the last decade

(Kuteyi & Winkler, 2022). Widespread use of the GSM in Kenya has led to an increase in logistics operations; over 90% of the population now has GSM cell signal access. And a public-private in Kenya's airline has significantly improved its logistics function, making Kenya's airline a top carrier in Africa. The most demanding part of the transportation route in East Africa lies with the Northern corridors. However, Kenya experiences some drawbacks in managing its logistics; the ports suffer from congestion, inefficient transhipment, performance, and low container capacity.

Ghana

The West African corridors comprise a network spanning more than 17,000 km with several transit corridors and a coastal corridor (Kuteyi & Winkler, 2022). Countries along these corridors experience similar logistic challenges; Ghana, one of the seven coastal countries in West Africa (Cote d'Ivoire, Guinea, Ghana, Togo, Senegal, Benin, and Nigeria), is faced with bureaucratic bottlenecks, poor infrastructure, inefficiency, and corruption (Kuteyi & Winkler, 2022).

Case Scenarios of Last-Mile Logistics in Sub-Saharan Africa

Tupuca is a last-mile delivery company in Angola that has expanded its operations to deliver much more than food; it also provides coal, petrol, fruit and vegetables, and even livestock to consumers living in Luanda, Angola (Eshkenazi, 2022). The future of last-mile logistics in Africa looks quite promising for Tupuca and its contemporaries as the continent is experiencing tremendous growth in its urban settlements; 21 out of the 30 fastest-growing metropolitan areas in the world are in Africa (Eshkenazi, 2022). This has many implications for the logistics industry, especially the last mile. These growing urban cities will experience an expanding middle class with disposable income and smartphones to engage in online ordering. And also, given the traffic situation due to the increasing population, consumers will prefer logistics companies to deliver their goods quickly using scooters.

Tupuca has over 140 drivers that make 17,000 deliveries every month to consumers who spend an average of $40 per order. Food delivery still accounts for most of Tupuca's revenue (Eshkenazi, 2022). Tupuca Livestock delivery feature was added to break down barriers between informal and formal markets, says the CEO Erickson Mvezi, as millions of the Luande residents are poor and living in the slums. To profitably fulfil this innovative delivery strategy, Tupuca entered a partnership with Roque Online. This startup employs an army of runners who visit markets to track down the best produce and livestock. These online services connect more sellers to buyers.

Case Scenario of Green Supply Chain Management and Logistics in Sub-Saharan Africa

The case of green supply chain management in Sub-Saharan Africa is the operation of an international organisation in South Africa called DB Schenker logistics, considered one of the global actors in the global logistics industry. Schenker started operations in South Africa in 1962 and has hired over 1000 employees today. DB Schenker Logistics has branches in Johannesburg, Durban, East London, Port Elizabeth, and Cape Town and serves over 5500 national destinations (Sandén Gustafsson & Göransson, 2014). The company believes that green logistics is imperative; companies that use natural resources are obligated to use these resources responsibly and keep the environmental impact as low as possible. DB Schenker in South Africa is given ecological targets and objectives from its headquarters in Germany. Targets include monitoring waste, recycling, environmental, and health and safety issues (Sandén Gustafsson & Göransson, 2014). They are also International Organization of Standardization (ISO) certified with the 9001, 14001, and 18001 certificates (Sandén Gustafsson & Göransson, 2014). Currently, DB Schenker has the following green logistics activities: emission compliant trucks and vehicles, regular checks and services, calculating carbon emissions, route optimisation, reverse logistics if required by the client, and implementing driver-training programmes to reduce fuel consumption. DB Schenker believes that implementing green logistics can be a cost saver if managed appropriately and make ecological sense, reduce water and electricity consumption, and improve vehicle performance.

Case Scenario of Drones Usage in Sub-Saharan Africa During the COVID-19 Pandemic

During COVID-19, a US company named Zipline began working with the government of Ghana in 2019. Today, it has six distribution centres in Ghana, reaching 2300 facilities and has partnered with Ghana's Health Ministry to deliver a range of essential medical products, including 1 million COVID-19 vaccines. The Silicon Valley-based company expanded from Rwanda, delivering blood products in 2016. A part of Ghana's COVID-19 response was using drones as Zipline's infrastructure was already in place when the pandemic stroke.

Conventionally, health supply chains in Ghana send products to facilities to ensure they don't have stock shortages. Still, the system has been inefficient as most facilities go out of stock or experience lots of waste due to product expiration. Using drones solves these problems: drones ensure products are delivered to facilities at the exact time they are needed. For example, while other countries across Africa had to reject COVID vaccines because they are too close to their expiration date, two-thirds of the COVID-19 vaccines distributed by Zipline in Ghana are one month away from expiration due to fast delivery time. And, while most missed opportunities for vaccination were related to stockouts, Zipline has reduced these instances by improving COVID-19 vaccine stock.

A study by IDinsight reveals that Zipline had a statistically significant impact on commodity availability, supply chain performance, and health. It was discovered that Zipline's services shortened vaccine stockout by 60%. The number of days those facilities were without critical medical supplies decreased by 21% and decreased the rate of people being turned down due to inventory issues by 42%. And the types of medicines and supplies stocked at health facilities also increased by 10% due to Zipline services.

Zipline warehouses products and processes orders placed by general health care workers and other customers and medical stocking orders via text, mobile, or web app. It is a robotics aeroplane manufacturer based in California, rethinking supply chains for vaccines, and other health products in undeveloped and underdeveloped areas. Zipline is supported by some of the most intelligent investors in the world, including Sequoia Capital, GV, SV Angel, Paul Allen, Jerry Yang, and Stanford University.

This shows how drones might be part of the solution to supply chain challenges in sub-Saharan Africa. Although Zipline is a dominant player in drone cargo delivery of health supplies, the technology is maturing, the industry is growing, and these findings highlight the potential for drones to deliver health products in near-real time.

Mitigation Strategies for Adopting and Adapting Eco-friendly Logistics Practices in Sub-Saharan Africa

Organisations undergo three phases to develop a more eco-friendly and sustainable supply chain management (Van Lakerveld & van Tulder, 2017). Organisations face various limiting factors in transitioning these phases that discourage successful sustainable supply chain practices. These phases are compliance, internal alignment, and external alignment.

Compliance

Compliance behaviour is often the first step organisations take towards sustainability. They often resort to finding answers to alleged claims by complying with international norms (Van Lakerveld & van Tulder, 2017). When confronted with a specific sustainability issue gaining attention of stakeholders and the government, the firm realises its reputation and competitive advantage are put at risk and quickly complies with the regulations. Examples of sustainability issues that put organisations at risk are child labour in production locations or oil spills. The compliance phase moves organisations from an inactive to a reactive business model, focusing on risk avoidance.

At this phase, sustainability within the supply chain is based on international standards and external stakeholder requirements (Van Lakerveld & van Tulder, 2017). The organisation translates these requirements to management systems or codes of conduct, which are shared with supply chain stakeholders; this then becomes the basis of their relationship with partners; if the supply chain partner does not comply with standards, they are rejected (Van Lakerveld & van Tulder, 2017). And through supervision, monitoring, and reporting, proper checks and balances are put in place. The compliance perspective is extrinsically motivated, not efficient; it's a reaction to an external trigger resulting from a liability-oriented attitude and a realisation that companies can do more in building a sustainable supply chain (Van Lakerveld & van Tulder, 2017).

Internal Alignment

The internal alignment phase describes when the organisation internalises the external expectations of stakeholders and the government on sustainability and CSR into the companies' supply chain management practices (Van Lakerveld & van Tulder, 2017). At this point, companies must hold themselves accountable for responding to their operations' social and environmental concerns and incorporate sustainability plans into their organisational strategy. Sustainability, in this case, becomes part of the long-term strategy internally and partly externally at this stage. Martinuzzi and Krumay (2013) defined this stage as strategic CSR, or 'rethink your business'. Organisations at this stage are intrinsically motivated to implement sustainability and not primarily by the desire to avoid risk. This shift from a reactive to an active attitude creates that internal alignment to advance sustainability within a company and, by extension, the chain (Tulder et al., 2016).

External Alignment

External alignment characterises a transition to a proactive approach. In this case, the company's entire supply chain is integrated into its sustainability plan while seeking opportunities to impact the chain and related communities positively. They work with different partners at this stage to create the intended effect while guiding their actions with established preconditions. Since the external alignment phase will require organisations to make a positive impact beyond their companies to society, it is therefore essential to align company goals with that of society. This supply chain management strategy focuses on shared responsibility in a broader sustainability context.

When it comes to screening for supply chain risks related to sustainability, CSR, and ESG, some common principles and best practices should be applied:

Monitor. Be sure you are monitoring your suppliers across key risk areas. Examples include health and safety issues, unpaid wages, underage labour, illegal overtime, pollution violations, bans, warnings, and investigations.

Quantify. Once monitoring is underway, highlight which suppliers have more robust CSR, sustainability, and ESG policies and practices. This way, you can single out those suppliers that might be more vulnerable and potentially cause legal, brand, or supply issues.

Mitigate. Work with the at-risk suppliers to develop joint plans to close gaps and ensure limited exposure to any trouble. If the risk is too significant, terminating the relationship and finding a new supplier might make sense.

Track. Maintain active tracking and report whatever mitigation plans you have in place to close gaps (Vakil, 2021).

Key Recommendations

1. Investors must devote substantial attention to sustainability issues with the urgent need to improve sustainable supply chains and long-term economic growth. This approach by investors will foster a long-term commitment to eliciting responsible supply chain ecosystems.
2. Global multinationals and governmental institutions need to develop an internal culture of supply chain management with a long-term view of convincing top management to curate and foster value creation based on responsible and ethical rules of creating value add.
3. The private and public sectors should leverage the tenets of the circular economy with a tandem aim of engendering value creation focused on returns of goods, waste management, and recycling of used goods. However, this strand of the decision should be geared towards innovation hinged on digitalisation.
4. People and leadership capabilities are critical to developing responsible chain management in sub-Saharan Africa; these are essential imperatives for quantifying, monitoring, mitigating, and tracking value flow within an accountable value chain.

Conclusion

Responsible supply chain management encompasses green purchasing, reverse logistics, eco-design, environmental performance, and eco-friendly legislation and regulatory practices (Epoh & Mafini, 2018). These components of an emergent responsible supply chain have been critical imperatives regarding competitive advantage for players in the global business ecosystem. There is an urgent drive for organisations to implement responsible supply chains eliciting the triple bottom line of people, planet, and prosperity in sync with the social dimensions of human capital, environment, and economic implications (Van Dam & Van Trijp, 2011). In this vain, business organisations implement and orchestrate global distribution, production, and service delivery with the supply chain ecosystem in connection with the interests of clients and suppliers in an evolving complex supply chain (Kannothra, Manning & Haigh, 2018). However, for an emergent supply chain to attain the level of the socially sustainable supply chain, it must connote a gamut of practices and initiatives that are relevant to and critical for global supply chain imperatives: health and safety programmes for employees, protections against child and slave labour, providing proper working conditions, supporting human rights, and sponsoring community impact programmes (Croom et al., 2018); this occurrence would accommodate the growing demands for customer-centric and environment-centric supply value chain the produces eco-friendly products and services that inhabit new customer demands.

A school of thought also contend that a responsible business status can be achieved when it maintains or regenerates natural, social, and economic capital beyond the value perimeter of the organisation in question (Freudenreich et al., 2019); another school of thought also argued that the concept of a responsible supply chain management could be regarded as evolving concept of business sustainability that strives to meet the needs of investors, employees, clients, and managers, without compromising its ability to satisfy the needs of future stakeholders in the long term (Jim-Yuh et al., 2019; Bacallan, 2000). Conclusively, responsible supply chain management seeks to enhance organisations' competitiveness by leveraging improvements via recalibration of the supply chain architecture, environmental concerns, and customers' needs in producing goods and services.

References

Bacallan, J. J. (2000). Greening the supply chain. *Business and Environment, 6*(5), 11–12.

Camilleri, M. A. (2017). The rationale for responsible supply chain management and stakeholder engagement. *Journal of Global Responsibility (Forthcoming).* Available at SSRN: https://ssrn.com/abstract=2923152

Cant, M. C., & Wiid, J. A. (2013). Establishing the challenges affecting South African SMEs. *International Business & Economics Research Journal, 12*(6), 707–716. https://doi.org/10.19030/iber.v12i6.7869

Croom, S., Vidal, N., Spetic, W., & Marshall, D. (2018). Impact of social sustainability orientation and supply chain practices on operational performance. *International Journal of Operations and Production Management, 38*, 2344–2366. https://doi.org/10.1108/IJOPM-03-2017-0180

Epoh, L. R., & Mafini, C. (2018). Green supply chain management in small and medium enterprises: Further empirical thoughts from South Africa. *Journal of Transport and Supply Chain Management, 12*. https://doi.org/10.4102/jtscm.v12i0.393

Abe Eshkenazi. (2022). *Last-mile delivery apps grow African economies one goat at a time*. Retrieved July 19, 2022, from https://www.ascm.org/ascm-insights/scm-now-impact/last-mile-delivery-apps-grow-african-economies-one-goat-at-a-time/

Freudenreich, B., Ludeke-Freund, F., & Schaltegger, S. (2019). A stakeholder theory perspective on business models: Value creation for sustainability. *Journal of Business Ethics, 1*(16), 1–17. https://doi.org/10.1007/s10551-019-04112-z

Gurzawska, A. (2020). Towards responsible and sustainable supply chains–innovation, multi-stakeholder approach and governance. *Philosophy of Management, 19*(3), 267–295. https://doi.org/10.1007/s40926-019-00114-z

Jim-Yuh, H., Kao-Yi, S., Joseph, C. P. S., & Gwo-Hshiung, T. (2019). Strengthen financial holding companies' business sustainability using a hybrid corporate governance evaluation model. *Sustainability, 11*, 582–608. https://doi.org/10.3390/su11030582

Kannothra C. G., Manning S., & Haigh N. (2018). How hybrids manage growth and social-business tensions in global supply chains: The case of impact sourcing. *Journal of Business Ethics, 148*, 271–290.

Kengne, B. D. (2016). Mixed-gender ownership and financial performance of SMEs in South Africa: A multidisciplinary analysis. *International Journal of Gender and Entrepreneurship, 8*(2), 117–136. https://doi.org/10.1108/IJGE-10-2014-0040

Kuteyi, D., & Winkler, H. (2022). Logistics challenges in sub-Saharan Africa and opportunities for digitalization. *Sustainability, 14*(4), 2399.

Martinuzzi, A., & Krumay, B. (2013). The good, the bad, and the successful – how corporate social responsibility leads to competitive advantage and organizational transformation. *Journal of Change Management, 13*. https://doi.org/10.1080/14697017.2013.851953

Pretorius, M. (2009). Defining business decline, failure and turnaround: A content analysis. *South African Journal of Entrepreneurship & Small Business Management, 2*(1), 1–16. https://doi.org/10.4102/sajesbm.v2i1.15

Sandén Gustafsson, H., & Göransson, H. (2014). *Green logistics in South Africa: A study of the managerial perceptions in the road transportation industry in South Africa.*

Tulder, R., & Seitanidi, M. M., Crane, A., & Brammer, S. (2016). Enhancing the impact of cross-sector partnerships. *Journal of Business Ethics, 135.* https://doi.org/10.1007/s10551-015-2756-4

Vakil, B. (2021, September 16). *Responsible supply chains: 'Tier 1' visibility no longer cuts it.* Retrieved March 17, 2022, from https://www.supplychainbrain.com/blogs/1-think-tank/post/33698-ensuring-responsible-supply-chains-going-beyond-tier-one

Van Dam, Y. K., & Van Trijp, H. C. M. (2011). Cognitive and motivational structure of sustainability. *Journal of Economic Psychology, 32,* 726–741. https://doi.org/10.1016/J.JOEP.2011.06.002

Van Lakerveld, A., & van Tulder, R. (2017). Managing the transition to sustainable supply chain management practices: Evidence from Dutch leader firms in Sub-Saharan Africa. *Review of Social Economy, 75*(3), 255–279.

14

Corporate Governance in Africa: Key Challenges and Running Effective Boards

Chris Ogbechie and Adebunmi Arije

Overview of Corporate Governance: Definition, Attributes, and Functions

The diverse and constantly changing nature of business globally has made corporate governance a nebulous concept. Although there is no single universally accepted definition of corporate governance, the understanding of the concept has been somewhat uniform. This concept has been explained in terms of its components, structure, principles, and purpose. O'Donovan (2003) defined corporate governance as an internal system encompassing policies, processes, and people, which serves the needs of shareholders and other stakeholders, by directing and controlling management activities with good business savviness, objectivity, accountability, and integrity. The corporate governance structure specifies the distribution of rights and responsibilities among different participants in the corporation, such as the board, managers, shareholders, and spells out

C. Ogbechie (✉) • A. Arije
Lagos Business School, Pan-Atlantic University, Lekki, Nigeria
e-mail: cogbechie@lbs.edu.ng; aarije@lbs.edu.ng

the rules and procedures for making decisions on corporate affairs (Gillan, 2006).

Corporate governance can be defined as the institutional, legal, and regulatory framework that governs the relationship between the managers and investors in a firm, whether it be private, publicly traded, or state-owned (African Development Bank, 2007). Corporate governance refers to the system of rules, practices, and processes by which a company is directed, governed, and controlled. The framework of laws, regulations, and customs shapes the organisation's strategic and operational decisions, as well as power distribution among different stakeholders. It also helps ensure that the other organisations' operation is transparent, law-abiding, accountable, responsible, and sustainable; corporate governance entails practically every sphere of management an organisation chooses to adopt in setting, achieving, and monitoring its goals and purpose.

Purpose of Corporate Governance

Irrespective of size and structure, corporate governance is an essential aspect of any organisation and plays a crucial role in ensuring organisational success and sustainability by governing the behaviour of the organisation and its management, as well as protecting all stakeholders' interests. In 2004, the Organization for Economic Corporations and Development (OECD) noted that the main purpose of corporate governance is to help build an environment of trust, transparency, and accountability necessary for fostering long-term investment, financial stability, and business integrity, thereby supporting stronger growth and more inclusive societies (OECD, 2004).

Good corporate governance ensures corporate success and economic growth by maintaining investors' confidence, lowering the cost of capital and minimising wastages, corruption, risks, and mismanagement, among others (Mishra et al., 2021). Responsible and transparent corporate governance provides the infrastructure to make good quality and ethical decisions that benefit all its stakeholders, become attractive to investors, build sustainable businesses, and enable them to create long-term value more effectively. Good corporate governance can help to promote long-term sustainable growth; protect the value of the company's assets and investments; enhance the reputation of the organisation, which can be beneficial for attracting new investors, customers, and business partners; minimise the risk of legal and regulatory violations; build trust and confidence among shareholders, employees, customers, and other stakeholders; increased investment; better employee retention; improved customer satisfaction; and an overall better reputation for the organisation.

On the other hand, when the principles of corporate governance are violated, it can have a range of negative consequences for the company, its shareholders, and other stakeholders. Some of the potential consequences of corporate governance violations include financial losses, reputational damage, legal consequences, loss of trust or even change in management, and/or board of directors. There is evidence of corporate governance failure cases that have had significant consequences on the organisation. Some examples are Enron (an energy company) total collapse in 2001, WorldCom (a telecommunication firm) in 2002, the famous Lehman Brothers, an investment bank, poor risk management led to their failure in 2008, Wirecard (German payment service provider) filed for insolvency in 2020 due to poor management.

Principles of Corporate Governance

The principles of corporate governance refer to the set of guidelines, rules, and practices that govern the actions and decisions of a company's board of directors, management, and shareholders and all other stakeholders. They are referred to as the foundation of a good governance structure because it entails the features that define its effectiveness. These principles are not exhaustive and differ among countries, sectors, or industries. Some of the main attributes of corporate governance are discussed as follows.

- Transparency: The company should disclose accurate and timely information to shareholders and other stakeholders, including financial reports and other relevant information.

- Accountability: The company should be answerable to all its stakeholders for its actions and decisions. This includes the accountability of the board and management to stakeholders.
- Fairness: The company should treat all stakeholders equally and should not engage in activities that would benefit one group of stakeholders at the expense of others.
- Independence: The company should have a board of directors that is independent of management and that is able to provide effective oversight of the company's operations.
- Ethical behaviour: The company should conduct its business in an honourable manner and adhere to all relevant laws and regulations.
- Long-term perspective: The company should have a long-term outlook when making decisions and should not make decisions that would benefit the company in the short-term but would harm it in the long term.

Other principles are stakeholder engagement, board diversity, performance evaluation, succession planning, shareholder rights, social and environmental responsibility, and a code of conduct. These attributes are used to evaluate the quality of corporate governance in a company and can be used to identify areas that need improvement.

Elements of Corporate Governance

Corporate governance principles and practices vary around the world; the elements may also differ based on the type, size, and structure of the organisation, sector, and region. Crowe Horwath in 2009 identified seven interrelated components: Board of directors and committees, legal and regulatory, disclosure and transparency, business practices and ethics, enterprise risk management, monitoring, and communication. Mishra et al., (2021) reported five elements of corporate governance: Strategic goals, employees, community, customers and suppliers, and compliance. Regardless of the specific corporate governance elements, corporate governance components can be grouped into two: internal and external components. Internal components are corporate governance mechanisms that are within the organisation's role. Examples of such are the board of directors, management, and employees. In contrast, external components are the corporate governance elements that are outside the power of the organisations. Such components include creditors, shareholders, governments, communities, customers, and suppliers.

Here are a few notes on key corporate governance elements.

- Board of Directors and Committees: the board establishes the direction and values of an organisation, oversees performance, and protects shareholder interests by using peer boards and best practices in the industry (Julien & Rieger, 2011).
- Management: these are mechanisms for effective oversight and control of the company's management. It is responsible for implementing the board's decisions and running the company's day-to-day operations.
- Shareholders: responsible for electing board members and controlling the company through their voting rights. The rights and equitable treatment of shareholders are consequential.
- Auditors: in charge of the transparency and integrity of the company's financial and non-financial reporting.
- Stakeholders: they include shareholders, employees, customers, governments, suppliers, and the community at large who impact and are impacted by the company's actions.
- Legal and regulatory: these are the legal boundaries within which a company operates. They encompass the requirements set forth by the company, governments (international, federal, and state), as well as industry associations.
- Business practices and ethics: Business practices are a company's operational tactics and measures to achieve its purpose and strategy. Ethics are the moral boundaries an organisation believes it should observe when pursuing competitive objectives.
- Monitoring: ensures the governance framework operates as intended and provides reporting to various levels of the organisation. At the most fundamental level, monitoring systems look at "what is" versus "what should be."

Models of Corporate Governance

Broadly, there are three main models of corporate governance: shareholder-centric, stakeholder-centric, and hybrid.

* Shareholder-centric model: This is also known as the "Anglo-American" model, and a strocharacterised in the rights and interests of shareholders characterises it. In this model, the board of directors is elected by shareholders and is responsible for making decisions that are in the best interests of the company's shareholders. This model is often associated with countries like the United States and United Kingdom.
* Stakeholder-centric model: This model is also known as the "Continental European" or "German" model and is characterised by a strong emphasis on the rights and interests of all stakeholders, including shareholders, employees, customers, and the community. In this model, a supervisory board often appoints the board of directors, representing all stakeholders' interests. This model is often associated with Germany, France, and other countries in continental Europe.
* Hybrid model: This model combines both shareholder-centric and stakeholder-centric elements. In this model, the board of directors is elected by shareholders, but is also responsible for considering the interests of all stakeholders. This model is often associated with countries like Japan, Australia, and Canada.

Some of the other corporate governance models are discussed as follows:

* The Asian model: commonly found in Asian countries such as Japan, China, Korea, and Singapore. The Asian model is often considered a hybrid model with key characteristics like a strong emphasis on long-term planning and stability, close relationships between companies and government, and greater use of insider control.
* The Latin American model: is characterised by a lack of transparency and weak shareholder rights.

- The African model: is mainly characterised by weak legal systems and a lack of transparency.
- The Middle Eastern model: is characterised by the concentration of ownership and control in the hands of a small number of large shareholders.
- Family-controlled model: the board of directors is often composed of family members, and decision-making is often based on the interests of the family rather than the company's shareholders.
- State-controlled model: the government appoints or controls a significant portion of the board of directors, and decision-making is often based on the government's interests rather than the company's shareholders.
- Islamic model: the board of directors is responsible for ensuring that the company's activities are in compliance with Islamic law and that the company's profits are distributed equitably.

Finally, note that these models are not mutually exclusive and different models can coexist within the same country depending on other factors. Also, a company's model may change over time as the company's operational environment or the country's business environment evolves.

Corporate Governance Across Sectors: Public, Private, and Social Sectors

Corporate governance in the public sector is focused on ensuring that public resources are used efficiently and that the government is accountable to citizens. This includes transparency in the use of public funds and oversight by elected officials and independent bodies. In the private sector, corporate governance maximises shareholder value and profitability. This includes transparency in financial reporting, decision-making, and oversight by the board of directors and independent auditors. Lastly, corporate governance in the social sector is focused on ensuring that an organisation's resources are used to achieve its mission and fulfil its social purpose. This includes transparency in financial reporting, decision-making, and oversight by the board of directors and independent auditors.

There are a few similarities between corporate governance in the public, private, and social sectors. All sectors strive to be transparent in their financial reporting and decision-making processes. They all aim to be accountable to their stakeholders, whether they are shareholders, taxpayers, funders, or clients. Conducting their activities in an ethical manner, adhering to all relevant laws and regulations, protecting the environment and the communities where they operate, proper identification, assessment, and management of potential risks, performance evaluation, as well as stakeholder engagement and fair treatment.

While there are similarities, it's important to note that the specifics of corporate governance practices, regulations, and expectations vary in the different sectors. Here are some of the key differences among the three sectors.

- Ownership: In the public sector, the organisation is owned by the government and controlled by elected officials. In the private sector, the organisation is owned by shareholders and controlled by the board of directors. In the social sector, the organisation is often owned by a combination of shareholders, donors, and stakeholders and is controlled by a board of directors.
- Decision-making: In the public sector, decision-making is often more centralised and bureaucratic and is subject to political influence. In the private sector, decision-making is often more decentralised and is driven by market forces. In the social sector, decision-making is often guided by the organisation's mission and values and is driven by the community's needs
- Performance evaluation: In the public sector, performance evaluation is often based on compliance with laws and regulations and on meeting specific policy goals set by the government. In the private sector, performance evaluation is often based on financial performance, such as profitability and return on investment. In the social sector, performance evaluation is often based on the organisation's impact on the community and its ability to achieve its mission.
- Stakeholder engagement: In the public sector, stakeholders include citizens, taxpayers, and other groups that may be affected by government policies. In the private sector, stakeholders include shareholders,

customers, employees, suppliers, and other groups that may be affected by the company's operations. In the social sector, stakeholders include clients, donors, volunteers, and other groups that may be affected by the organisation's activities.
- Transparency and reporting: Public sector organisations are often subject to more stringent transparency and reporting requirements than private sector organisations, and their activities and financials are subject to more public scrutiny. Social sector organisations may also have specific reporting requirements, depending on the nature of their activities and funding.

The above-mentioned distinctions are generalisations, and there might be variations and overlap between sectors; for example, many private organisations have a social purpose or are socially responsible and thus have some features of governance similar to the social sector. Additionally, the corporate governance practices and regulations in different countries may also vary.

Corporate Governance in Africa

Corporate governance in Africa was not given serious attention until the beginning of the 1980s. Since then, the African corporate governance landscape has witnessed significant and progress. However, the pace of the progress has not been uniformed among the countries on the continent. For example, some countries, such as South Africa, Mauritius, Botswana, and Cape Verde, have well-developed corporate governance systems and regulations in place. In contrast, the corporate governance in Nigeria, Kenya, and Ghana has improved greatly but is yet to be considered developed. Other countries like Zimbabwe and Mozambique are at the other extreme and corporate governance is still embryonic.

The concept in Africa is experiencing significant evolvement with the different reforms across the other countries. In Nigeria, the Corporate Governance Code for public companies was introduced in 2010, and the Nigerian Stock Exchange has been working to improve corporate governance practices by listing companies that meet its standards. The Capital

Markets Authority launched the Corporate Governance Code in Kenya in 2009. At the same time, the Ghana's Securities and Exchange Commission has implemented several measures to improve corporate governance, including introducing a Corporate Governance Code for public companies in 2013. The Johannesburg Stock Exchange in South Africa has also implemented few measures to improve corporate governance, including the introduction of a Corporate Governance Code for listed companies in 2002. In 2017, Egypt introduced Corporate Governance Code for public companies through its Capital Market Authority. Although there are few cases of strong compliance and enforcement, the major problems with the reforms in these countries have been poor implementation and weak enforcement. In some cases, implementation of the code is even voluntary.

Generally, the African corporate governance model is one that is often characterised by weak legal systems and a lack of transparency. However, individually, the dominant model practised across African countries differs. The Anglo-American model characterised by a strong emphasis on transparency, accountability, and independent directors is mostly found in countries such as South Africa and Kenya. The Continental European model, based on the principles of stakeholder primacy and the integration of ownership and control, is dominant in countries such as Egypt and Morocco. The Hybrid model is characterised by different governance practices depending on the type of company, sector, and region leads in countries such as Nigeria and Ghana.

Furthermore, corporate governance in Africa, on the whole, is not as developed as it existed in the developed parts of the world. This is due to differences in their social, cultural, legal, and economic environments. According to NEPAD Africa Peer Review Mechanism (APRM) country reports, several factors undermine corporate governance in Africa. Some of which include the lack of progress in economic and political governance, lack of enforcement, and the existence of large informal sectors. Based on these, African countries have also had their fair deal of corporate governance failures, across different sectors and industries, with severe consequences. These African organisations include South African Airways, Satyam Computer Services, Zimbabwe Iron and Steel Company, National Bank of Ethiopia, and Ecobank.

Challenges of Corporate Governance in Africa

Corporate governance practices in Africa have been improving in recent years, but challenges still need to be addressed. Several social, economic, legal, historic, cultural, and political factors have been identified as impediments to corporate governance development in Africa. Specifically, these factors include lack of transparency, awareness and accountability, weak investor protection, institutions and regulation, corruption, weak institutions, and lack of independent directors.

* Weak legal and regulatory frameworks: Many African countries have weak legal and regulatory frameworks that do not effectively enforce corporate governance principles, leading to poor governance practices.
* Lack of transparency and accountability: Many African companies lack transparency and accountability, making it difficult for shareholders and other stakeholders to hold management accountable for their actions.
* Limited access to information: Shareholders and other stakeholders often have limited access to information about a company's financial performance and governance practices, making it difficult to make informed decisions.
* Corruption: Corruption can undermine corporate governance by allowing individuals or groups to use their positions of power for personal gain at the expense of shareholders and other stakeholders. This can lead to poor decision-making, mismanagement of resources, and a lack of accountability. Corruption is a significant issue that undermines corporate governance in countries such as Angola, Guinea, and South Sudan. This can include bribery, embezzlement, and nepotism, which can lead to poor decision-making and mismanagement of resources.
* Ownership structure: Unclear or concentrated ownership structures can lead to a lack of transparency and accountability, as well as a lack of oversight of management. This can make it difficult for shareholders to hold management accountable for their actions. In countries such as Egypt, Morocco, and Tunisia, the ownership structure of companies is often concentrated in the hands of a small group of individuals or families, which can lead to a lack of transparency and accountability.

- Unsatisfactory judicial procedures: Ineffective or corrupt judicial systems can make it difficult for shareholders and other stakeholders to seek redress for governance-related issues and can limit the ability of regulators to enforce governance principles. In countries such as Ethiopia, Democratic Republic of Congo, and Somalia, the judicial system is often weak, corrupt, or ineffective, making it difficult for shareholders and other stakeholders to seek redress for governance-related issues and limiting the ability of regulators to enforce governance principles.
- Lack of enforcement: A lack of effective enforcement of corporate governance laws and regulations can make it difficult to hold companies and individuals accountable for poor governance practices. This can create an environment in which governance principles are not taken seriously and companies can operate without adequate oversight. In countries such as Nigeria and Ghana, the lack of effective enforcement of corporate governance laws and regulations is a significant challenge, making it difficult to hold companies and individuals accountable for poor governance practices.
- Political interference: Political interference in the affairs of companies can undermine corporate governance principles, leading to poor governance practices. Political interference: In countries such as Sudan, South Africa, and Zimbabwe, political interference in the affairs of companies can undermine corporate governance principles, leading to poor governance practices.
- Limited shareholder participation: Shareholder participation in governance is limited in Africa, which can lead to a lack of oversight and accountability. Shareholder participation in government is limited in many African countries such as Ethiopia, Kenya, and Tanzania, which can lead to a lack of leadership and accountability.
- Cultural and societal factors: Cultural and societal factors can play a role in corporate governance practices in Africa, with traditional values and practices sometimes conflicting with modern governance principles.
- Limited stakeholder engagement: Many African companies do not engage with stakeholders effectively, making building trust and promoting good governance practices difficult.

- Limited resources: Many African companies lack the resources to implement effective corporate governance practices, such as hiring independent directors or establishing internal audit functions.

Addressing Corporate Governance Challenges in Africa

The corporate governance challenges in Africa are diverse and not peculiar to the continent. It is important to keep in mind that corporate governance is a continuous process, and it requires a consistent effort to improve, monitor, and enforce it. Addressing these challenges will require a comprehensive approach that requires long-term commitments and cooperation between governments, companies, investors, and other stakeholders. It is important to note that each country has its specific context, and what works in one country may not be appropriate or effective in another. Hence, it's important to tailor solutions to the specific context of each country. Several initiatives and organisations further promote good governance on the continent.

These organisations typically work to promote the adoption of best practices, raise awareness of the importance of good governance, and provide training and education to corporate governance professionals and stakeholders in Africa. Examples of such organisations on a continent-wide basis are The African Institute of Corporate Citizenship (AICC), The African Centre for Corporate Governance (ACCG), The Centre for Corporate Governance in Africa (CCGA), The Corporate Governance Network for Africa (CGNA), and The African Corporate Governance Forum (ACGF). On a regional level, there are The Corporate Governance Institute of West Africa (CGWA), The Corporate Governance Institute of East Africa (CGEA), and The Institute of Directors in Southern Africa (IoDSA). In terms of country-specific organisations, there is The Institute of Corporate Governance of Nigeria (ICGN), The Corporate Governance Forum of Tanzania (CGFTA), The Corporate Governance Institute of Namibia (CGIN), The Corporate Governance Association of Uganda (CGAU), The Corporate Governance Africa (CGA), The Centre for Corporate Governance and Ethics (CCGE) in South Africa, and The Corporate Governance Association of Kenya (CGAK).

The attention of these organisations, governments, and other regulatory agencies in Africa seeking to confront corporate governance challenges can be geared towards the following.

- Legal and regulatory reform: Improving legal and regulatory frameworks to enforce corporate governance principles effectively is critical. This can include strengthening laws and regulations related to transparency, accountability, and good faith, as well as ensuring that there are effects effective enforcement mechanisms for creation and training: Providing education organisations individuals and organisations on corporate governance principles and best practices can help to promote good governance practices. This can include training for boards of directors, management, and shareholders, and education for the general public on the importance of good governance.
- Stakeholder engagement: Encouraging engagement between companies and their stakeholders, such as shareholders, customers, employees, and the community, can promote transparency and accountability. This can include providing shareholders with information on the company's performance and governance practices and allowing them to vote on important issues.
- Independent directors: Appointing independent directors to boards of directors can promote transparency and accountability, as they are not beholden to management or other insiders and can provide an independent perspective on the company's performance and governance practices.
- Auditing and monitoring: Regularly auditing and monitoring a company's financial performance and governance practices can help ensure that they are being managed transparently and accountable. This can include internal and external audits and monitoring by regulators and other oversight bodies.
- International standards: Encouraging African companies to adopt international corporate governance standards can help to improve transparency and accountability, and to make it easier for companies to raise capital and do business internationally.
- Stronger governance institution: Establishing or strengthening institutions such as the Securities and Exchange Commission, the Central

Bank, and other regulatory bodies that oversee corporate governance, to promote transparency, accountability, and good governance.
- Corporate governance codes and guidelines: Developing and implementing corporate governance codes and guidelines can help to promote best practices and provide a framework for companies to follow. This can include codes of conduct for boards of directors and management and guidelines for shareholders and other stakeholders. With these, corporate governance ratings and indices can be developed. Developing and publishing corporate governance ratings and indices can help to promote transparency and accountability by providing information on the governance practices of companies.
- Board evaluation: Regularly evaluating the board of directors' performance can help promote transparency and accountability. It can allow shareholders and other stakeholders to provide feedback on the board's performance.
- Encourage responsible investment: Encouraging responsible investment can help to promote good governance practices by aligning the interests of investors with those of other stakeholders, such as employees and the community.
- Innovative solutions: Encouraging the use of new technologies such as blockchain, digitalisation, and artificial intelligence can improve transparency and accountability in corporate governance.

Running an Effective Boards: Emphasis on Africa

Meaning, Functions, and Characteristics of Board Effectiveness

Although in the narrow sense, boards or boards of directors are just intermediaries engaged by the shareholders (owners of the organisation) to help oversee and checkmate the activities of the management employed to watch over their resources and investments. However, they are indisputably the key player and the focal point in an organisation's governance. It is a fact that the board's composition, capability, and character greatly influence every organisation's competitiveness and performance. The board's influence comes from the leadership their leadership and oversight role in organisational.

Boards all over the world have been subjected to constant scrutiny in terms of their structure, processes, operations, and strategies. This is evident in the introduction, revision, and reforms of codes of corporate governance and laws. Moreover, from experience, major stakeholders are no longer comfortable with having a board just for its sake or for fulfilling regulators' requirements. They now seek that the board is effective in the discharge of its duties. This is true for every organisation, whether small or large; for-profit or not-for-profit; private or public, national or multi-national.

Basically, the board's functions can be grouped under four main tasks: monitoring, service, strategy, and resource provision (Amaral-Baptista & de Melo, 2010). Some of the specific functions of a board in an organisation include providing a competitive edge and access to resources, increasing efficiency and performance, and creating greater value. The board also protects shareholders' wealth through good governance and strategic direction of the organisation. The boards sometimes provide the link between the firms and their external stakeholders. Therefore, an effective board performs its responsibilities diligently and is result driven.

In Africa where the level of 'VUCA' is considered high, having an effective board becomes an obligation for any organisation aiming to achieve its purpose, create value, and succeed. Identifying the key features that distinguish a board in terms of competence and effectiveness has been of great concern for investors, shareholders, and other stakeholders. This is because no universally accepted and recognised characteristics exist among the numerous lists available. However, some basic attributes that can be identified are openness, integrity, transparency, enthusiasm, commitment, and accountability.

From experience, effective boards also have respectable, experienced, and accountable members who clearly understand their assignments and are committed to getting the job done. High board diversity in terms of age, gender, background, education, skills, and experience is also an attribute that has distinguished boards over time. The diversity in board composition brings a different perspective to the discussion or approaches the problem from a new angle. Similarly, it is essential that the directors are focused and dedicated with a shared passion for the organisation's overall success. More importantly, effective boards are often with many neutral and independent members with little or no connections with owners and management. This enables them to present sincere and unquestionable opinions towards the organisation's progress.

Drivers of Effective Boards

Due to the important and germane roles that the board performs, promoting and enhancing the effectiveness of the board has been a significant concern to all stakeholders. In addition, the numerous corporate scandals all over the world arising from negligence and incompetence of boards have now, more than ever, resulted in an increasing demand for board effectiveness. There is, therefore, the need to consider the several factors and forces that influence the extent to which a board can be effective. These factors are elements that influence everything about the board, starting from the recruitment of members to the overall behaviour of the board. These forces can be broadly grouped into internal and external drivers. Both internal and external drivers of board effectiveness are equally important and significantly impact an organisation's success through their influence on the board. Each of the internal and external drivers is examined in some detail below.

The internal drivers include the board's characteristics (such as size, age, diversity, meeting frequency, and others), the organisation's codes of conduct, resource availability, adequate information, good communication, and well-established monitoring and evaluation. The kind of relationships between the board of directors, the management, and other stakeholders of the organisation also affect how effectively the board will perform its duty. The internal drivers can strengthen, correct, modify, or even inhibit the effectiveness of a corporate board. At the same time, the internal drivers are, in most cases, under the board's control and can thus be influenced by the board to achieve their aims and objectives.

On the other hand, the external drivers are the forces that enhance or discourage the effectiveness of boards. They include the rules, institutions, laws, and regulations imposed by the government, regulatory agencies, and professional bodies. The generally acceptable standards, global best practices, market conditions, and societal expectations are external factors that can affect the board's effectiveness.

In Africa, where there are no strong institutions and well-regulated markets, the external drivers have in the past encouraged ineffective boards. However, given the severe consequences of having too numerous ineffective boards, the recent calls for stringent punishments in the form of legal and criminal sanctions against the boards have helped improve board effectiveness. Again, the recent urge to meet up with industry-specific standards and international best practices has also encouraged board effectiveness on the continent. Lastly, on the part of governments, agencies and regulators, laws and regulations have been reviewed to ensure and promote competent boards. Some of these actions include the King III code that emerged in South Africa and the revision of the Securities and Exchange Commission (SEC) code in Nigeria, among others.

Dimensions of Board Effectiveness

According to Cossin and Caballero (2014), board effectiveness has four pillars. The first dimension in ensuring the effectiveness of a board is to consider the quality, focus, and dedication of board members. The board members must be of high quality with the right level of expertise, competencies, and knowledge required to perform their tasks. Training and development programmes can also be introduced, where necessary, to ensure that the desired quality of the board members is achieved and maintained. The training for boards should include, among other things, the education and evaluation of members along the established knowledge standards, roles, and dedication to the organisation (Cossin & Caballero, 2014).

In addition, the board must also ensure that a quality workforce is recruited in the organisation, from the executive management to the lower cadres. An effective board must also put efforts into the retention of quality staff by providing good compensation, showing genuine concern about staff welfare and keeping up to date regarding obtainable best practices in both the domestic and international labour markets.

Another important pillar of board effectiveness is the quality of information and information architecture a board has. A great board makes the right or great decisions. The quality of genuine and relevant information a board has access to will largely influence the decisions such a board makes. Therefore, a board aiming at success must source for and be furnished with quality internal and external information about the business, the industry, and other related issues. This will help understand and track the business and its key value drivers. The board must be open to information derived from both formal and informal sources, not only from internal sources but also from necessary external sources.

The board structure and processes are the third dimension when evaluating its effectiveness. To a large extent, board structure and processes have greatly evolved due to the overall corporate governance refinement. Having largely independent members and well-managed board diversity regarding opinion, experience, personality, and genre greatly impacts effectiveness. Other aspects of the structure that must be evaluated are the frequency and timing of board's and committees' meetings, agenda setting and decision-making processes. When it comes to processes, boards are often advised to adopt and implement several dynamic processes as opposed to the simple straight running of the board. The board must be tactically involved in strategy, succession planning, and stakeholder engagement, encourage internal audit and control adequacy and conduct a genuine self-assessment. It is, therefore, fundamental for the board to regularly benchmark its structures and processes against the standards and best practices.

The fourth pillar is the group dynamics and governance structure. Fundamentally, this pillar is linked to the culture of the board. A board may operate functional, efficient, and active dynamics and governance structure based on its culture. The energy level, behaviour, values, and relationship among members are some of the dynamics that must be checked to promote board effectiveness.

Challenges of Board Effectiveness: Focus on Africa

In every corporate organisation globally, the boards have numerous challenges that must be overcome to ensure effectiveness. The level and extent to which these challenges influence effectiveness differ among countries, sectors, and businesses. However, the prevalent structure and conditions in which organisations operate in many African countries make the challenges more pronounced and have a stringent lasting impact. Some of these challenges emanate from the organisations, and others are the results of the economic and social conditions of the countries.

* Corporate culture problem: the perceived and obtainable culture of any organisation has a lot of impacts on the organisation. A strong and healthy culture makes companies more valuable and resilient. Similarly, a poor organisational culture reduces an organisation's values and performance. It can also have other severe negative impacts like lots of legal obligations, scandals, or even total closure of the firm. Bearing this in mind, the board is expected to set the tone regarding the culture from the top and, at the same time, ensure strict adherence to it. Measures such as constant discussion and enforcement of good behaviour and 360-degree feedback results for executives can be adopted to ensure a healthy culture.
* Social issues: businesses are now, more than ever, expected to be involved in social issues, and those that operate in Africa are no exception. Responsible corporate boards in Africa, where several social issues like poverty, inequality, and abuse are on the rise, are often overwhelmed. Effective and strategic boards are, thus, expected to design creative means of addressing these issues while still attending to their primary roles. Boards must understand that to succeed in the long term, they must focus on both financial performance and positive contributions to society. Incorporating social issues into company strategy makes organisations purpose-driven, with numerous benefits. Again, the approaches adopted in addressing these issues must be sustainable as investors, especially institutional investors, now emphasise sustainability, focusing on society's economic, social, and governance aspects.

And as such, strategic boards must have this in mind will making decisions. Accountable and transparent boards now provide an annual sustainability report detailing their efforts and impacts.

- Workplace diversity: globally, the workforce has never been as diverse as it is currently, where there are simultaneously four generations of workers in the workplace. Managing this tricky situation is tedious enough for boards as different generations require different policies. In Africa, board members not only deal with this issue, but other diversities such as ethnicity and religion are also prominent in the workplace. This makes addressing diversity cumbersome, but an effective and strategic board must recognise its presence and deal strategically with it.
- Risk and uncertainty: the risk and uncertainty level all over the world is high but higher in Africa. These risks include economic, financial, reputational, and other threats. Boards must understand and evaluate the different risks and strategically work around them. To be effective, the board must ensure an appropriate awareness level exists in the organisation; the board must ensure that a clear risk-management policy is published and that the risk-management processes adopted work effectively.
- Institutions: institutions govern all the relationships and connections between different players in an organisation and institution can be formal and informal. According to Oman et al. (2004), institutions include corporate laws, securities laws, accounting rules and guidelines, generally accepted business best practices, and fundamental business ethics. The influence of these institutions on the board's effectiveness can be either positive or negative. In Africa, the rules and laws that boards have to deal with are mostly blurred, cumbersome, inconsistent, and sometimes conflicting. It is, however, important for boards to properly understand these rules and seek expert interpretation where necessary.
- Corruption: the incidence of corruption in many African societies is high and at a level that has penetrated almost all aspects of the society. The boards in Africa are also not exempt from this situation. This is evident in the series of scandals rocking corporate organisations as a result of board corruption. At the same time, corruption in society also affects the functioning of the board itself. Boards in Africa that want

to excel and distinguish themselves from others must first ensure their members and organisation are free from corruption. Thereafter, such boards can devise means of tactically dealing with societal corruption.

Navigating Through the Complexity: Focus on Africa

Boards need to understand how to manoeuvre through the several challenges they must deal with to deliver on their task and gain the trust of the stakeholders. Some of the means through which boards, especially in Africa, can manoeuvre their way through the identified complexities are as follows:

- Leadership: deciding the appropriate leadership is one of the most critical decisions a board must always make. The board chair and management team are sensitive positions that the right individuals must occupy. The importance of having leaders with deep knowledge of the business and all it entails, good leadership skills, and other necessary qualities at the helm of affairs can never be overemphasised. Good leadership provides guidance and direction in the organisation. Therefore, boards must ensure the boards, committees, management, and department have credible and responsible leaders as chairpersons, management executives, and heads. Sustainability in leadership should also be paramount in the board's minds as soon as good leadership is established. This can be done by developing leadership in pipeline programmes, attending training, and developing viable succession plans for board members and the top management team.
- Focus on strategy: the board must be strategic in its dealings to overcome the challenges, create value, and achieve its aim. It must also be actively involved in the strategy development of the organisation. Their meetings are expected to be used for strategic issues and generative thinking. The responsibilities of the board regarding strategy are to set the direction, formulate, approve, track, and review the strategy. At the same time, their focus on strategy should ensure sustainability.

- Reinvention and innovation: the world is ever-evolving, and so are the challenges and opportunities that abound in ensuring board effectiveness. Thus, the board must keep reinventing the board's and organisation's structure, operations, and processes to stay afloat and create great value. The board should formulate policies that encourage customer-led innovation.
- Technological adoption: Technological advancement has affected all aspects of human endeavour, from learning to working and others. It will, therefore, be impossible for boards looking to navigate through the complexities and risks in the world not to consider technological adoption. An effective board that wants to succeed must encourage and be involved in the company's digital strategy.
- Stakeholder engagement: as much as engaging stakeholders is encouraged in all regards, boards must be able to classify their stakeholders considering their power and interest level. This will assist the board in knowing who deserves what. Some stakeholders require minimal effort; some only need to be informed and satisfied, while others are the key players that must be toyed with.
- Assessment of board effectiveness: a review of the board and its directors' effectiveness must be done regularly. This activity has been increasing globally due to its numerous challenges (Andersen, 2018). This can be ascribed to the benefits of board evaluation which include improving board and organisation performance, enhancing corporate governance and benchmarking against national and global best practices, attracting the right investors, promoting trust and transparency, and improving the relationship among the board, management team, and other stakeholders. Board evaluation should never be one size fits, rather a bespoke approach based on the attributes of the organisation and its board (Andersen, 2018). However, there are undoubtedly important elements of the board, such as leadership, composition, structure, culture, strategy, performance, and remuneration, germane (Andersen, 2018; Berghe & Levrau, 2013). This assessment can be done by self (board), internal monitoring and evaluation unit, or external auditors. There are also already existing swift software packages that can be employed to assess board performance.

Summary

Corporate governance came into the limelight in Africa in the 1980s, and since then it has constantly evolved and progressed. Almost all African countries have had in place codes of conduct for corporate organisations in their different countries. Although there are few cases of strong compliance and enforcement, the major problems with the reforms in these countries have been poor implementation and weak enforcement. In some instances imply, the Implementation of the code is even voluntary. Consequently, the development of corporate governance among these countries differs.

Several challenges discourage good corporate in Africa, including poor economic and political governance, lack of enforcement, ownership structure, poor stakeholders' education, and the dominance of informal sectors. Several initiatives and organisations that been developed to encourage good governance in Africa. These efforts have been focused on encouraging stakeholder engagement, performance evaluation and international standards, and advocating for legal and regulatory reforms.

The board of directors is a major element of corporate governance that is responsible for the overall effect of the corporate governance system in any organisation. This position of the board as a focal point in corporate governance has subjected it to scrutiny, and stakeholders, especially the shareholders, are no longer comfortable with an ineffective board. However, it must be recognised that the two main drivers of board effectiveness are internal and external. The internal drivers include the board's size, age, meeting frequency, and composition. In contrast, the external drivers are the rules, institutions, laws, and regulations imposed by the government, regulatory agencies, and professional bodies.

African boards, like their counterparts around the globe, encounter numerous challenges, such as corporate culture problem, social issues, poor institutions, corruption, workplace diversity, and others. To become effective, these challenges must be overcome through visionary and resilient leadership, reinvention and innovation, technological adoption, stakeholder engagement, and board evaluation.

Key Recommendations

Poor corporate governance and board ineffectiveness undoubtedly affect the overall well-being of organisations, their shareholders and other stakeholders, their domicile country, and their economy. Therefore, responsible and good corporate governance, as well as board effectiveness, must be encouraged. This chapter suggested the different approaches that can be adopted to navigate the challenges in volatile and uncertain environments. Some of these recommendations are to:

* improve state governance and institutions: this will go a long way in addressing the issues of implementing and enforcing corporate codes and encouraging board effectiveness. It will also help protect against corruption, abuse of power, and mismanagement of resources.
* develop systems and processes that will assist in effectively monitoring implementation and compliance with the established rules.
* adopt standardised evaluation methods and approaches.
* educate and train all stakeholders to promote their engagement in the corporate governance process.

References

African Development Bank. (2007). *African Development Bank corporate governance strategy [online]*.

Amaral-Baptista, M., & de Melo, M. A. (2010). Factors for board effectiveness from the perspective of strategy implementation: Proposal of an instrument. *Corporate Ownership and Control, 8*(1), 709–719.

Andersen, K. (2018). Board evaluation: A powerful tool for enhancing board performance. *Journal of Corporate Governance, 10*(1), 2074–2087.

Berghe, L. V. D., & Levrau, A. (2013). Promoting effective board decision-making, the essence of good governance. In *How to make boards work* (pp. 211–267). Palgrave Macmillan.

Cossin, D. D., & Caballero, J. (2014). *The four pillars of board effectiveness*.

Gillan, S. L. (2006). Recent developments in corporate governance: An overview. *Journal of Corporate Finance, 12*(3), 381–402.

Julien, R., & Rieger, L. (2011). *Strengthening corporate governance with internal audit.* Crowe Horwath LLP.

Mishra, B. P., Biswal, B. B., Behera, A. K., & Das, H. C. (2021). Effect of big data analytics on improvement of corporate social/green performance. *Journal of Modelling in Management, 16*(3), 922–943.

O'Donovan, G. (2003). *Change management - A board culture of corporate governance.* Mondaq Business Briefing.

OECD, O. (2004). The OECD principles of corporate governance. *Contaduría y Administración*, (216), 183.

Oman, C. P., Fries, S., & Buiter, W. (2004). *Corporate governance in developing, transition and emerging-market economies.* OECD Publishing.

15

Concluding Chapter (Summary)

Rose Ogbechie and Marvel Ogah

During the fifteen years of teaching Business Ethics and Leadership at the Lagos Business school, I realised how important it is to write this book on responsible business practices in Africa. A book focused on helping managers see how important it is to make responsible business decisions and achieve sustainability in their businesses. From my interactions with hundreds of top corporate executives of various organisations, I have discovered that many believe that making responsible business decisions and taking responsible actions is crucial for businesses to remain sustainable. However, many find it challenging to give enough voice to their values due to the structural, economic, and ethical challenges of doing business in Africa.

While it can be acknowledged that the operating business environment in Africa can be uniquely demanding and exigent, leaders who want long-term business sustainability must aim to make responsible

R. Ogbechie (✉) • M. Ogah
Lagos Business School, Pan-Atlantic University, Lekki, Nigeria
e-mail: rogbechie@lbs.edu.ng; mogah@lbs.edu.ng

business decisions and take responsible actions to help the organisation. Globally many organisations have collapsed because of unethical business decisions made by their top executives. Some others suffered corporate disrepute because of irresponsible business decisions. For example, in Nigeria, many organisations and banks also collapsed as a result of irresponsible and unethical business decisions. Many of those could have been avoided if managers had not acted out of their selfish interests.

Businesses do not operate in a vacuum. Different stakeholders contribute to a business, and leaders must consider all stakeholders' interests in business decisions. This book is focused on helping managers see how important it is to make responsible business decisions and how to go about them. It cuts across different business areas, including marketing, advertising, pricing, human resources management, leadership, business ethics, waste management, corporate governance, etc. In summary, the first two chapters expose us to business issues in Africa with case studies from Rwanda, Nigeria, Libya, and also in South Africa; these business challenges, risks, and opportunities were exploited by the authors, and it shows how business sustainability, growth, and development can be achieved. Chapter 4 addresses the issues of sustainability in business; it buttresses that making strategic plans and taking critical steps to protecting the future of a business within the industry and environment of its operation is what sustainability in business means, and businesses in Africa must achieve this to remain competitive. The next sections of the book introduce chapters that discuss various other stakeholders and business engagement of firms in Africa; Chap. 5 exposes how consumers are key business stakeholders and consumer-centric organisations need to be developed in Africa in order to protect consumers and also reach consumer satisfaction through good marketing practices and products.

Chapter 6 reminds business managers the role of responsible advertising in reaching out to potential consumers. It emphasises that issues such as promoting unhealthy or harmful products, exploiting cultural values, and perpetuating negative stereotypes have negative consequences for the business. Still, adverts must fulfil ethical obligations to promote their businesses. Chapters 7 and 8 addressed responsible pricing and responsible financial accounting strategies, respectively, each reemphasising the need for African business organisations to be transparent and accountable. Prices must be set not to get excessive profits but to meet consumer needs. Chapter 9 creates the need for desirable and suitable workplace behaviour and careers based on the employees' abilities to proffer culturally sensitive strategies for business operations process and success. Chapter 10 introduces ethical leadership, a form of leadership that combines ethics and business practices that promotes responsible decision-making and leadership in the organisation; unethical leadership has been catastrophic form businesses and organisations round the world. Another important issue in the African business world was explained in Chap. 11, which has to do with waste management. Responsible African business leaders must be prepared to control and manage their ecosystems regarding the impact of the issues that concern the ethos of the circular economy especially creating products that are not harmful to the environment and tends to preserve it for the future. The discussion in the next chapter (Chap. 12) focused on enhancing Corporate Social Responsibilities in emerging business environments in Africa. It can expose how Corporate Social Responsibility (CSR) is a tool that can be applied to reduce risks, build brand equity, elevate market performance, and drive business sustainability, its importance for business sustainability in Africa, and how African organisations have done this. Chapter 13 addresses responsible logistics and supply chain challenges in businesses in Africa; it shows how to adopt eco-friendly logistics practices and sustainable supply chain architecture towards the people and the environment. The final chapter addresses corporate governance in Africa, its challenges, and how to run effective boards in African organisations. It proposes that corporate governance in Africa can be strengthened through legal and regulatory reforms; education and training; stakeholder engagement; auditing and monitoring, encouraging international meeting standards, and practising global best practices.

It is expected that managers will find this very useful in navigating the various challenges that they encounter in business. The emphasis is to build businesses that would withstand the test of time. This means building strong brands responsibly. It entails ensuring that leaders live up to their responsibilities to the different stakeholders and that they take responsibility for their actions. Leaders have the power and capacity to make a positive difference. They can make a difference in the lives of their employees by treating them with dignity and value. They can make a difference in the lives of their customers by ensuring that they offer them value and products that are not harmful to them. They can make a difference in the lives of the shareholders by helping them grow their investments responsibly. They can make a difference in the lives of the community by ensuring that they create a social impact. They can make a difference in the lives of the environment by ensuring they avoid actions that are harmful to the environment. This way, all the stakeholders would have positive experiences that would make them remain loyal to the organisation.

This book would help leaders see that business is not all about profit maximisation but rather about profit optimisation. It would help them learn to have a purpose for their existence and aim to create long-term value. Organisations that have a purpose are more likely to be successful than those with no purpose. This is because they have something much more than selfish interest driving them. Leaders of such organisations would tend to give it all as they have a purpose and want to make a difference. Leaders have only one choice, and this is to make profits responsibly. This choice is not negotiable because leaders must endeavour to improve the people they interact with rather than impoverish them. They must endeavour to leave the environment better than before. They should focus on fulfilling their responsibilities to the people and planet while making profits. This is the only way to achieve long-term sustainability.

Index[1]

A

Accounting, 5–6, 141–165, 242, 285, 292
Adventure, 103
Advertising, 4, 94, 95, 103–120, 132, 200, 292
African business, 1–2, 4, 7–8, 11–31, 41–56, 142, 143, 145, 149, 150, 152, 157, 160, 164, 205–221, 292, 293
African Continental Free Trade Area (AfCFTA), 23, 31
African model, 271
African values, 183
Agricultural waste, 210
Anglophone, 183
Aristotle, 107, 108, 190, 198
Asian model, 270
Audacious, 116

B

Bankruptcy, 65, 76
Behavioural, 6, 171, 172, 192
Bribery, 191, 200, 275
Broadcast, 105, 115
Business ethics, 89, 191, 285, 292

C

Carbon emissions, 66, 74, 76, 250, 255
Cardinal virtues, 107, 198
Categorical Imperative, 109
Christian, 116
Circular economy, 7–8, 74, 76, 205–221, 260, 293
Climate change, 20, 66, 74, 82, 96, 142, 149, 150, 154, 157, 159, 184, 196, 200, 203, 216

---

[1] Note: Page numbers followed by 'n' refer to notes.

Commercial waste, 206
Community, 4, 21, 27, 42, 43, 43n1, 46, 47, 50, 52–56, 65, 67, 82, 88, 93–96, 113, 141, 145, 146, 152, 153, 156, 157, 161, 165, 177, 196, 199, 214, 218, 227, 230, 233–235, 237–239, 241, 243, 259, 261, 268–270, 272, 278, 279, 294
Competitive analysis, 137
Competitive pricing, 131
Conflict management, 172
Consumer education, 86, 87, 91, 93
Consumer empowerment, 81
Consumer protection, 87, 93
Contingency model, 72
Corporate citizenship, 224, 230
Corporate culture problem, 284, 288
Corporate governance, 9–10, 19, 148, 149, 156, 157, 196, 224, 240, 265–289, 292, 293
Corporate Social Responsibility (CSR), 8–9, 66, 67, 92, 93, 149, 150, 196, 223–244, 251, 252, 258, 259, 293
Corruption, 29, 152, 199, 200, 209, 215, 225, 238, 253, 254, 266, 275, 285, 286, 288, 289
Cost-plus pricing, 131
Cultural humility, 6, 174–176, 185
Customer-centric, 3, 89–91, 96, 261
Customer satisfaction, 3, 5, 83, 90–91, 96–97, 134, 267
Cyber-security, 19

D

Decision-making, 145, 149, 159, 176, 196, 202, 271, 272, 275, 293
Decision-making processes, 158, 272, 283
Degradation, 146, 150, 205, 216, 230
Deontological ethical theory, 107–109
Destructive behaviours, 111, 241
Digital, 21, 22, 45, 51, 83, 86, 89, 90, 105, 106, 158, 163, 176, 287
Digital age, 118, 184
Digital marketing, 105
Digital technology, 19, 21–22, 31, 120

E

Eco-design, 260
Economy pricing, 132
Ecosystem, 7, 151, 161, 260, 293
Effective communication, 201
Empathy, 192, 194, 197, 200
Enron, 7, 190, 191, 267
Entrepreneur, 2, 13, 20, 22, 26, 42–46, 49–52, 54–56, 75, 180
Environmental, 5, 6, 14, 15, 27, 65, 68, 87, 93, 96, 142, 145–151, 154–161, 163, 164, 184, 187, 206, 207, 209, 214, 216, 219, 225–228, 230, 233, 235, 249–253, 255, 258, 261, 268
Environmental performance, 147–149, 154–158, 260

Environmental, social, and governance (ESG), 149, 156, 159, 251, 252, 259
Environmental sustainability, 66–67, 74, 76
Ethical, 4, 7, 24, 48, 74, 85, 106, 110, 111, 114–115, 118, 120, 141, 152, 170, 174, 189, 190, 192, 194–202, 226, 228–230, 235, 236, 238, 240, 243, 249–251, 260, 266, 272, 291, 292
Ethical behaviour, 190, 268
Ethical leadership, 7, 189–203, 293
Ethical responsibilities, 196, 198
Ethical theory, 107–110
Ethnographic, 91
European Commission, 44n2

Fairness, 120, 176, 189, 193, 199, 241, 243, 268
Family-controlled model, 271
Federal Trade Commission (FTC), 110, 111
Financial sustainability, 67, 75
First National Bank (FNB), 113
Fortitude, 107, 108, 120
Francophone, 183

Gaseous waste, 206
Gender, 48, 73, 115, 172, 280
Gender balance, 73
Gen Z, 171, 185
Globalisation, 162, 180, 191, 231

Government, 5, 11, 14, 16–18, 21, 22, 25, 28–31, 43n1, 47, 49–53, 55, 56, 65, 66, 69, 70, 76, 82, 85, 86, 88, 89, 93, 96, 120, 146, 148, 150–153, 155, 162–164, 178, 187, 199, 209–215, 219, 220, 226, 233, 234, 237, 239, 240, 243, 244, 256–258, 269–272, 276–278, 282, 288
Green accounting, 161
Green energy, 74, 76
Green operation, 9
Green purchasing, 260
Group dynamics, 283

Harvard model, 73
Hazardous waste, 207, 212
Honesty, 114, 192, 197, 198
Human dignity, 73, 112
Humane, 193
Humanitarian, 25, 27, 224
Hybrid, 76, 270
Hybrid model, 270, 274

Illiteracy, 12, 91
Impact investing, 161
Independence, 73, 268
Industrial waste, 206
Infrastructure, 2, 6, 12, 14, 15, 19, 22, 28, 29, 43n1, 44–46, 52, 55, 56, 83, 85, 144, 148, 158, 159, 163, 209, 214, 253, 254, 256, 266

Institutional framework, 209, 210, 219
Integrated reporting, 142, 149, 155, 161, 164
Intellectual capital, 67–68
International Integrated Reporting Framework (IIRF), 148
Islamic model, 271

J

Jesus Christ, 116
Justice, 107, 108, 189, 193, 194, 241, 243

K

Kantian theory, 109

L

Leadership, 7, 8, 10, 12, 13, 24, 25, 30, 90, 171, 186, 192, 197–199, 201, 217, 220, 224, 260, 276, 280, 286–288, 292, 293
Limited resources, 54, 85, 145, 234, 244, 277
Limited stakeholder engagement, 276
Liquid waste, 206
Livelihoods, 11, 22, 218, 221, 225, 238
Logistics, 9, 55, 249–261, 293

M

Management, 14, 71, 126, 142, 171, 190, 205, 234, 249, 265

Marketing Mix, 3, 4, 93, 105, 125, 126, 134
Marketplace, 15, 21, 45, 111, 230, 241
Middle Eastern model, 271
Mining waste, 207
Morality, 24, 191
Moral standard, 116, 189, 191
Multinational, 63, 75, 85, 88, 89, 91, 92, 94, 174, 219, 238, 239, 249, 260

N

Nigerian, 19, 27, 28, 69, 85, 112, 113, 182, 201, 210, 238, 239, 252
Non-hazardous waste, 207
Non-recycled, 85

O

Organisational culture, 90, 172, 175, 184, 284
Overconsumption, 82
Ownership, 43, 201, 239, 271, 272, 274
Ownership structure, 275, 288

P

Penetration pricing, 131
Perception/perceptions, 84, 104, 107, 111, 126, 129, 135, 194, 197, 241
Performance evaluation, 268, 272, 288
Phygital, 83
Physiological, 84, 177–179

Plato, 190
Political interference, 276
Post-apartheid, 41–56
Post-pandemic, 1, 90, 176, 185
Premium pricing, 131–132
Pricing, 4–5, 86, 125–137, 200, 292
Profit maximisation, 134, 195, 235, 294
Prudence, 107, 108, 120, 198
Psychosomatic, 119
Purchasing behaviours, 127, 130

Recycle/recycled, 74, 95, 207, 218, 219
Refurbish, 74
Regulatory, 4, 10, 12, 19, 118, 120, 145, 150, 154–157, 159, 224, 225, 238, 239, 243, 249, 252, 260, 266–269, 275, 278, 279, 282, 288, 293
Religious insensitivity, 115–116
Responsible advertising, 4, 103–120, 292
Responsible logistics, 9, 249–261, 293
Responsible marketing, 88, 93, 97
Responsible pricing, 4–5, 125–137, 292
Return on assets, 133
Return on investment (ROI), 272
Reverse logistics, 255, 260
Risk and uncertainty, 285
Rurality, 43n1, 46

Sachetisation, 84
Sales maximisation, 134

Seaports, 252
Self-actualisation, 73, 177, 178
Self-esteem, 84, 183
Shareholder-centric model, 270
Social accounting, 146, 161
Social and environmental accounting (SEA), 5, 141, 142, 145–165
Social disasters, 224
Socialisation, 112
Social issues, 154, 183, 214, 227, 230, 231, 242, 284, 288
Socio-economic, 6, 15, 17, 21, 30, 31, 41, 186, 215, 240
Solid waste, 206, 207, 209–215, 220
Stakeholder-centric model, 270
Stakeholder engagement, 10, 149, 158, 268, 272, 278, 283, 287, 288, 293
Stakeholder Theory (ST), 66, 232–236, 241, 242
Standardisation, 65, 158, 159
Startups, 44, 255
State-controlled model, 271
Sub-Sahara/Sub-Saharan Africa, 4, 8, 83, 84, 86, 90, 94, 126, 127, 129, 132–133, 136, 142, 163, 164, 210–220, 252–260
Supply chain, 9, 16, 19, 30, 69, 75, 144, 162, 249–261, 293
Supply chain management (SCM), 250–252, 255–256, 258–261
Survival-based theory, 12, 24, 25
Sustainability, 2–5, 8, 14, 47, 49, 51, 63–76, 82, 126, 132, 136, 141–143, 145–149, 151, 153–164, 186, 191, 201, 202, 251, 252, 257–261, 266, 284–286, 291–294

Sustainable, 3, 9, 10, 21, 64, 65, 75, 82, 85, 96, 111, 127, 135, 142, 143, 145, 147, 150–154, 157–164, 184, 195, 200, 202, 203, 207, 210, 220, 244, 250, 251, 257, 258, 260, 261, 266, 284, 291, 293
Sustainable businesses, 3, 7, 66–71, 142, 145, 149, 160–164, 169, 181, 183, 185, 187, 202, 266
Sustainable finance, 161
Sustainable growth, 2, 12, 156, 225, 267
Sustainable supply chain management, 154, 162, 257

T

Technological adoption, 10, 287, 288
Technological innovation, 218
Technology, 9, 19, 21–22, 31, 44, 45, 51, 68, 93, 106, 120, 132, 143, 149, 158, 159, 163, 164, 171, 185, 187, 219, 221, 257, 279
Temperance, 107, 108, 120
Transparency, 5, 74, 92, 94, 96, 141, 147, 149, 150, 154, 157, 158, 160, 162, 250–252, 266–271, 273–275, 278–280, 287
Tupuca, 254, 255
Twitter, 69

U

Unethical, 4, 5, 7, 74, 92, 114–116, 118–120, 136, 152, 190, 192, 199–201, 225, 229, 250, 251, 292, 293
Unsustainability, 68
Utilitarian ethical theory, 107, 109–110

V

Value-based leadership theory, 12, 24–25
Value-based pricing, 132, 133, 135
Value creation, 31, 70, 235, 244, 260
Values, 19, 42, 65, 84, 111, 125, 151, 190, 214, 224, 249, 266
Virtue, 106–108, 189, 198
Volatile, 12, 25, 69, 170, 237, 242, 289

W

Waste management, 7–8, 74, 154, 205–221, 260, 292, 293
Workplace diversity, 285, 288
WorldCom, 7, 190, 191, 267

X

Xenophobic, 52